# LAMBETH PALACE LIBRARY

*Treasures from the Collection of the Archbishops of Canterbury*

# LAMBETH PALACE LIBRARY

*Treasures from the Collection of the Archbishops of Canterbury*

Edited by Richard Palmer and Michelle P. Brown

SCALA

# Contents

# Foreword

In 1647, two years after the execution of Archbishop Laud, with the see of Canterbury still vacant, Parliament ordered a survey to be made of Lambeth Palace. Crossing the Thames to Lambeth Stairs and entering the Palace, the surveyors reached the central cloister court. Above it, arranged on all four of its sides, they found Lambeth Palace Library and it evidently made an impression; the surveyors recorded it as 'the greate library of the Archbishopp-ricke of Canterbury'.

This was not the usual description of the Library. Founded in 1610 by the will of Archbishop Bancroft, it was dedicated to serve not only the Church and the Archbishops of Canterbury but also 'the Kings and Common wealth of this Realme', and, when Parliament commandeered its keys in 1643, it was named as 'the publick library belonging to the see of Canterbury'. It is this special role as one of England's earliest public libraries, enhanced by successive Archbishops for the benefit of all, which has characterised the Library throughout its history.

Today the Library is more active then ever, preserving the written and printed heritage of the Church and making it accessible as a source of perspective on the present and an aid to the better ordering of the future. Founded to benefit both Church and nation, the Library now serves a wider public throughout the world, not least through its electronic catalogues and online resources. This book celebrates 60 of its treasures, giving some indication of the range and significance of the Library as a whole. Yet the collection is more than the sum of its parts; the real treasure is the Library itself, a unique institution in the life of the Church and the English people which is now 400 years old.

Archbishop Bancroft bequeathed his collection to his successors, the Archbishops of Canterbury, for ever. I am the 30th recipient of his benefaction, and with it his charge to care for the Library and facilitate its descent from age to age in public service. Happily, the Library has long been maintained on behalf of the Archbishop by the Church Commissioners, whose faithful provision for its needs deserves acknowledgement here, as does the outstanding professionalism and welcoming approach of the Librarian and staff. The Library also benefits from the guidance of its Trustees and from public goodwill, focused through its Friends. With this support, Lambeth Palace Library enters its fifth century with confidence, continuing its service to the Church and to all who may benefit from the historic collections in its care.

+ Rowan Cantuar:

*Rowan Williams, Archbishop of Canterbury*

*Half-title and contents pages:* Border details from MS 186; A London Liturgical Psalter, ff. 1r and 109r (see no. 17)
*Frontispiece:* Detail from MS 209; The Lambeth Apocalypse, f. 8r (see no. 9)
*Opposite:* Portrait of an archbishop from MS 209; The Lambeth Apocalypse, f. 52v (see no. 9)

# Lambeth Palace Library and its Collections

1. (*opposite*) Photograph of the interior of the Great Hall, Lambeth Palace Library, 2009

2. (*below*) The will of Archbishop Bancroft, 20 October 1610. Probate copy, 12 November 1610

Lambeth Palace Library was founded in 1610 by the will of Richard Bancroft (1544–1610), Archbishop of Canterbury (figs 2–3). Bancroft amassed a personal library of printed books and manuscripts which was outstanding, not only in quantity but also in the richness and diversity of its contents.[1] In his will he bequeathed the collection, housed in his study over the cloister at Lambeth, 'to the Arch-Bishops of Canterbury successively for ever'.[2]

Bancroft was far from the first Archbishop of Canterbury to form a library at Lambeth. As scholars and patrons of learning, Archbishops had always needed access to a range of books. The library of Thomas Cranmer (1489–1556) was described by John Strype as 'the storehouse of ecclesiastical writers of all ages … open for the use of learned men'.[3] Matthew Parker (1504–75) gathered an astonishing corpus of Anglo-Saxon and other manuscripts, and made Lambeth a centre for manuscript studies and even for book production.[4] The library of John Whitgift (1530?–1604), the largest private collection of his generation, comprised some 6,000 volumes.[5] All of these, however, were personal collections, subject to dispersal or removal from Lambeth on the deaths of their owners. Bancroft was the first Archbishop to perceive the need for a permanent library and even he was unsure whether his intention could be fulfilled, given the difficulty in law of binding his successors to preserve the collection. Accordingly, he made his bequest conditional, recognising that establishing the Library needed the support of his successor and that of the King. If their efforts proved unavailing, the collection was to pass to the proposed Chelsea College, or, failing that, to Cambridge University Library.

In the name of God Amen I Richard Bancroft by the providence of god Archbishop of

Tenore presentium nos Thomas Nevile

Edmundus Woodhall Registrarius

3. (*left*) *Richard Bancroft* (1544–1610), Archbishop of Canterbury
English school, seventeenth century

4. (*below*) *George Abbot* (1562–1633), Archbishop of Canterbury
English school, seventeenth century

5. (*opposite left*) Catalogue of the library of Archbishop Bancroft: preface signed by Archbishop Abbot, 15 October 1612

6. (*opposite right*) Catalogue of the library of Archbishop Bancroft: the north side

Bancroft's successor proved to be the Bishop of London, George Abbot (1562–1633), who was 'blown over the Thames to Lambeth' in 1611 (fig. 4). Notwithstanding his Evangelical sympathies, Abbot shared the Calvinist, episcopalian outlook of Bancroft, and his appointment to Canterbury was in line with Bancroft's desire and expectation.[6] More importantly, Bancroft and Abbot were fellow bibliophiles and book collectors. They supported literary projects such as the Authorised Version of the Bible (MS 98 in the Library is one of the few surviving drafts of part of it), and they shared a friendship with the greatest library patron of the day, Sir Thomas Bodley, whose library had opened its doors at Oxford in 1602. Bancroft had made no secret of his intention to found a Library, and it is likely that the project was discussed, perhaps when Bancroft and Abbot dined with Bodley at his house at Fulham.[7] Happily, too, the King was James I, an author with an admiration for scholarship. It is thanks to Abbot and to James I that Bancroft's intention was carried into effect, and it was they who determined its character as a public collection.

The circumstances of the founding of the Library were related by Abbot in a preface to a catalogue of Bancroft's collection compiled in 1612 (fig. 5). He related that, in bequeathing his 'greate and famous librarie of bookes of divinity and of many other sortes of learning', Bancroft had appealed to James I to find a way to safeguard the collection for posterity. The King, 'conceaving it to be a monument of fame within his kingdome, and of greate use to himselfe and his successors, as well as to the Church of God', sought counsel of his solicitor, Francis Bacon. Bacon's advice was that the best security for the collection lay in the production of a catalogue as an enduring record of all its contents. In concluding his preface, Abbot appealed to his successors, 'as they will answere unto me and my Predecessor in that fearefull day of God', to preserve the Library with diligence, enabling it 'to descend from age to age, and from succession to succession, to the service of God and his Church, of the Kings and Common wealth of this Realme, and particularly of the Archbishops of Canterbury'.[8] With these words Abbot impressed upon the Library its public character, as one of England's earliest public libraries, which has endured to the present day.

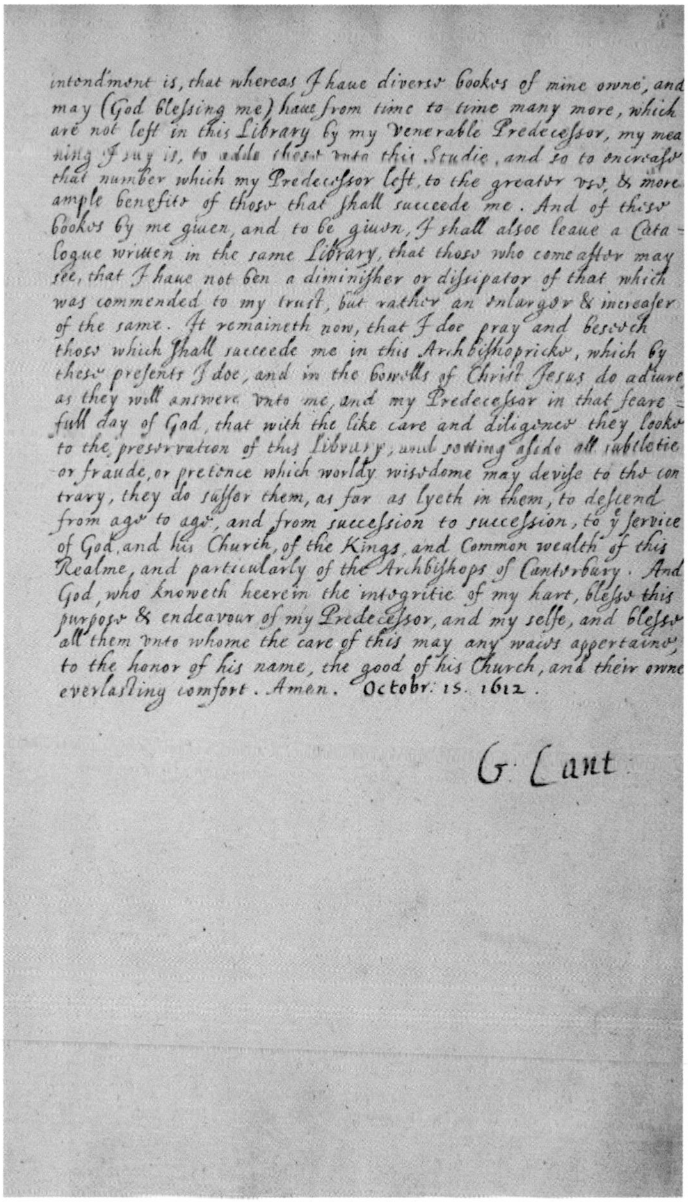

intendment is, that whereas I haue diverse bookes of mine owne, and may (God blessing me) haue from time to time many more, which are not left in this Library by my Venerable Predecessor, my meaning I say is, to adde those vnto this Studie, and so to encrease that number which my Predecessor left, to the greater vse & more ample benefite of those that shall succeede me. And of these bookes by me giuen, and to be giuen, I shall alsoe leaue a Catalogue written in the same Library, that those who come after may see, that I haue not ben a diminisher or dissipator of that which was commended to my trust, but rather an enlarger & increaser of the same. It remaineth now, that I doe pray and beseech those which shall succeede me in this Archbishopricke, which by these presents I doe, and in the bowells of Christ Jesus do adiure, as they will answere vnto me, and my Predecessor in that feare full day of God, that with the like care and diligence they looke to the preservation of this Library; and setting aside all subtletie or fraude, or pretence which worldy wisedome may devise to the contrary, they do suffer them, as far as lyeth in them, to descend from age to age, and from succession to succession, to ye service of God, and his Church, of the Kings, and Common wealth of this Realme, and particularly of the Archbishops of Cantorbury. And God, who knoweth heerein the integritie of my hart, blesse this purpose & endeavour of my Predecessor, and my selfe, and blesse all them vnto whome the care of this may any waies appertaine, to the honor of his name, the good of his Church, and their owne everlasting comfort. Amen. Octobr: 15. 1612.

G. Cant

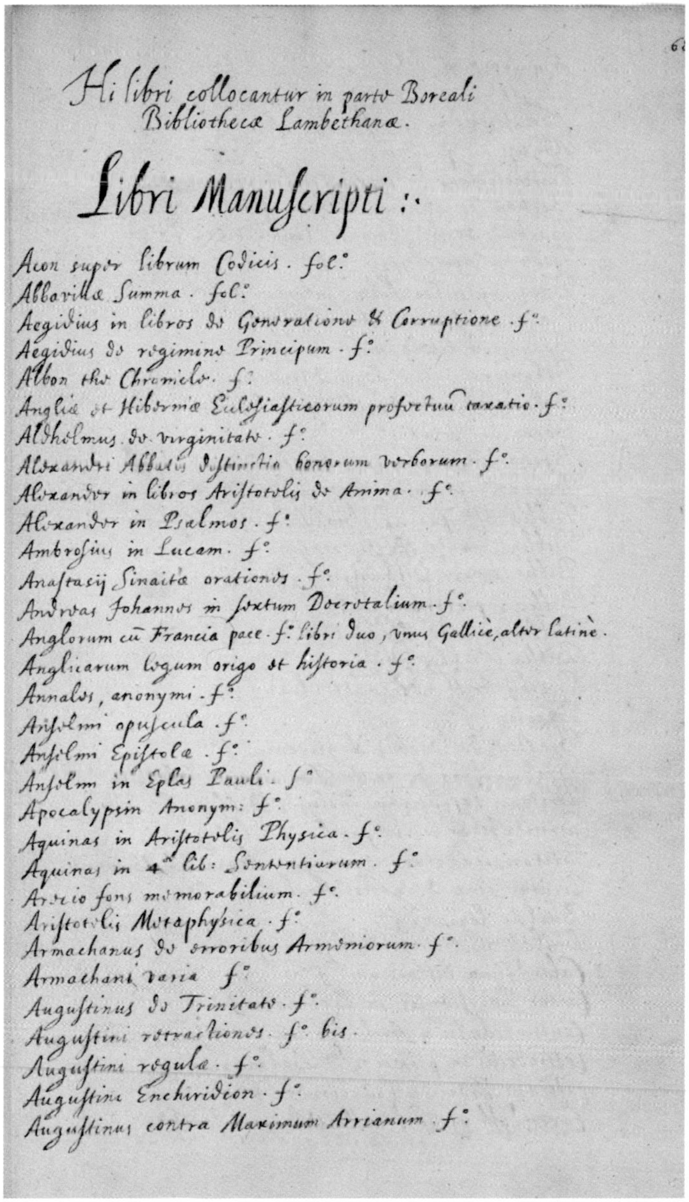

Hi libri collocantur in parte Boreali
Bibliothecæ Lambethanæ.

Libri Manuscripti :

Acon super librum Codicis. fol.
Alborillæ Summa. fol.
Aegidius in libros de Generatione & Corruptione. f.
Aegidius de regimine Principum. f.
Albon the Chronicle. f.
Angliæ et Hiberniæ Ecclesiasticorum proventuum taxatio. f.
Aldhelmus de virginitate. f.
Alexandri Abbatis distinctio bonorum verborum. f.
Alexander in libros Aristotelis de Anima. f.
Alexander in Psalmos. f.
Ambrosius in Lucam. f.
Anastasij Sinaitæ orationes. f.
Andreas Johannes in Sextum Decretalium. f.
Anglorum cum Francia pace. f. libri duo, unus Gallice, alter Latine.
Anglicarum legum origo et historia. f.
Annales, anonymi. f.
Anselmi opuscula. f.
Anselmi Epistolæ. f.
Anselmus in Eplas Pauli. f.
Apocalypsis Anonymi. f.
Aquinas in Aristotelis Physica. f.
Aquinas in 4m lib: Sententiarum. f.
Arecio fons memorabilium. f.
Aristotelis Metaphysica. f.
Armachanus de erroribus Armeniorum. f.
Armachani varia. f.
Augustinus de Trinitate. f.
Augustini retractationes. f. bis.
Augustini regula. f.
Augustini Enchiridion. f.
Augustinus contra Maximum Arrianum. f.

### The Founding Collections

The catalogue of 1612 gives a picture of Bancroft's collection and its arrangement around four sides of the Palace cloister. On the west side were Bibles and commentaries, patristics, Protestant and Catholic theology and controversies; on the south side sermons, scholastic writings, law and the humanities; on the east side history; and on the north side manuscripts, Protestant and Catholic liturgy, Puritan works and dictionaries.[9] In all, the catalogue recorded some 5,600 printed books and over 470 manuscripts (fig. 6).

Bancroft acquired a large number of volumes from the Royal Library, as many as 500, if Patrick Young, librarian to James I, is to be believed.[10] Among them are books from the collection of Henry VIII, including the Nuremberg Chronicle (no. 21 in this volume) and a treatise on indulgences commissioned by Katherine of Aragon (no. 24). Others were owned by Henry's children, including a copy of William Lily's Latin grammar, printed on vellum in 1540 and bound in crimson silk, with an illustration of the feathers of the Prince of Wales to represent its owner, the future Edward VI (fig. 7). A Venetian atlas (no. 29) may also have served in Edward's education. Other caches of books came to Bancroft from noblemen such as Robert Dudley, Earl of Leicester, including the Aldine Aristotle (no. 32), and John, 6th Baron Lumley, including 'the St Albans Chronicle' (no. 18) and the Arundel Choirbook (no. 25). Bancroft also acquired books from scholars, including John Foxe, the martyrologist, and Robert and Thomas Wakefield, both Hebraicists.

7. (*below*) [William Lily], *Institutio Compendiaria Totius Grammaticae* (London, 1540) The emblem of Edward, Prince of Wales

More numerous, however, were the books which Bancroft acquired from the dissolved monastic libraries. Among books recorded in this volume are the MacDurnan Gospels from Christ Church, Canterbury (no. 1); Aldhelm's treatise on virginity from Waltham Abbey (no. 2), and Hugh of Fouilloy's advice on the monastic life from Buildwas Abbey (no. 7). However, many other houses are represented in the Lambeth collection, including St Augustine's, Canterbury, the place of origin of Aldhelm's treatise, and also the source of the Library's oldest manuscript (MS 414, an Augustinian *florilegium* and other texts from the first quarter of the ninth century), and Llanthony Priory, near Gloucester, from which Bancroft acquired a hoard of around 120 manuscripts (no. 8).

However, the largest source of Bancroft's books was the library of his predecessor, John Whitgift, of whose will Bancroft was one of the executors. Some 2,000 to 3,000 books passed from Whitgift to Bancroft, including the Gospels in Church Slavonic (no. 33), sufficient in themselves to suggest the benefit which an Archbishop might gain from the retention of his predecessors' books at Lambeth.

In his preface to the Bancroft catalogue, Archbishop Abbot announced his intention to bequeath his own books to enhance the Library. In his lifetime he housed his collection alongside the Bancroft volumes, distinguished by protruding vellum tabs with the initials 'G. C.' (George Cantuar). In so doing he adopted the subject arrangement of the Bancroft catalogue for his own books, and from this it appears that the two Archbishops collected in similar fields.[11] However, the proportion of works on history and humanities – subjects well represented in Bancroft's library – was even higher in Abbot's, which included many works of contemporary European literature and on the history and affairs of France. Whereas Bancroft preferred plain calf bindings stamped with his arms or his initials 'RB', Abbot had a liking for more elaborate bindings; a good number of his books are gilt-tooled with corner pieces surrounding his armorial, as in the case of Nathaniel Brent's English translation of Paolo Sarpi, *The Historie of the Council of Trent* (London, 1620) (fig. 8). Abbot ensured that a separate catalogue of his books was compiled, and from this it appears that, by the time of his death in 1633, there were some 2,667 books, including some fifty manuscripts.[12] In total, the joint Bancroft–Abbot collection comprised some 9,000 books and manuscripts. It was one of the largest libraries in the country at a time when England could boast few libraries and even fewer with any claim to public status.

The purpose of the Library was not stated explicitly by Bancroft or Abbot, but may be discerned. It was founded in an era when the Elizabethan religious settlement was under attack, on the one hand from militant Roman Catholicism, and, on the other, from the Puritans, who sought a more radical reformation of Church discipline and practice. In this age of fierce controversy, theological differences were argued in print, and libraries were founded as

8. Paolo Sarpi, *The Historie of the Council of Trent* (London, 1620) Armorial binding for Archbishop Abbot

literary arsenals. This is true of the Lambeth Library as it is of the Bodleian, and it may be noted that Bancroft bequeathed his collection, if his foundation were to fail at Lambeth, to Chelsea College, an abortive project, which, according to Thomas Fuller, was 'intended for a spiritual garrison, with a magazine of all books for this purpose; where learned divines should study and write ... against the papists'.[13]

Bancroft and Abbot also sponsored the project of Bodley's librarian, Thomas James, for the collation of the works of the Church Fathers. This involved the comparison of manuscripts and printed texts to expose supposed falsifications by Roman Catholic theologians. The principal tools for this were the medieval manuscripts, scattered after the Dissolution of the Monasteries, which Bancroft and like-minded collectors sought to recover and preserve. Archbishop Parker had used his library as an ideological resource to show that in Anglo-Saxon times the English Church operated with relative independence of Rome, and also boasted a married clergy, a vernacular Bible and even an understanding of the Eucharist which accorded with his own. Bancroft, who built his reputation as the hammer of the Puritans, made a similar appeal to history. He sought especially to prove that the governance of the Church by bishops could be traced back to the Apostles, and strove to uphold the 'old and Apostollical forme of Church government under her excellent Majestie, by Archbishops or Arch-builders, and Bishops, practised in the Apostles times, approved by all the ancient Fathers and generall Councils, and continued in this land since the time that it first professed Christianity'.[14] Bancroft and Abbot both borrowed chronicles and other historical manuscripts from the collection of Sir Robert Cotton.[15] In the Lambeth Library too, alongside the various classes of divinity, history was the largest single category, comprising 1,671 books at the time of Abbot's death in 1633.[16]

The arrangement of the Library in its early days, with sections of Protestant liturgics, Catholic liturgies, Protestant commentaries, Catholic commentaries and so on, further indicates its nature as a library of controversy. So too does the section of Puritan books, reflecting Bancroft's work as a polemical author and his active engagement in censorship of the press and the suppression of prohibited books. The Library preserves the only complete surviving set of Marprelate tracts of 1588–89 with their scurrilous attacks on the bishops, whose printers and authors Bancroft hounded so effectively.[17] The first of the tracts, *Oh read over D. John Bridges*, known as the Epistle, and which includes an attack on 'the Pope of Lambeth', is full of Bancroft's underlinings (fig. 9). Bancroft did not normally write in his books, but his sparring with John Penry, who was implicated in the production of the Marprelate tracts and eventually executed in 1593, drove him to exasperation. One of the Library's copies of John Penry, *A briefe discovery of the untruthes and slanders contained in a sermon ... by D. Bancroft* [Edinburgh, 1590] is interleaved with Bancroft's furious manuscript rejoinders (fig. 10).[18]

These and many other works in the Library, including Bancroft's tracts on witchcraft (no. 38), reflect the agendas of the Archbishops who owned them. When Bancroft noted on his copy of Robert

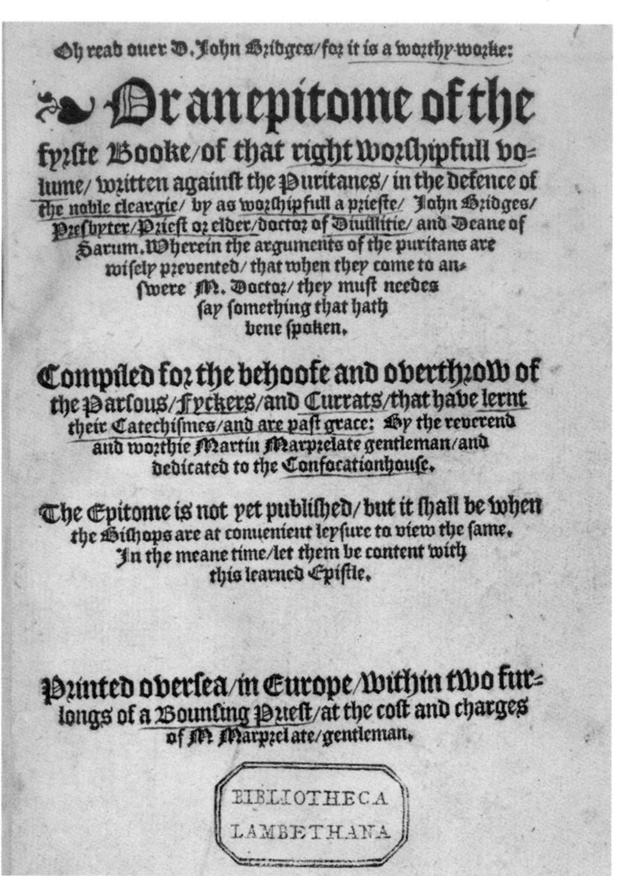

Oh read ouer D. John Bridges/ for it is a worthy worke:
Or an epitome of the
fyrste Booke/ of that right worshipfull vo-
lume/ written against the Puritanes/ in the defence of
the noble cleargie/ by as worshipfull a prieste/ John Bridges/
Presbyter/ Priest or elder/ doctor of Diuillitie/ and Deane of
Sarum. Wherein the arguments of the puritans are
wisely preuented/ that when they come to answere M. Doctor/ they must needes
say something that hath
bene spoken.

Compiled for the behoofe and ouerthrow of
the Parsons/ Fyckers/ and Currats/ that haue lernt
their Catechismes/ and are past grace: By the reuerend
and worthie Martin Marprelate gentleman/ and
dedicated to the Confocationhouse.

The Epitome is not yet published/ but it shall be when
the Bishops are at conuenient leysure to view the same.
In the meane time/ let them be content with
this learned Epistle.

Printed ouersea/ in Europe/ within two fur-
longs of a Bounsing Priest/ at the cost and charges
of M. Marprelate/ gentleman.



9. (*left*) *Oh read over D. John Bridges … Compiled … by the reverend and worthie Martin Marprelate*, 1588

10. (*below*) John Penry, *A briefe discovery of the untruthes and slanders contained in a sermon by … D. Bancroft* [Edinburgh, 1590], interleaved with Bancroft's handwritten responses

Harrison, *Three formes of catechisme* [Middelburg, 1583] that it was given him by the Lord Chief Justice of the Common Pleas at Bury [St Edmunds] assizes on 6 July 1583, he was not recording a gift from a fellow bibliophile, but documenting his investigation there of a subversive Brownist tract. Two laymen who had distributed books by Browne and Harrison were arrested as a result and put to death.[19] A copy of Henry Jacob's petition to James I for the toleration of puritan congregations, its margins crammed this time with James I's angry notes, was no doubt forwarded by the King to the Archbishop for his attention, although Jacob was safe in exile in Zeeland.[20] Similarly, the presence in Abbot's collection of Nathaniel Brent's translation of *The Historie of the Council of Trent* reflects Abbot's masterminding of this publication. It was Abbot who sent

10

ceiues you, thinking belike, that wheresoeuer wee
read of any called Elders in the Scriptures, wee
presently take the place, as making for the Eldership
vnder the Gospell. Wee thinke farre otherwise then
so, because wee finde the Gouernours of the Common wealth, as well as the rulers of the Church, to
be called Elders by the spirit of God. (Reade Genesis 50.7. Iosuah 6. 11.)
Whatsoeuer then you say of false Prophets, (as
you speake much of them in your Sermons) the
reader seeth, that at your first assault of the cause of
Christs Gouernement, you haue manifested your
selfe to bee of their number, that speake euill of the
thinges they knowe not, which the holy Ghost ma-
keth to be a marke of these false teachers, by whom (2.Pet.2.13.)
the way of truth in the latter ages, should bee euill
spoken of.
But heere you will saye, that wee ground something for the proofe of the Eldershippe vppon the
place of Math. 18. Tell the Church, &c. and that
wee bring in the Iewishe Synagogue for some purpose in this question. True it is, wee doe so: And
because you neither knowe, as it appeareth, what
wee inferre, nor weare able to aunswere them, being made knowen vnto you, therefore you did wise-
lie to set downe in our name, your owne absurdi-
ties, which of themselues, with out any confuter,
desire for shame to be buried vnder the earth. That
which we affirme is this. And we appeale vnto the
conscience of the reader, whether wee speake the
truth or not. First we prooue that the offices of Pa-
stors, Doctors, Elders, &c. are perpetually to continue in the Church, because the Lord hath apointed
them

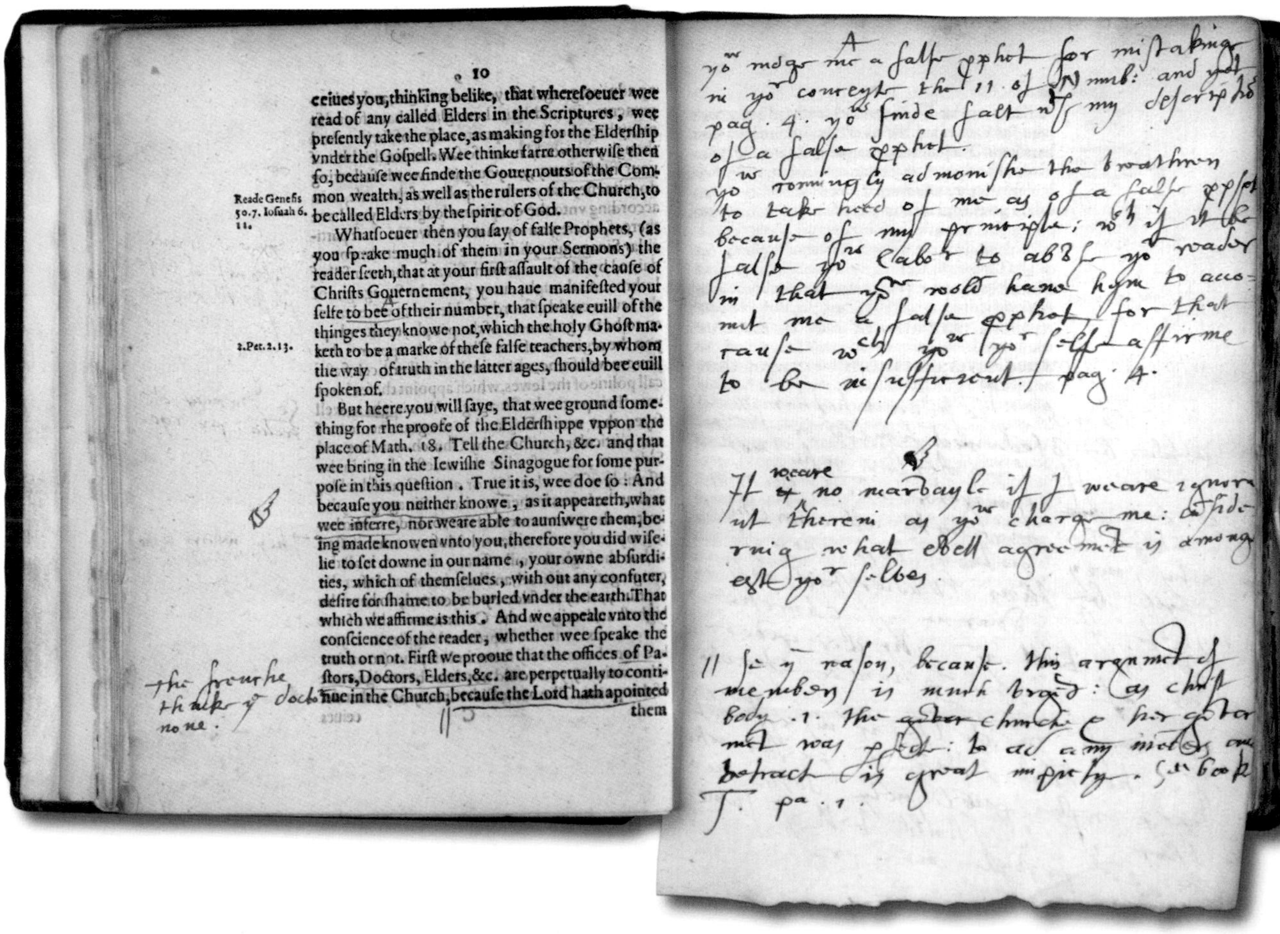

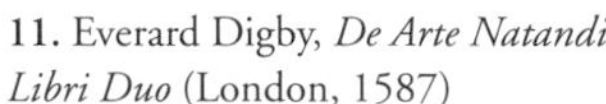
**11.** Everard Digby, *De Arte Natandi Libri Duo* (London, 1587)

Brent to Venice in 1618 to secure Sarpi's manuscript, which was intended, according to the preface which Brent addressed to Abbot, 'to remoove an erroneous opinion of the infallibilitie of this pretended Councell'.

Many books such as this came to the Archbishops as presentation copies, often from authors in search of patronage. More than 50 books are recorded with dedicatory prefaces addressed to Bancroft, and over 80 in the case of Abbot.[21] Such books would naturally be presented. Abbot, who was himself the author of *A Briefe Description of the Whole World*, owned several editions of one of the great travel books of the age, *Purchas his Pilgrimage*, in fine armorial bindings and with dedications to Abbot by the author, who was his chaplain.[22] Many books with no printed dedication were also received as gifts, including, in all probability, some of the more unusual items in the collection, such as Bancroft's copy of the first English manual on how to swim (fig. 11), by Everard Digby, an aspiring clergyman,[23] and Abbot's copy of the account of the circulation of the blood by William Harvey, who was one of the Archbishop's tenants and a participant in his funeral procession.[24] Examples of this kind throughout the Library's history indicate the special interest of its books resulting from their ownership and use by successive Archbishops.

**From Laud to Peter the Great**

Abbot's successor William Laud (1573–1645) collected manuscripts on a huge scale, and was so munificent a benefactor of the University of Oxford that he doubled the number of the manuscripts in the Bodleian Library. Yet his contribution to the Lambeth Library was insignificant, perhaps because of a want of sympathy with its founders, or because his personal collection had been plundered by the time of his death. At Lambeth there are only a dozen or so of Laud's books, but among them two are worthy of note. One is a copy of John Selden, *De iure naturali* (London, 1640). It contains a presentation inscription from Selden to Laud, indicating a friendship which was soon to prove invaluable for the Library. The other is a lavish manuscript on the laws and privileges of the clergy, finely written on vellum and illuminated with archiepiscopal heraldry (fig. 12). Laud commissioned this in 1637, as his diary reveals. Its title page displays the arms of the sees held successively by Laud, as well as a portrait of the compiler, the herald and archivist William Ryley (d. 1667).

In 1641 Laud was sent to the Tower of London accused of high treason, and in the following years Lambeth was put to new use as a prison. Parliament took pains, however, to secure the 'publick library', and began to consider its fate.[25] In 1644 a proposal was made in the House to Commons to transfer the collection to Sion College, the library of the City of London clergy. However, no action was taken to put this into effect. According to verses written a decade later by Matthew Poole, it was Cambridge University which objected to the banns by which Parliament sought to marry Lambeth to Sion:

> *When Lambeth-Sea of Books was to forsake*
> *Its ancient Seat, and a new Channel take*
> *Our Senate did espouse those choice Remains*
> *to Sion-House, Cambridge forbad the Banes.*
> *'Twas doubtful where that walking Library*
> *Would fix; Both places were resolved to try*
> *their Titles; but at last did thus agree*
> *To send it to the Universitie ...*[26]

12. *(opposite)* The title page of MS 323, *Iura et Privilegia Clero Anglicano Adiudicata* (extracts on the rights and privileges of the English clergy from the records of Parliament), commissioned by Archbishop Laud in 1637

A petition from Cambridge was laid before the House of Lords in 1646, citing the will of Richard Bancroft, which had named Cambridge University Library as a potential recipient if the foundation failed at Lambeth.[27] The inspiration for the petition had come from John Selden, who, as a member of the parliamentary committee for dealing with sequestered books, was in a position of influence. Parliament gave its consent, and in March 1647 agreed that Abbot's books should be included in the grant with those of Bancroft.

The arrival in Cambridge of more than 9,000 Lambeth books must have been sensational; not long before, in 1629, Cambridge University Library possessed barely 1,000.[28] The transfer necessitated new bookcases and catalogues and new shelf marks, which remain important for the understanding of the collection. Thus endowed, the University Library was said to rival the Vatican and the Bodleian collections, but the restoration of the monarchy and the archbishopric of Canterbury meant that the work was soon undone. Letters from Archbishop Juxon in 1662, and from his successor Gilbert Sheldon in 1663, thanked the University for its careful preservation of the collection and solicited its return to Lambeth.[29]

Archbishop Sheldon (1598–1677) welcomed the collection back to Lambeth in 1664. The Library was restored to its place in the galleries around the cloister, presumably in new bookcases, as John Aubrey attributed to his friend Stafford Tyndale the design of Sheldon's 'new Library'.[30] Tyndale, 'that most ingenious Gent.' as John Evelyn described him, had served as Secretary to Sheldon while Bishop of London, and had accompanied him to Lambeth.[31] Sheldon proved to be the third great benefactor of the Library. Annexed to his will was a catalogue of books designated for the 'publique library', and a list made in 1691 shows that the bequest included at least 788 printed books, mainly of folio size.[32] Among them, and still on the Lambeth shelves, were such early books as John Gower's *Confessio amantis*, printed by Caxton in 1483, but more typically the bequest updated the collection by adding the theological and biblical literature of the day, including the massive polyglot Bible edited by Brian Walton and the *Lexicon heptaglotton* of Edmund Castell.

Sheldon was also a significant donor of manuscripts. Foremost among them were the Carew manuscripts. Bound in 42 volumes, these comprise the papers of George Carew (1555–1629), 1st Earl of Totnes, relating to his ruthless military and administrative career in Ireland, including a survey of the Londonderry plantation (no. 39), and also his collections for Irish history. Sheldon was also the donor of most of the 110 manuscripts which now comprise MSS 245–324 and 490–521, many of which are also of Carew provenance.[33] Here may be found manuscripts on ordnance and coinage, heraldry and genealogy, politics and European diplomacy, all reflecting Carew's involvements. There is likewise a volume of Elizabethan and Jacobean voyages to the Americas and elsewhere (MS 250), including Carew's journal of the expedition to Cadiz in 1596. Also among these Sheldon manuscripts is a manuscript copied from Caxton's edition of the *Dictes* with a celebrated portrait of the family of Edward IV (no. 16). A major archival series was also acquired in 1662, when Parliament entrusted the ecclesiastical records of the Commonwealth period to the Archbishop for public use.[34]

The translation to Canterbury in 1678 of William Sancroft (1617–93) brought to Lambeth a scholar who became engrossed with the collection. He left an indelible mark on the Library through his radical rearranging and rebinding of the manuscripts and through the lists of contents in his own hand, which he left on their flyleaves.[35] Archbishop Sancroft also employed the earliest recorded Lambeth Librarian, Paul Colomiès (1638–92), a native of La Rochelle and a prolific author. Colomiès produced a new shelf list of the Library in 1684, with new shelf marks indicating a rearrangement of the collection, but even this was not immune from Sancroft's handwritten improvements and corrections.[36]

Under Sancroft the Library became a centre for scholarship, one of its principal users being his chaplain, Henry Wharton (1664–95). Wharton drew on the collection for his *Anglia sacra* (London, 1691), and also compiled a new catalogue of the manuscripts, the first in which they are numbered sequentially (MS 580). Gifts from donors other than the Archbishops began to appear (no. 43). John Evelyn found the Library 'exceedingly improved' when he paid a return visit in 1687 and had access to the manuscripts, now in a

LAVS DEO
CANTVARIENSIS
RELIGIO
PIETAS
IVRA ET PRIVILEGIA
CLERO ANGLICANO
ADIVDICATA
EX
Parliamentorum Rotulis
deprompta
M.DCXXXII
ANTIQVITAS
INDVSTRIA
VERITAS
ACAD; OXON
BATH ET WELLEN
LONDON
MENEVEN
ACAD: CANTABRIG

separate room.[37] In the following year he remarked in a letter to Pepys that the Lambeth Library 'ebbs and flows like the Thames running by it, at every Prelat's succession or translation'.[38] His comment was to prove prophetic. Sancroft had resolved to leave his private collection of nearly 6,000 books to his successors and, as Wharton recorded, had already placed them in the public collection at Lambeth. Then came his deprivation from office and, in May 1691, an order from the Queen to leave Lambeth House within ten days.[39] In disgust, Sancroft removed his books, ultimately to Emmanuel College, Cambridge, where they remain. Yet, despite this loss, the Lambeth Library could still impress. When Tsar Peter the Great visited in 1698 he declared that nothing in England had astonished him as much; he had never thought there were so many books in all the world.[40]

### The Library in the Eighteenth Century

The primacy of Thomas Tenison (1636–1715) brought a new period of growth in the Library. Tenison had already proved himself a patron of learning by founding a public library at St Martin-in-the-Fields. During his archiepiscopate from 1695 to 1715 the Library at Lambeth was populated by writers and antiquaries such as John Strype, Humphrey Wanley and Samuel Pepys (see no. 43), while a fragment of a loan register shows loans to Tenison himself and to clergymen such as Peter Allix and Thomas Sprat, Bishop of Rochester.[41] Tenison ensured that the Library was in the care of scholarly librarians, from 1696 Edmund Gibson (1669–1748), afterwards Bishop of London, and, from 1706 or 1707, Benjamin Ibbot (1680–1725), afterwards a Boyle lecturer and opponent of deism. Gibson's scholarly engagement with the collection may be seen in his catalogue of its manuscripts.[42]

In his will Tenison bequeathed to the Library all the printed books and manuscripts which he had already placed in the 'publick library', if Gibson and Ibbot saw fit to retain them there, as well as others of their choice from his private collection.[43] As a result the Library was handsomely enhanced, not only with theological books, but also with precious documents on British history. The Tenison manuscripts (MSS 639–928) include major Tudor and Stuart collections, such as the papers of Anthony Bacon as secretary for foreign affairs to Robert Devereux, 2nd Earl of Essex (MSS 647–662), the Shrewsbury Papers (MSS 694–710, see no. 35), and the papers of Thomas Murray as secretary to Charles I while Prince of Wales (MSS 663–669). Tenison also presented the papers of Henry Wharton (MSS 577–595), while the records of the Society for the Propagation of the Gospel (no. 45) reflect an aspect of his work and mission as Archbishop. Among printed books he gave the personal prayer book of Elizabeth I (no. 34).

The Library's records, although still meagre in the eighteenth century, are sufficient to show the work of the Library under a regular succession of Librarians.[44] These included David Wilkins, afterwards distinguished as the editor of the *Concilia*, who completed a new catalogue of the manuscripts, based on Gibson's, in 1720, and Andrew Coltee Ducarel, Librarian to five Archbishops from 1757 to 1785 (fig. 14). On his appointment Ducarel enthused: 'Thus it has pleased Providence to commit to my care the greatest manuscripts collection in this kingdom as far as related to ecclesiastical affairs'.[45] Although blind in one eye, Ducarel compiled 48 volumes of indexes to the Archbishops' registers (no. 31). In his time the Library gained in importance as a record repository, having in its care not only the registers, but also archival series such as the medieval court rolls of the Archbishops' estates, the *Carte Miscellanee*, and records of Convocation. It also fell to Ducarel to arrange and bind the Gibson Papers, which had been received in 1748, being largely papers of Archbishop Tenison, bequeathed by him to Gibson to be placed at his discretion in the Library. Ducarel's correspondence also illustrates mundane aspects of life in the Library, including the problems of cobwebs, damp and dirt in the 'lower library' around the cloisters, and the need for more shelving in the manuscripts library above.[46]

Fragmentary loan records for the years from 1708 to 1756 show the daily borrowings by the Archbishops and their families and chaplains, and by clergymen and other visitors. Thomas Birch, who received a friendly welcome from Archbishop Herring – 'Libraries were collected for such folk as you' – mined the Bacon Papers for his *Memoirs of the Reign of Queen Elizabeth*, (1758).[47] Horace Walpole

**13.** (*opposite, from left to right*) The arms of Archbishops John Whitgift, Richard Bancroft, George Abbot and Gilbert Sheldon, centrepieces from armorial bindings in the Library

**14.** (*right*) *Andrew Coltee Ducarel* (1713–85)
Engraving by Francis Perry (1757, wording revised 1784) after Antonio Soldi (1746)

borrowed MS 265 and published its portrait of the family of Edward IV (no. 16).[48] David Maichel, a visitor from Tübingen who published his *Lucubrationes Lambetanae* in 1729, was even permitted to borrow the Lambeth Bible.[49] Such liberality sometimes went awry. Among books lost from the Library was Matthew Parker's *De antiquitate* (no. 36), missing in 1720 and recovered with the aid of Richard Trevor, Bishop of Durham, in 1757.

Not every Archbishop left books to the Library, but one whose benefaction matched that of Tenison in scale was Thomas Secker (1693–1768), Archbishop from 1758. Secker's close involvement with the Library may be seen in his account book, which records his payments for the Librarian's salary, books and book binding, and likewise in his oversight of his Librarian, Ducarel, whose work he sometimes criticised.[50] In his will Secker bequeathed all those of his books which the Library lacked. No less importantly, the Library received his personal and administrative papers, both domestic and foreign, including series relating to the Society for the Propagation of the Gospel, the American Colonies and Protestants overseas. The records of Queen Anne's Commission for Building Fifty New Churches were also deposited in the Library in 1759.

### The Library under the Ecclesiastical Commissioners

The nineteenth century opened positively with the purchase in 1806 of the Greek manuscripts collected by J. D. Carlyle (no. 4). The Archbishop responsible was Charles Manners-Sutton (1755–1828), whose papers relating to the insanity of King George III are also described in this volume (no. 50). Librarians issued the first printed catalogues. Henry John Todd published a catalogue of the manuscripts in 1812, and descriptions of the early printed books were produced by Samuel Roffey Maitland in 1843 and 1845. The major development, however, was a change of venue. The Library around the cloister was old, dilapidated and so cold that it was said that none but Captain Parry, the Arctic explorer, and his crew, could possibly use the collection (fig. 15).[51] In 1829 Archbishop Howley commissioned Edward Blore to undertake the reconstruction of parts of the Palace. The buildings around the cloister were demolished and the Library was transferred to the Great Hall, built for Archbishop Juxon in 1663.[52] The Hall served as the Library's reading room, while a muniment room for the manuscripts and records was constructed over an adjoining archway.

In its new setting the Library was described in 1849 as 'replete with comfort ... completely warmed at pleasure by two grand fireplaces, one at each end of the room'.[53] There was, all the same, a cloud on the horizon. The Library had always been financed from the revenues of the Archbishops' estates, and this continued after 1836, when the revenues passed into the control of the Ecclesiastical Commissioners. The Commissioners' power to maintain the Library was confirmed by Act of Parliament in 1866,[54] but the extent of the financial provision remained to be decided. The Commissioners considered £150 per annum sufficient for the salary of the Librarian and all of the Library's costs; Archbishop Charles Thomas Longley (1794–1868) demurred. Longley had employed an outstanding historian as Librarian – William Stubbs, afterwards Bishop of Oxford. When Stubbs left Lambeth in 1866 to become Regius Professor of Modern History at Oxford, Longley found that the salary available for a successor would be no more than that of 'one of the menial servants of the British Museum'. In the public row which followed in 1867 Longley was driven to the extreme step of closing the Library. The result was a flurry of concern 'at a moment when the whole world of letters is watching with anxiety the fate of this remarkable library', including a leader in *The Times* and a rejoinder from the Archbishop written under the pseudonym *Vindex*.[55]

This storm in the Lambeth teacup was calmed by an Order in Council of 7 August 1869, whereby, along with the provision of £150 per annum, the Commissioners undertook to maintain the fabric of the Library, and to set in hand a programme of conservation for the books and manuscripts which had fallen into disrepair.[56] On this basis the Library was reopened, but the question of the annual provision for the Library remained unresolved, and Longley recorded a formal protest against its inadequacy.[57] The issue was to overshadow two librarianships of epic length, those of Samuel Wayland Kershaw from 1868 to 1910 and Claude Jenkins from 1910 to 1952.

Records of the re-opened Library show the continued public appreciation of its collections. The Library was open for three days each week from 1869, and for five days from 1880 (fig. 16). A readers' book records the daily visits, and there are registers of requests for loans for study, publication or exhibition, each request approved by the Archbishop of the day.[58] The Archbishops continued to make use of the Library and Archbishop Benson 'ransacked' its shelves in search of materials for his judgement in the Lincoln Trial held in the Library in 1889.[59] In addition there were regular visits from societies and individuals, among them the Poet Laureate, Alfred Tennyson, the Prince and Princess of Wales, and Frederick William, Crown Prince of Germany. During such visits Kershaw displayed many of the treasures recorded in this volume, including the Lambeth Bible (no. 6), which he took to be a fine example of German art.[60]

Yet, despite the splendour of its historic collections, the Library was losing both pace and purpose. There were few notable gifts and bequests at this time and, with almost no funds for the purchase of printed books, the collections became increasingly antiquated. Kershaw owed his appointment to the absence of a salary appropriate to a better-qualified librarian. Archbishop Tait seems to have tried to unseat him in 1869, and then pursued a different remedy by appointing honorary librarians and honorary curators to enhance his endeavours.[61] The most notable was John Richard Green, the historian, who was honorary librarian from 1869 to 1877.[62]

Claude Jenkins was a far greater scholar than his predecessor, but was obliged to supplement his salary with other employment. Eventually he ran the Library by post from Oxford, where he became Regius Professor of Ecclesiastical History in 1934. His librarianship is remembered in large part for the achievements of others, the catalogue of the medieval manuscripts by M. R. James, and the history of Canterbury administration by his deputy at Lambeth, Irene Churchill.[63]

The Commissioners' provision for the Library rose gradually, but remained woefully inadequate. From 1910 to 1928 the costs of the Library outstripped the Commissioners' grant in every year, leaving the balance to be met by the Archbishop and, even more, from the Librarian's own pocket. In 1929 it was reported that the Library was draughty and bitterly cold, as fuel was too expensive; the staff consisted of the Librarian and a boy, but Jenkins could not afford a boy old enough to carry the heavier books.[64]

This situation was brought to an end by what has come to be regarded as a message from on high. In 1941 fire bombs fell on the Great Hall, damaging or destroying towards 10,000 printed books and throwing the whole library into chaos.[65]

### The Post-War Renaissance

The disaster which befell the Library in 1941 might well have brought about its extinction. Instead, it led to what has been described as 'virtually a second foundation'.[66] This outcome owed much to the initiative of Archbishop Geoffrey Fisher (1887–1972) and to generous support from the Pilgrim Trust, which in turn spurred on the Church Commissioners (as the Ecclesiastical Commissioners became known in 1948) to develop the Library on a new basis. The Library's role was redefined in 1953 as the main special library for the history and affairs of the Church of England,

**15.** (*left*) The old Library around the cloisters at Lambeth Palace
Engraving by B. Roffe after F. Nash, published in E. W. Brayley and W. Herbert, *A Concise Account … of Lambeth Palace* (London, 1806)

**16.** (*below*) The Library in the Great Hall of Lambeth Palace Library, 1886
Published in *The Graphic*, 31 July 1886, p. 113

17. *Morton's Tower, Lambeth Palace*, second half of the eighteenth century
Unknown artist

with an enlarged responsibility as a record repository and research centre for the archiepiscopal records of Canterbury and similar material. This redefinition of the Library's purpose was accompanied by the formation of a Library Committee to bring expert advice to bear on its affairs, and by the appointment of a new Librarian, Reginald Dodwell, and staff to assist him.[67]

The restoration of the Great Hall (see fig. 1) and the construction of a new reading room and strongroom were completed between 1946 and 1951. The task which confronted the new Librarian was nevertheless formidable. The printed books lay in vast quantities in the crypt of the Palace Chapel, in various states of damage and disorder. A bindery had to be established to restore them and a team of cataloguers established to produce a new catalogue. The development of the Library as a record repository brought the transfer into its care of the huge archives of the Faculty Office, Vicar General and the Court of Arches (no. 48). Morton's Tower (fig. 17), the Tudor gatehouse of the Palace, was shelved to accommodate them and the Library's first archivist was appointed. By 1957, when Dodwell moved to Trinity College, Cambridge, the extent of the transformation in the Library was becoming apparent and Archbishop Fisher could describe it as 'a joy to behold'.[68]

On these foundations Dodwell's successor, Geoffrey Bill, built a remarkable edifice. During his long service from 1958 to 1991 the Library gained recognition as the principal record office of the Church of England and as a research centre of international standing. He was also the first Librarian to leave a memoir of his time in office, enlivened by his characteristic sardonic humour.[69]

One of the achievements of these years was the foundation in 1964, with the encouragement of Archbishop Michael Ramsey, of the Friends of Lambeth Palace Library. Thereafter, year by year, the Friends richly enhanced the collection through the purchase of rare books and manuscripts, often joining with other national funds and charities to make spectacular acquisitions, including the Talbot Papers (no. 35), the Fairhurst Papers (no. 37) and the early liturgical books from the library of Lord Kenyon (of which no. 28 is one example).[70] The number of manuscripts in the Library had almost trebled by the time of Bill's retirement in 1991. Archives also reached the Library in profusion, among them the Fulham Papers (correspondence of the Bishops of London), and papers of leading churchmen such as George Bell, Bishop of Chichester (no. 58) and societies such as the Incorporated Church Building Society (no. 52). The correspondence and papers of the Archbishops of Canterbury, which had accumulated in the Palace in ever greater quantities from

the 1860s onwards, also entered the Library. Bound in thousands of volumes, they became one of the most frequently consulted series in the Library's care.

Acquisitions on this scale required increased resources for cataloguing and for the delivery of services to readers, who arrived at Lambeth in ever-increasing numbers. Fortunately, the Church Commissioners took a more enlightened view than their predecessors of the nineteenth century, and resources were also augmented by the ingenuity of the Librarian and the support of the Library Trustees, who were established in 1955, primarily to raise funds for the Library's benefit. An impressive series of catalogues emerged as a result, published and unpublished, including seven catalogues of

**18.** Register of benefactors of Sion College Library from 1629 to 1703, with section of chain attached

manuscripts by Geoffrey Bill and others by his tireless Deputy, Melanie Barber. Facilities for readers were enhanced by the construction in 1988 of a new reading room and strongroom, funded entirely by donations, and itself a reflection of the place which the Library had gained in public esteem.

In more recent years the Library has not wavered from the path on which it entered in its post-war revival. The Friends have continued to enhance the collection in rich measure (nos 22, 44, 57) and archives such as that of the Mothers' Union (no. 55) are still received and made accessible for all to use. When called upon, the Library has helped more widely in preserving the written and printed heritage of the Church, as in 1996, when it took under its wing the early collections from Sion College (fig. 18), the historic library of the clergy of the City of London (nos 23, 26, 47). Today, through its online catalogues and other electronic resources, the Library serves a wider public than ever before, but its mission of service remains the same, enabling the collections to descend, as Archbishop Bancroft intended, 'to the service of God and his Church, of the Kings and Common wealth of this Realme, and particularly of the Archbishops of Canterbury'.

*Richard Palmer*
*Lambeth Palace Library, London*

NOTES

1. J. P. Carley, 'A Great Gathererer Together of Books: Archbishop Bancroft's Library at Lambeth (1610) and its Sources', *Lambeth Palace Library Annual Review*, 2001, pp. 51–64.
2. M. R. James, 'The History of Lambeth Palace Library', *Transactions of the Cambridge Bibliographical Society*, vol. 3, no. 1, 1959, pp. 1–31.
3. E. G. W. Bill, 'Lambeth Palace Library', *The Library*, 5th series, vol. 21, 1966, pp. 192–206. See also David Selwyn, *The Library of Thomas Cranmer* (Oxford, 1966).
4. R. Palmer, 'Lambeth Palace Library and its Early Collections' in D. Ganz and J. Roberts (eds), *Lambeth Palace and its Anglo-Saxon Manuscripts* (London, 2007), pp. 6–16. See also no. 36 in this volume.
5. D. Pearson, 'The Libraries of English Bishops', *The Library*, 6th series, vol. 14, 1992, pp. 221–55.
6. P. Welsby, *George Abbot, the Unwanted Archbishop* (London, 1962); S. M. Holland, 'George Abbot: "The Wanted Archbishop"'. *Church History*, vol. 56, 1987, pp. 172–87. Bancroft also made Abbot an overseer of his will.
7. R. Palmer, 'In the Steps of Sir Thomas Bodley: The Libraries of Lambeth Palace and Sion College in the Seventeenth Century', *Lambeth Palace Library Annual Review*, 2006, pp. 53–67.
8. M. R. James, op. cit., pp. 2–3.
9. The catalogue is now in Library Records, LR/F/1, with a second contemporary copy at LR/F/2. For an analysis of its contents, see Ann Cox-Johnson, 'Lambeth Palace Library 1610–1664', *Transactions of the Cambridge Bibliographical Society*, vol. 2, 1954–58, pp. 105–26.
10. J. P. Carley, op. cit.
11. A. Cox-Johnson, op. cit., p. 108, gives an analysis of the number of Bancroft and Abbot books in each section of the classification.
12. The Library holds two copies of the Abbot catalogue (LR/F/3 and 4).
13. R. Palmer, 'In the Steps of Sir Thomas Bodley', op. cit.
14. S. B. Babbage, *Puritanism and Richard Bancroft* (London, 1962), pp. 35–36.
15. C. Tite, *The Early Records of Sir Robert Cotton's Library* (London, 2003).
16. A. Cox–Johnson, op. cit., p. 108.
17. C. S. Clegg, *Press Censorship in Elizabethan England* (Cambridge, 1997), Chapter 8.
18. This copy has the shelf mark 1588.11.01. Bancroft's copy of John Penry, *An humble motion* [1590] is also full of Bancroft's marginalia (shelf mark 1590.31.02).
19. S. B. Babbage, op. cit., p. 21. Bancroft's copy of Harrison's tract (shelf mark 1560.1.03) is the only one in England, reflecting its effective suppression.
20. Henry Jacob, *To the Right High and Mightie Prince, Iames …* [Middelburg, 1609]. Shelf mark 1609.42.

21. F. B. Williams, *Index of Dedications and Commendatory Verses in English Books Before 1641* (London, 1962).
22. The editions of 1614 (shelf mark 1614.24) and 1617 (1617.19).
23. Everard Digby, *De Arte Natandi Libri Duo* (London, 1587). Shelf mark 1587.17. Recorded in the Bancroft catalogue (LR/F1/f.49r).
24. William Harvey, *Exercitatio Anatomica de Motu Cordis* (London, 1625). Shelf mark **VP101, with Abbot's armorial binding.
25. A. Cox-Johnson, op. cit., is the principal source for what follows.
26. Samuel Clarke, *The Lives of Sundry Eminent Divines* (London, 1683), p. 55.
27. J. C. T. Oates, *Cambridge University Library, A History. From the Beginnings to the Copyright Act of Queen Anne* (Cambridge, 1986), Chapter 10, 'The Lambeth Library at Cambridge'.
28. Ibid., p. 212. The precise date of the arrival of the Lambeth books at Cambridge is not known; Oates considered that it occurred in the academic year from 1648 to 1649.
29. Ibid., Chapter 12, 'The Work Undone, 1659–64'.
30. John Aubrey, *The Natural History and Antiquities of the County of Surrey*, 5 vols (London, 1718–19), vol. 1, pp. 9–10.
31. John Evelyn, *The Diary*, ed. E. S. de Beer, 6 vols (Oxford, 1955), vol. 3, p. 349. Tyndale was subsequently drowned in the Thames.
32. For Sheldon's will, see MS 577, ff. 66v–69r. The list of 1691 is found in LR/F/10. Some duplicates were sold by Sancroft to purchase other books, which may explain books published after his death which still have Sheldon's armorial bindings.
33. M. R. James, 'The Carew manuscripts', *English Historical Review*, vol. 42, 1927, pp. 261–67.
34. D. M. Owen, *Charters in Lambeth Palace Library: A Catalogue of Lambeth Manuscripts 889 to 901 …* (London, 1968), pp. 3–4.
35. N. R. Ker, 'Archbishop Sancroft's Rearrangement of the Manuscripts of Lambeth Palace', in E. G. W. Bill, *A Catalogue of the Manuscripts of Lambeth Palace Library, MSS 1222–1860* (Oxford, 1972), pp. 1–51.
36. On Colomiès, see *Oxford Dictionary of National Biography*, vol. 12 (Oxford, 2004). His shelf list is LR/F/10.
37. John Evelyn, *The Diary*, op. cit., vol. 3, p. 527; vol. 4, p. 560. The manuscripts room appears to have been on an upper floor above the west side of the gallery around the cloister. A building on this site, with a river frontage between the Great Hall and the Lollard's Tower, has been attributed to Sheldon (*V. C. H., Surrey*, vol. 4, 1967, p. 46). The manuscripts room may therefore have been part of Sheldon's reinstatement of the Library.
38. John Evelyn, *Memoirs*, ed. W. Bray, 2 vols (London, 1819), vol. 2, p. 247.
39. MS 2214, f. 25r.
40. Cited from Macaulay's *History of England* by Claude Jenkins, 'The Historical Manuscripts at Lambeth', *Transactions of the Royal Historical Society*, 3rd series, vol. XI, 1917, pp. 185–97.
41. Strype's use of Lambeth sources was investigated by S. R. Maitland. See Cambridge University Library, Add 119–45. On Wanley, see the references to Lambeth in *Letters of Humfrey Wanley*, ed. P. L. Heyworth (Oxford, 1989). The fragment of the Lambeth loan register 1708–56 is in LR/D/5.
42. LR/F/39.
43. *The Last Will and Testament of … Thomas Tenison* (London, 1716), pp. 24–25.
44. On the Librarians, A. C. Ducarel, *The History and Antiquities of the Archiepiscopal Palace of Lambeth* (London, 1785), pp. 63–76. W. J. Thoms, 'Lambeth Library and its Librarians', *Notes and Queries*, 4th series, vol. 1, 1868, pp. 9–10, 48–50.
45. R. Myers, 'Dr Andrew Coltee Ducarel, Lambeth Librarian, Civilian, and Keeper of the Public Records', *The Library*, 6th series, vol. 21, 1999, pp. 199–222.
46. MSS 1163 and 2214.
47. John Nichols, *Literary Anecdotes of the Eighteenth Century*, 9 vols (London, 1812–16), vol. 5, p. 289.
48. Ibid., vol. 4, pp. 700–01.
49. LR/D/5.
50. Secker's account book is MS 1483. His letter in 1758 criticising Ducarel's failure to arrange the Gibson Papers prior to binding them is in MS 2214, ff. 22–23.
51. *The Athenaeum*, no. 2451, 17 October 1874, pp. 513–14. The remark, referring to Sir William Edward Parry, is attributed to Sir Nicholas Harris Nicolas, who drew upon Lambeth wills for his *Testamenta Vetusta*, 1826.
52. The work on the Library is described as complete in *Gentleman's Magazine*, May 1830, pp. 393–94.
53. Beriah Botfield, *Notes on the Cathedral Libraries of England* (London, 1849), p. 189.
54. Ecclesiastical Commissioners Act, 1866 (29 and 30 Victoria Chapter III), section 7.
55. *The Times*, 16 September 1867, p. 6; 19 September 1867, p. 10. *Notes and Queries*, 3rd series, vol. 12, 1867, p. 325; 4th series, vol. 1, 1868, p. 9. There is further documentation in Lambeth Palace Library, Tait Papers, vol. 163 and MS 4549, ff. 177–82.
56. Ecclesiastical Commissioners for England, *22nd report*, 1870, pp. 653–55. The programme of conservation is documented in LR/A/4.
57. Lambeth Palace Library, Tait Papers, vol. 163, f. 268.
58. LR/C/2, a readers' book, 1864–96; LR/B/2–3, books of loans, 1862–1909.
59. A. C. Benson, *The Life of Edward White Benson*, 2 vols (London, 1899), vol. 2, p. 355.
60. LR/D/4, visitors' book, 1870–1940. See also S. W. Kershaw, *Art Treasures of Lambeth Palace Library* (London, 1873).
61. Lambeth Palace Library, Tait Papers, vol. 163, ff. 168–235. A document signed in 1871 by J. R. Green and W. S. Simpson as honorary librarians is in LR/A/4. A list of honorary curators appointed in 1870 is in LR/C/2.
62. Lambeth Palace Library, Tait Papers, vol. 97, ff. 126–31; vol. 163, ff. 1, 90–96, 218–21.
63. M. R. James, *A Descriptive Catalogue of the Manuscripts in the Library of Lambeth Palace. The Mediaeval Manuscripts* (Cambridge, 1932). I. J. Churchill, *Canterbury Administration*, 2 vols (London, 1933).
64. LR/J/11/1 and 3. The Commissioners' annual grant rose to £250 per annum in 1880, to £350 in 1910 and £550 in 1914. It remained at this level into the 1930s. In 1927 the cost of the Library was £743, of which £184 was provided by the Librarian and £9 by the Archbishop.
65. LR/J/10, Records of the Library in wartime, 1939–45.
66. Lambeth Palace Library, *Catalogue of an Exhibition of Recent Gifts and Accessions* (London, 1960), p. 4.
67. R. Palmer, 'Reginald Dodwell, Lambeth Librarian 1953–58' in G. R. Owen-Crocker and T. Graham (eds), *Medieval Art: Recent Perspectives* (Manchester, 1998), pp. 224–30.
68. *Lambeth Palace Library. A Short History* (London, 1957).
69. MS 4435.
70. *Far Above Rubies: An Anniversary Celebration of Forty Years of Gifts from the Friends of Lambeth Palace Library* (London, 2004).

BROUGHTON'S DICTIONARY OF RELIGIONS
1756
NOVARINI ELECTA SACRA
1629
CEREMONIES AND RELIGIOUS CUSTOMS
PICART VOL. I
PICART VOL. II
PICART VOL. III
PICART VOL. IV
PICART VOL. V
PICART VOL. VI-VII
PRAESTANTIUM AC ERUDITORUM VIRORUM EPISTOLAE
1704
BIBLIOTHECA PATRUM DE LA BIGNE
I
II
IV
1624
1624
1624
OPERA OMNIA
MUIS
1650
DE FESTIS
TOM I
TOM II
TOM III
TOM IV
1698
GRATII FASCICULUS RERUM BROWN
TOM II
1690
1690
BIBLIOTHECA PATRUM
TOM I. II. III
TOM. IV
TOM. V P. II
TOM. V P. III
TOM. VI
1618
1618
1618
1618
1618
1618
TRACTATUS CONTRACTUUM
BIBLIOTHECA PATRUM
TOM. X. XI
TOM. XII P. I
TOM. XII P. II
TOM. XIII. XIV
TOM. XV
1618
1618
1618
NOVA BIBLIOTHECA VETERUM PATRUM SUPPLEMENTUM
I
II

AMBROSII OPERA
TOM. 4 5
ATHANASII OPERA
TOM. I
ATHANASII OPERA
TOM II
1601
BIBLIOTH. LOND.-BELG.
BIBLIOTHECA PATRUM
TOM IX P II
1618
DE CIVITATE DEI AVGVSTINVS
1570
AUGUSTINI SERMONES
AUGUSTINI OPERA
I - II
1576
BASILII MAGNI OPERA

# TREASURES

# 1 The MacDurnan Gospels

**MS 1370; Pocket Gospel Book**
Ireland, Armagh?; second half of the ninth century
Latin and Old Irish; vellum; 160 x 110 mm; ff. 216
Illustrated: (*opposite*) binding, upper board; (*right; detail and overleaf, top left*) ff. 4v–5r, St Matthew Evangelist miniature and Chi-rho page; (*overleaf, bottom left*) ff. 3v–4r, King Athelstan dedication inscription and thirteenth-century Crucifixion miniature; (*overleaf right*) f. 72r, decorated Incipit page of St Mark's Gospel

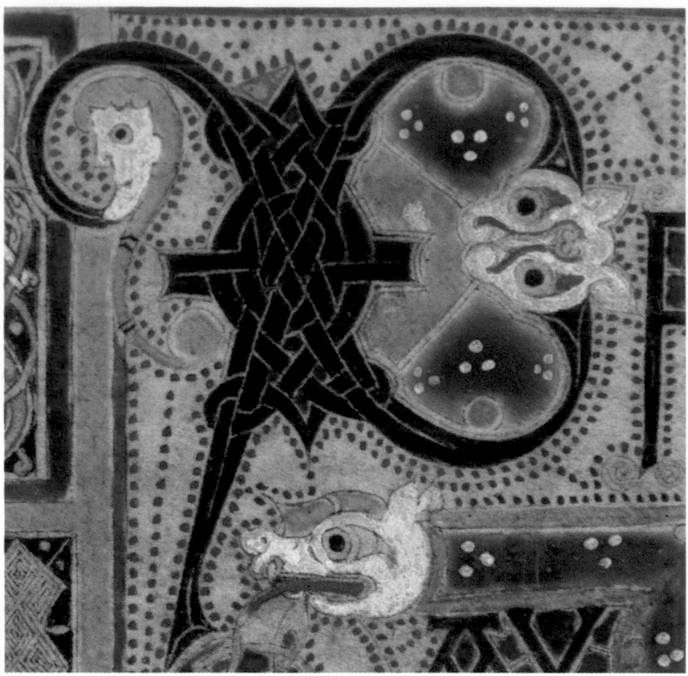

This is one of the finest of the pocket-size Gospel Books manufactured in Ireland during the early Middle Ages and is a masterpiece of 'Insular' book production (i.e. of the islands of Britain and Ireland, *c.*600–900). Each Gospel is introduced by a miniature depicting the relevant Evangelist as author and by a decorated Incipit page bearing the opening words of each Gospel, and the Nativity in Matthew (Chi-rho page). There is also a four-symbols page (f. 1v) in which each Evangelist is represented by his symbol from the apocalyptic vision of Ezekiel: Matthew, the Man; Mark, the lion; Luke, the calf or bull; John, the eagle. These are arranged around a cross, in the manner of other famous earlier Insular Gospel Books, the Book of Durrow, the Lichfield Gospels, the Trier Gospels, the Book of Kells and the Book of Armagh. The volume lacks the usual prefatory Canon Tables (a concordance system devised in the fourth century by Eusebius), but the numbers of the 'Ammonian' sections into which the Gospel texts were divided for means of comparison are nonetheless marked in the adjacent margins of the manuscript and set within orange cartouches.

The book is written in an expert Insular minuscule (lower case), the assured calligraphic nature of which led palaeographer Ludwig Bieler to attribute it to Ferdomnach (d. 846), master scribe of the Book of Armagh (*c.*807). Scholarly consensus, however, favours a date later in the century and, given the conservative nature of Irish scribal tradition, this is not untenable. The style of decoration likewise recalls eighth-century Insular art, but this endures in other Armagh Gospel Books into the twelfth century and a late ninth-century date was favoured by eminent art historian Françoise Henry.

A colophon (f. 3v) was added for King Athelstan of Wessex (reigned 924–939), recording his gift of the volume to Christ Church, Canterbury. It also commemorates the book's former owner, Maelbright MacDurnan (Mael Brigte mac Tornain), Abbot of Armagh (*c.*888) and Raphoe, who died in 927. Athelstan was a renowned collector of books from pre-Viking England, the Celtic areas and the Carolingian Empire. Charters were entered into the volume at Canterbury during the early eleventh century (ff. 69v, 114v, 114r, 115r and on a leaf now in the British Library, Cotton MS Tiberius B.iv, f. 87).

Archbishop Matthew Parker commissioned its current fine gold-tooled binding by the MacDurnan Gospels Binder. A prominent early bibliophile and connoisseur, Parker was probably also responsible for the insertion of four thirteenth-century Psalter miniatures (ff. 4, 71, 116, 171), bringing the scheme of decoration into line with later medieval illumination. In 1754 the book was owned by Archbishop Herring, but by 1755 had passed to Francis Howel, a mathematical instrument maker in London. It was probably acquired for Lambeth by A. C. Ducarel (Librarian from 1757 to 1785).

*Michelle P. Brown*
*Institute of English Studies, University of London*

L. Bieler, 'Insular Palaeography: Present State and Problems', *Scriptorium* 3 (1949), p. 276
P. McGurk, 'The Irish Pocket Gospel Book', *Sacris Erudiri* 8 (1956), pp. 249–70
N. R. Ker, *Catalogue of Manuscripts Containing Anglo-Saxon* (Oxford, 1957; revised edn 1990), no. 284
F. Henry, *Irish Art During the Viking Invasions, 800–1020 AD* (London, 1967), no. 97 and pl. 1
J. J. G. Alexander, *Insular Manuscripts, 6th to the 9th Century. A Survey of Manuscripts Illuminated in the British Isles*, vol. 1 (London, 1978), no. 70
S. Keynes, 'King Athelstan's Books', in *Learning and Literature in Anglo-Saxon England: Studies Presented to Peter Clemoes*, ed. M. Lapidge and H. Gneuss (Cambridge, 1985), pp. 153–89
P. R. Robinson, *Catalogue of Dated and Datable Manuscripts c.888–1600*, 2 vols (London, 2003)
D. Ganz and J. Roberts, *Lambeth Palace Library and its Anglo-Saxon Manuscripts* (London, 2007), pp.24–26, illustrated p. 25
C. A. Farr, 'Irish Pocket Gospels in Anglo-Saxon England', in *Anglo-Saxon Traces*, ed. J. Roberts and L. Webster, forthcoming

+ MÆIELBRIĐUS MAC
DURNANI · ISTŪ · TEXTŪ
· PER · TRIQUADRŪ · DO
DIGNE · DOGMATIZAT ·
925 + AST · AETHELSTANUS ·
ANGLOSÆXNA · REX · ET
RECTOR · DORUERNENSI
METROPOLI · DAT · ÆVŪ ·

# 2 Praising Virginity and Learning Latin

**MS 200, part II (ff. 66–113); Aldhelm, *De virginitate* (prose version)**
Canterbury, St Augustine's Abbey; second half of the tenth century
Latin; vellum; 275 x 200 mm; ff. 48 in a volume of ff. 229
Illustrated: (*below*) Aldhelm presenting his tract to a group of nuns, and the opening of the text, ff. 68v–69r; (*opposite; details*) ff. 94v and 97v, two penwork initials

Aldhelm, Abbot of Malmesbury, then Bishop of Sherborne (639–709/10), was the first Englishman to leave a significant body of writings. His most influential work, judged by the number of surviving copies (19), was a prose treatise on virginity (he also produced a companion-piece in verse). Having discussed virginity in general terms, Aldhelm offered biographies of distinguished celibates, first male (from Old Testament patriarchs to Christian martyrs and confessors), then female (starting with the Virgin Mary), ending, after a diatribe against vanity, with a request for prayers from his readers. These, the dedication and envoi reveal, were nuns, ten of whom he mentions by name. Lauding a chastity appropriate to Anglo-Saxon noblewomen and celebrating the heroism of past worthies in the face of adversity, Aldhelm wrote with broad relevance to the early Anglo-Saxon Church. However, the

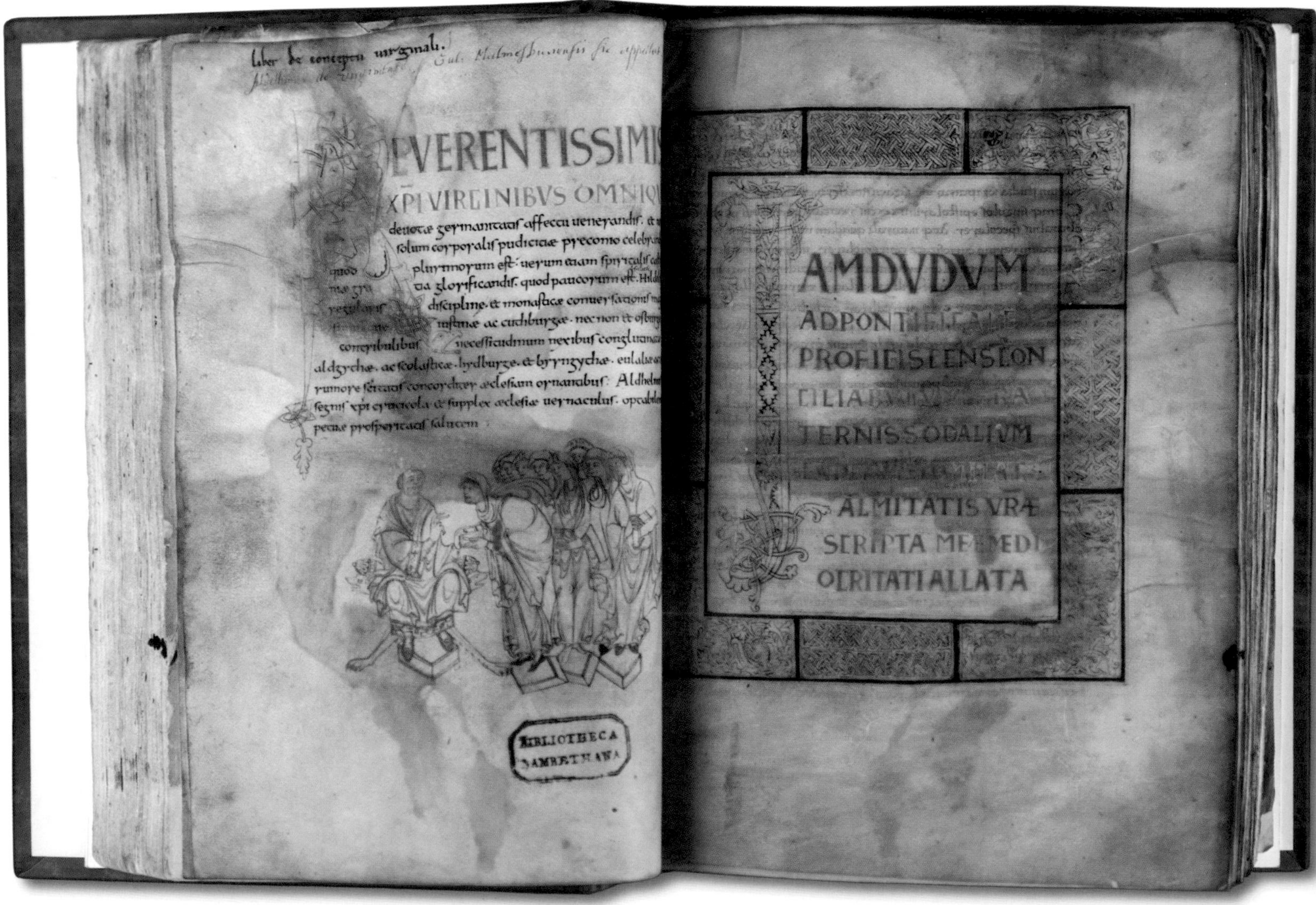

text's fiercely complicated Latin – characterised by long, digressive sentences and arcane vocabulary – made it challenging to read. Indeed, the surviving copies, with a rich tradition of explanatory glossing, suggest that it was often studied more for its language than its content.

The work enjoyed its greatest popularity, the surviving manuscripts indicate, around the millennium at Canterbury. While most of the copies were made at Christ Church (the cathedral), where it was evidently adopted as a 'school' text, this one, the earliest, was written at St Augustine's Abbey; the paucity of glosses suggests that it was a 'library' rather than a 'school' book. Active from the second quarter of the tenth century, the scriptorium of St Augustine's produced library books to a high standard, developing distinctive styles of handwriting and decoration.

The script of the present volume is an elegant synthesis of indigenous and continental traditions (Anglo-Saxon square minuscule and Caroline minuscule respectively), and each chapter is headed by a pen-work initial formed of beast and bird heads, woven into the letter form. Between the Preface (above) and the start of the text proper (opposite) is a depiction of the author – a rare feature for a library book at this date, but here a balanced part of a grand first opening. An enthroned Bishop Aldhelm places his work in the receptive hands of the first of a group of nuns, evoking those named in the Preface. The final woman also holds a book – perhaps alluding to the other version of *De virginitate*, or as a means of showing the studiousness of the tract's original audience. Presenting Aldhelm as a spiritual authority and donor rather than as simply an author, this frontispiece highlights the inspirational dimension of a text that celebrated values central to Benedictine monasticism, which was then in the early stages of a revival. The idea of a portrait was reprised a few years later in a copy of the verse *De virginitate*, made at Christ Church, in which Aldhelm is shown as author and donor. However, the drawing in the present manuscript has the distinction of being not only the earliest image of Aldhelm, but also the first depiction of any English author.

This manuscript was owned by Waltham Abbey by the fourteenth century (inscriptions, ff. 66v–67r) and came to Lambeth via Archbishop Richard Bancroft.

*Richard Gameson*
*Durham University*


T. A. M. Bishop (ed.), *Codex Leidensis Scaligeranus* 69 (Amsterdam, 1966)
E. Temple, *Anglo-Saxon Manuscripts, 900–1066. A Survey of Manuscripts Illuminated in the British Isles*, 2 (London, 1976), no. 39
M. Lapidge and M. W. Herren (eds), *Aldhelm, The Prose Works* (Cambridge, 1979)
S. Gwara (ed.), *Aldhelmi Malmesbiriensis Prosa de Virginitate*, 2 vols (Turnhout, 2001)

# 3 An Anglo-Saxon Glossed Psalter

**MS 427; glossed Gallican Psalter**
England, south-west?; first half of eleventh century
Latin with Old English gloss; vellum; 212 x 158 mm; ff. 213
Illustrated: (*below*) f. 5r, Psalm 1; (*opposite*) ff. 53v–54r

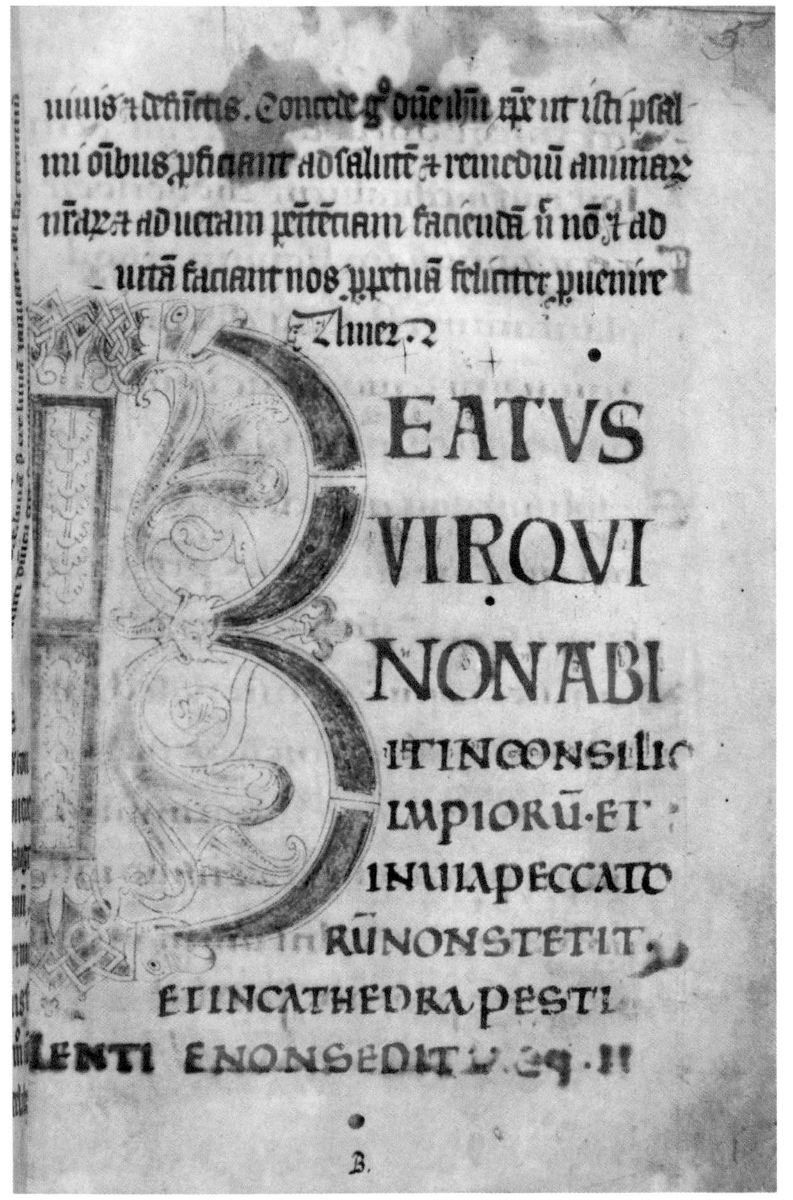

This manuscript is traditionally known as 'the Lambeth Psalter'. It contains Jerome's Gallicanum edition of the Psalter (ff. 5–182v), a confessional prayer (ff. 182v–183v) and fifteen canticles (ff. 184–202v), written in English caroline (Carolingian) minuscule and all, except Psalm 151, glossed in Old English (i.e. with explanatory notes or commentary). The prefatory materials (ff. 1–2) are more closely written than ff. 5–202, which are likely therefore to have been laid out with glosses in mind. The page dimensions would have been greater before trimming. Apart from the initial that opens the Psalter, there is little decoration, save for the use of red for biblical *tituli* (titles) and capitals at the beginning of verses. Yet, this little book is an important witness to psalter scholarship in its day, abreast with up-to-date readings. The text's collations with St Jerome's Hebraicum recension of the Psalter, signalled by enclosure between obelus (÷) and two dots (:), may have been the scribe's own work. Soon after the main text was written, further scholarly information was added: Latin glosses; emendations; and Christian *tituli*.

Although the smallest of the Anglo-Saxon glossed psalters, Lambeth 427 is the most fully and most intelligently equipped with vernacular glosses and is therefore an important witness to English in the early eleventh century. The glossator draws together English words and phrases from a range of glossed psalters; he adds readings from Jerome's Romanum and the Vetus Latina, up-to-date readings and critical signs. The construe marks were written later than the glosses, helping the reader follow the continuous glossing in vernacular word order. Overall it is a sophisticated package, designed for reading, rumination and perhaps teaching in English as well as Latin.

Annotations and additions show that the book continued to be used until the seventeenth century. Among the additional leaves are late eleventh- to early twelfth-century lunar prognostications and tables (ff. 3–4) and a sixteenth- or seventeenth-century supply leaf (after f. 77) with partial English gloss (Pulsiano 1991 and 1997; Ganz and Roberts 2007, illustrated p. 47). A fifteenth-century quire (ff. 203–08) is followed by two leaves (ff. 210–11) from a lost Old English 'History of the Kentish royal saints' (Ker 1957, no.

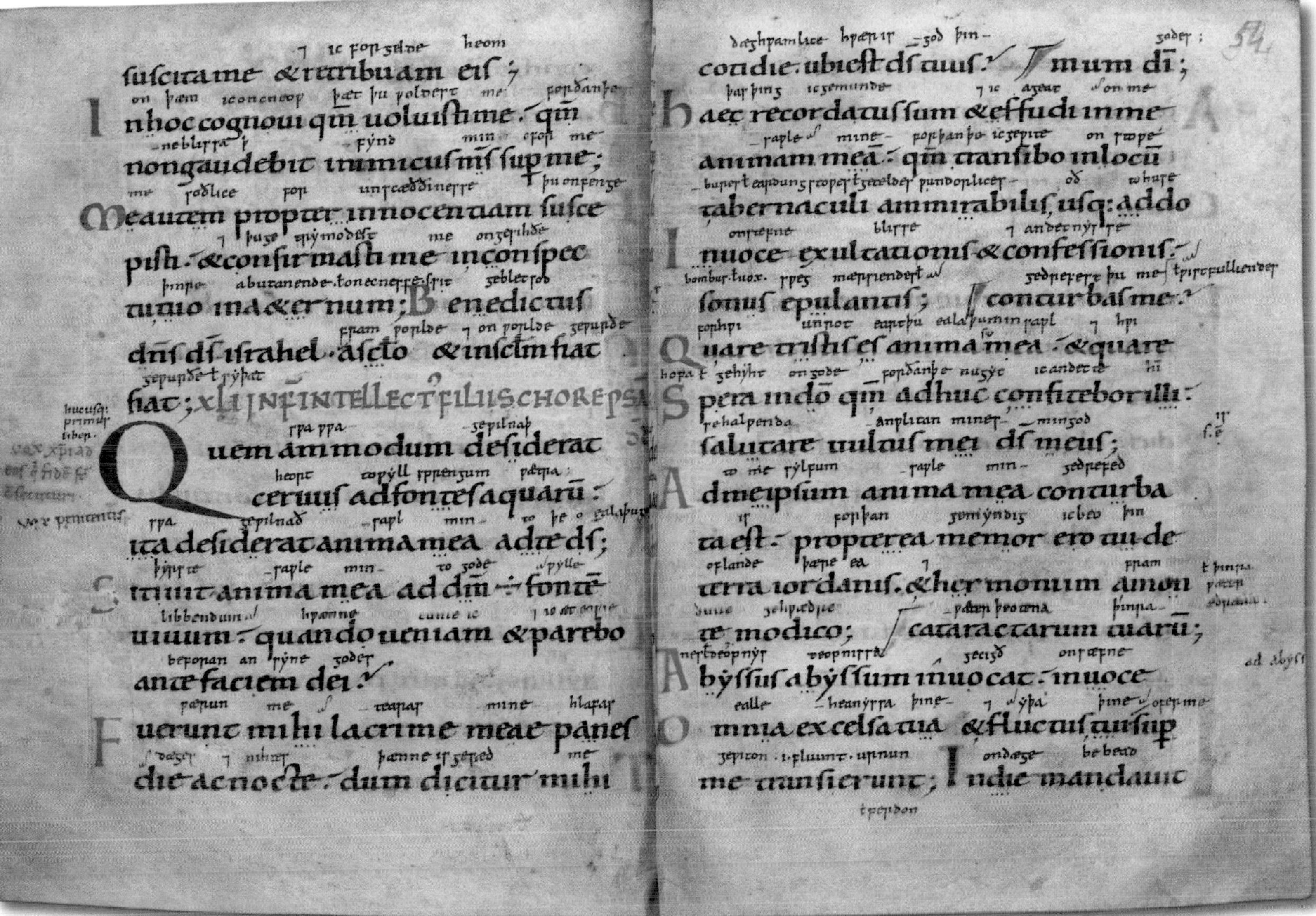

281; Ganz and Roberts 2007, illustrated p. 59). These important eleventh-century fragments, from waste materials used in rebinding this manuscript in the fifteenth century or earlier, are perhaps from a manuscript that once also contained the *Finnsburh Fragment*, a notable Old English poem, known only through its publication by Hickes (1705).

The place of origin is unknown, although there is a strong case for Winchester. It was at Llanthony by the fifteenth century (press-mark, f. 209) and was probably acquired for Lambeth by Archbishop Bancroft.

*Jane Roberts*
*Institute of English Studies, University of London*

G. Hickes, *Linguarum veterum septentrionalium thesaurus* (Oxford, 1705), pp. 192–93
*Der Lambeth Psalter: eine altenglische Interlinearversion des Psalters in der Hs. 427 der erzbischöflichen Lambeth Palace Library*, ed. U. Lindelöf, 2 vols, Acta Societatis Scientiarum Fennicae, 35/1 and 43/3 (1909; 1914)
N. R. Ker, *Catalogue of Manuscripts Containing Anglo-Saxon* (Oxford, 1957), no. 280–82
M. J. Swanton, 'A Fragmentary Life of St Mildred and Other Kentish Royal Saints', *Archaeologia Cantiana* 91 (1976 for 1975), pp. 15–27
P. P. O'Neill, 'Latin Learning at Winchester in the Early Eleventh century: The Evidence of the Lambeth Psalter', *Anglo-Saxon England* 20 (1991), pp. 143–66
P. Pulsiano, 'The Old English Gloss of the Lambeth Psalter and its Relations', *Neuphilologische Mitteilungen* 92 (1991), pp. 195–210
P. Pulsiano, 'A Middle English Gloss in the Lambeth Psalter', *ANQ: American Notes and Queries* 10.1 (1997), pp. 2–9
D. Ganz and J. Roberts, *Lambeth Palace Library and its Anglo-Saxon Manuscripts* (London, 2007), pp. 45–48
J. Roberts, 'The Finnsburh Fragment, and its Lambeth Provenance', *Notes and Queries* 253 (2008), pp. 122–24

IC XC

# 4 Greek Manuscripts

Collection of manuscripts, tenth to seventeenth century, including:

**MS 1187; Gospel lectionary**
Eleventh century, 256 x 186 mm
Illustrated: (*opposite*) binding of red silk over wooden boards, with metal corner pieces depicting the Evangelists and a crucifix in the centre

**MS 461; Anti-Catholic treatise by George Scholarios**
*c.*1450–54; 187 x 141 mm, ii, 305 ff.
Illustrated: (*below; detail*) f. 1r, with signature of Meletios Pegas (1549–1601), Patriarch of Alexandria

Lambeth's collection of 53 Greek manuscripts, dating from the tenth to the seventeenth centuries, is the fruit of continued Anglican contact with the Orthodox world. The largest number are New Testament texts or lectionaries, with theological works, a few Classical authors, and two post-Byzantine texts. The one Old Testament manuscript, an Octateuch with biblical commentaries dating from the twelfth century, was copied for Leo Nikerites, Duke of Cyprus.

The first Greek manuscript to enter the Library was donated by Archbishop Abbot; MS 461, an anti-Catholic treatise entitled *On the Causes of the Schism* by George Scholarios (later Ecumenical Patriarch Gennadios II), was possibly a gift to Abbot from Patriarch Cyril Loukaris and may have come into Loukaris's possession when he succeeded Meletios I Pegas as Patriarch of Alexandria in 1601. The title page bears at its foot the monocondyle (interlaced cursive), signature of Meletios.

A significant cache of manuscripts was acquired by Archbishop Manners-Sutton in 1806 following the death of the Revd J. D. Carlyle, Professor of Arabic at Cambridge. Carlyle had spent the years from 1799 to 1801 travelling in the eastern Mediterranean while chaplain to the British Ambassador to the Sublime Porte. He visited numerous libraries, bringing back a haul of 37 manuscripts (MSS 1175–1207 and MS 1214), though some were later returned to Jerusalem. Carlyle's object had been to collect biblical texts with a view to collating them and publishing a new edition of the Bible. The Library holds some fruits of this work in MSS 1223, 1224, 1255 and 1259, supervised by the Classical scholar Charles Burney.

Fourteen Greek manuscripts were acquired in 1996 with the library of Sion College, London. Four were gifts of Sir Paul Pindar, possibly acquired during his time as Ambassador in Constantinople from 1611. In 1777, Edward Payne donated five volumes inherited from his great-uncle Thomas Payne, chaplain at Constantinople.

About a third of the volumes retain their original Byzantine bindings, from coarse cloth or leather to velvet-covered boards with embossed metal furnishings. Most of the volumes contain interesting decoration, such as MS 1176 with its miniatures of the Evangelists and rubbed but colourful depictions of the Nativity and the Resurrection, and Arc L40.2/G5 with its vignettes of the story of Dives and Lazarus. Some contain fascinating idiosyncrasies; instructions for finding buried treasure (MS 1199, f. 144v), a shopping list, a sighting of Halley's comet, a diagram of the celestial spheres, names of the months in Arabic and details of ownership. All are a testament to the close links between the Orthodox Church and the Church of England and remain a vital tool for Greek scholarship.

*Clare Brown*
*Lambeth Palace Library, London*

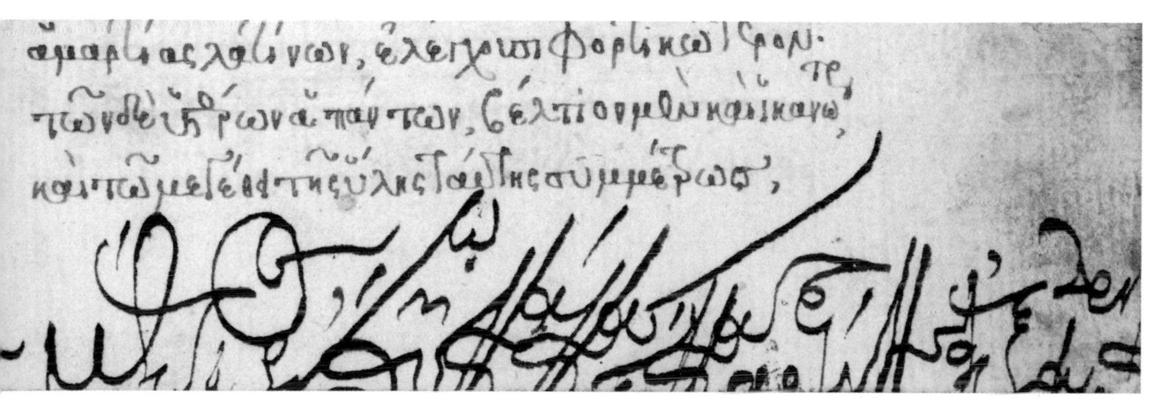

H. J. Todd, *An Account of Greek Manuscripts, chiefly Biblical, which had been in the possession of the late Professor Carlyle, the greater part of which are now deposited in the Archiepiscopal Library at Lambeth Palace* (London, 1823)
*The Greek Manuscript Collection of Lambeth Palace Library: An Exhibition held on the Occasion of the 21st International Byzantine Congress, London, 22–23 August 2006* (London, 2006)

# 5 Collecting Anselm

**MS 224; Anselm's collected treatises and letters, compiled by William of Malmesbury**
Malmesbury; *c.*1120–24
Latin; vellum; 285 x 193 mm, ff. ii, 213
Illustrated: (*below; detail*) f. 40r, opening of Anselm's treatise *Cur Deus Homo*; (*opposite*) f. 152r, letters to Anselm from King Henry I and Pope Paschal II

**MS 59; Anselm's collected letters**
Christ Church Canterbury; *c.*1125–30
Latin; vellum; 363 x 265 mm; ff. ii, 278

Born *c.*1033, Archbishop Anselm died at Canterbury in 1109. In his lifetime he had published more than a dozen treatises of theology and philosophy, as well as devotional works and letters intended to develop a monk's vocation. He had also gained international fame for the stand he took against the royal control of episcopal appointments, which had taken him into exile twice in the reigns of King William II (r. 1087–1100) and King Henry I (r. 1100–35). In the decade after his death his sermons and addresses were collected by his disciples. His former secretary, Eadmer, wrote two accounts of his life: one in hagiographical terms, including miracles attributed to Anselm; the other in historical terms, documenting the career of the Archbishop as a defender of the Church.

These two manuscripts provide direct testimony to the consolidation of Anselm's writings for a new generation in the 1120s.

The earlier of the two, MS 224, was written in the 1120s. It is a compilation of Anselm's treatises and a collection of his letters made by William of Malmesbury (*c.*1090–*c.*1143), monk of Malmesbury, scholar and historian. In the course of his career William arranged for many texts to be copied, and he was often personally involved in writing such copies, as he was in this example. Much of the book is in William's own hand, recognisable from many examples elsewhere, while the remainder is written by the copyists who worked with him. William brought together in one volume treatises which he had probably found as booklets and he compiled a systematic collection of letters from various sources. One such source was Eadmer's account of Anselm's career, which included some 60 letters, but William also used at least two other collections of letters.

The later and larger volume, MS 59, contains the major collection of Anselm's letters, made at Christ Church Cathedral Priory in Canterbury and copied towards the end of the 1120s. It is one of three closely related copies of this collection but, unlike the others, this one remained at Canterbury until the Dissolution. The letter collection, when first copied, occupied ff. 1r–159v and was followed by a few leaves on which some disjointed passages of Anselm's teaching had been copied, now ff. 187r–190. At an early date, however, additional leaves were inserted as ff. 160–181 and the original blank end-leaves were moved to become ff. 182–186. These leaves were used to include some additional letters, documents and more passages of Anselm's teaching, including some duplicate copies. The distinctive Christ Church handwriting and the evidence of access to Anselm's papers persuaded Dom F. S. Schmitt, Anselm's twentieth-century editor, that this manuscript was a prototype of the letter collection made under Anselm's own direction. Greater understanding of the development of the Christ Church hand and comparison with other copies now shows this belief to be incorrect.

*Richard Sharpe*
*Wadham College, Oxford*

N. R. Ker, 'William of Malmesbury's Handwriting', *English Historical Review* 59 (1944), pp. 371–76
F. S. Schmitt, 'Die unter Anselm veranstaltete Ausgabe seiner Werke und Briefe: die Codices Bodley 271 und Lambeth 59', *Scriptorium* 9 (1955), pp. 64–75
R. W. Southern, *Anselm. A Portrait in a Landscape* (Cambridge, 1990), pp. 470–81
R. M. Thomson, *William of Malmesbury* (Woodbridge, 2003), pp. 86–88

93 Henricus dei gratia rex anglorum anselmo archiepiscopo cantuarie salutem. In die sancti georgii apud tonebrigge michi fuerunt delate littere reposite in tuo sigillo. Et per eas michi mandasti talia unde multum miror: quia quod feci credo me per te fecisse. Et in die ascensionis domini habebo omnes barones meos simul congregatos et per consilium eorum ita convenienter tibi respondebo quod cum tecum locutus fuero non credo me esse inde blasphematum. Et quicquid fiat alias, scito quia tu et quicquid ipsi fecerint, per omnes terras tuas in pace permanserint.

94 Suo reverendo domino henrico gratia dei regi anglorum anselmus archiepiscopus cantuarie fidele servitium cum orationibus. Gratias ago deo et dignationi vestre que in litteris suis promisit se convenienter responsuram michi de hoc unde precatus eam fueram in litteris meis de sacerdotibus anglie. Et oro dominum cuius consilium manet in eternum ut ipse vobis consulat respondere et facere quod illi placeat, et unde fideles dilectores anime vestre gaudeant. De hoc autem quod legi in litteris vestris quia creditis vos facere per me quod facitis: pro certo scitote mi domine quia non est per me. Quin contra deum facerem si per me esset. Quapropter adhuc precor magno et fideli affectu, quatinus in tali incepto nullius consilio persistatis.

95 Henricus rex anglorum anselmo archiepiscopo salutem et amicitiam. De hoc quod michi mandasti de sacerdotibus scias scias quod ita decenter feci ut opinor secundum quod facere debui. Nec tibi sit incognitum brevi intervallo temporis me consiliaturum. Et ex quo tecum loquutus fuero: tibi quod commisi in hac re omnipotentis dei et tuo consilio dirigam. Teste Waldrico cancellario apud merlebergam.

96 Paschalis episcopus servus servorum dei venerabili fratri et illustrissimo rotomagensi episcopo salutem et apostolicam benedictionem. Licet cause tue qualitas patientiam nostram plurimum gravet, pre reverentia tamen fratris nostri cantuariensis episcopi et dilectione latoris presentium filii nostri willelmi qui pro te apud nos vehementer intercesserunt paterna penes te benignitate movemur. Causam itaque tuam eidem fratri cantuariensi episcopo commisimus, ut quod ipse indulserit indulgeamus, eo nimirum intuitu ea conditione, ut malos consiliarios quorum instinctu multas pravitates incurristi a tua familiaritate repellas.

97 Pascalis episcopus servus servorum dei venerabili fratri anselmo cantuariensi archiepiscopo salutem et apostolicam benedictionem. Quod anglici regis cor ad apostolice sedis obedientiam omnipotentis dei dignatio inclinavit: eidem miserationum domino gratias agimus in cuius manu regum corda versantur. Hoc nimirum tue caritatis gratia tuarumque orationum instantia factum credimus ut in hac parte populum illum cui tua sollicitudo presidet miseratio superna respiceret. Quod autem et regi et nobis quodam obnoxium videntur adeo condescendimus eo affectu et compassione factum noveris ut eos qui iacebant erigere valeamus. Qui enim stans iacenti ad sublevandum manum porrigit, numquam iacentem eriget nisi et ipse curvetur. Ceterum quamvis casui propinquare inclinatio videatur, statum tamen rectitudinis non amittit. Te autem frater in christo

reuersi sunt p tribus & familias in
tabernacula sua. In diebȝ illis n̄ erat
rex in isrl. s; unusquisq; qd rectu sibi
uidebat. hoc faciebat. Explicit liber
sopthim id est iudicum. habet uersus
mille septingentos. Incip capl libri ruth.

I Facta fame intra iude elimelech de bethleem iuda
abiit cum uxore sua noemi & duobȝ filiis intra
moabitide causa uictualium q mortuo filii acci-
pientes uxores & ipsi mortui sunt.

II Noemi reuertente ad patriā ruth nurus deserere
noluit. que perueniens in bethleem iuda perexit in
agrum booz ad colligendas spicas.

III Booz dat licentiam ruth ut de agro ei colligat spi
cas & hora uescendi cū messoribȝ comedat; peo

res usq; ad dauid. Explicitunt capitula.

Incipit prefatio Sci Ieronimi prbi
in librum ruth.

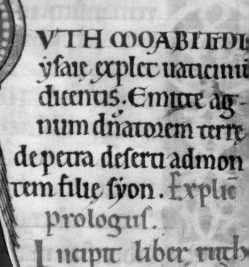

RUTH MOABITIDI
ysaie explet uaticinium
dicentis. Emitte agnum dnatorem terre
de petra deserti ad montem filie syon. Explic
prologus.

Incipit liber ruth

# 6 The Lambeth Bible

**MS 3; Bible, vol. 1 only**
South-east England, Canterbury?; *c.*1150–70
Latin; vellum; ff. 328, 518 x 353 mm
Illustrated: (*opposite; detail*) f. 130r, panel depicting Ruth and Boaz with text and initial 'R' above; (*right; detail*) f. 198v, initial 'V' depicting Isaiah sawn in two; (*overleaf left*) f. 285v, scenes from the Book of Daniel; (*overleaf right*) 198r, Jesse Tree (Isaiah xi), prophecy of the coming of Christ; (*front cover*) f. 6r, Jacob's ladder (Genesis 28)

Sets of enormous manuscript Bibles, in Latin, were produced for many monasteries throughout western Europe in the twelfth century. The fashion for such books derives from the reforms of Gregory VII (Pope from 1073 to 1085), who re-affirmed the centrality of the entire Bible in religious and monastic life. These monumental manuscripts were probably used for reading aloud in church and refectory, and they undoubtedly became competitive symbols of a monastery's prestige, wealth and visible commitment to the ancient Scriptures. Professional illuminators were sometimes employed to embellish the manuscripts, which were often on a scale beyond the modest domestic skills of the monks.

About a dozen giant Bibles survive, in part or entirety, from Romanesque England, of which the finest are undoubtedly the Bury Bible (*c.*1130–40; Corpus Christi College, Cambridge, MS 2), the Lambeth Bible (*c.*1150–70) and the Winchester Bible (*c.*1160–80; still in Winchester Cathedral). All three were principally painted by secular or itinerant craftsmen. The Bury Bible was made by a professional painter and metal worker recorded there as Master Hugo. The hand of the main artist of the Lambeth Bible is found also in fragments of a Gospel Book made for the abbot of Liessies in Hainault before 1147 (Société Archéologique, Avesnes). The Winchester Bible illuminators may even have worked on frescoes in north-east Spain. All these painters probably travelled from place to place seeking work.

No one knows where the Lambeth Bible was illuminated, except that it was undoubtedly in south-east England. Its obvious expense suggests a community of some wealth and status. By 1538, it was apparently at Lenham, in Kent, a parish connected with St Augustine's Abbey, Canterbury, and it is certainly possible that it was intended for St Augustine's, the oldest monastery in southern England. This is the the conclusion of default reached by Dorothy M. Shepard (2007), mainly by elimination of obvious possibilities. However, there is no trace of it in the extensive surviving inventories of that abbey.

When the Bible entered Lambeth Palace Library in the foundation bequest in 1610, it comprised two volumes of rather different appearance: Genesis–Job (MS 3) and Psalms–Revelations (MS 4). In 1924, Eric Millar realised that MS 4 was a later mismatch and that the original volume two of the Lambeth Bible was a mutilated remnant owned by All Saints' Church, Maidstone (now Maidstone Museum, MS P.5). MS 4 has consequently been sidelined, although it may, or may not, still have a bearing on the provenance of the Lambeth–Maidstone set.

Like many giant Romanesque Bibles, the Lambeth Bible was left partially unfinished. The funding may have dried up, or the artist may have died or moved on. Other illuminations have been cut out or lost. Nonetheless, the six huge paintings and 24 historiated initials which remain are among the most beautiful of the twelfth century. The style reflects the new fascination with Byzantine art. Figures with sad faces and swirling draperies step through their roles, as if re-enacting biblical history in a graceful and silent ballet.

*Christopher de Hamel*
*Corpus Christi College, Cambridge*


E. G. Millar in *Bulletin de la Société Française de Reproduction de Manuscrits à Peintures* 8 (1924), pp. 15–31, pls 2–10

C. R. Dodwell, *The Great Lambeth Bible* (London, 1959)

C. M. Kauffmann, *Romanesque Manuscripts, 1066–1190. A Survey of Manuscripts Illuminated in the British Isles* 3 (London, 1975), no. 70, pp. 99–100, ills. 192–95 and figs 30, 32 and 36

D. M. Shepard, *Introducing the Lambeth Bible* (Turnhout, 2007) manifestissima pdicatione annotat. Explicit plog.

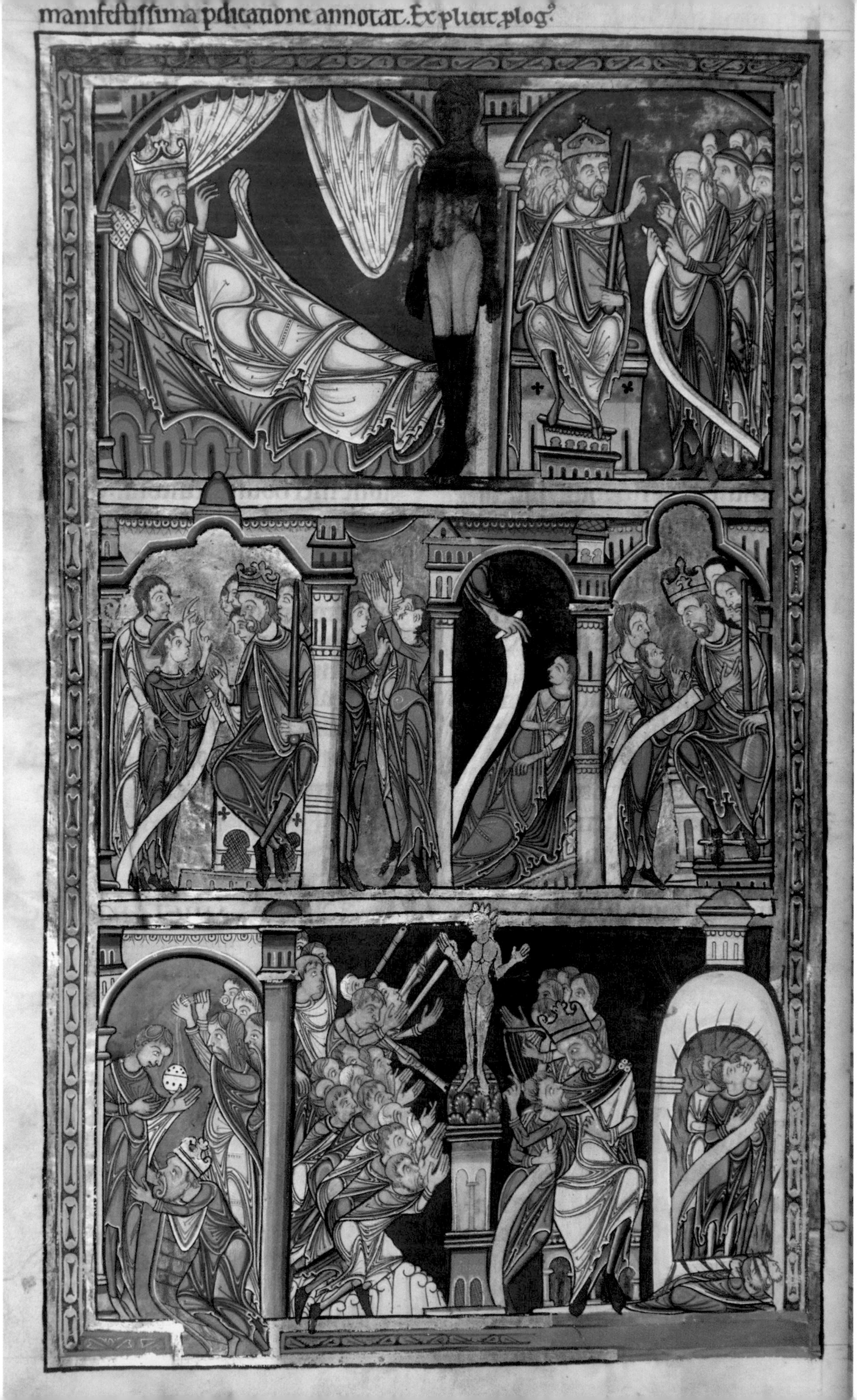

ABBAS
hic manet indignitate:
Sed cum caritate.
Volens
Dominatur.
iudice volens.
hec rota: est re
ligiosi uita.
Axis stridet: dum
fr p peccatis dolet:
Axis silet: dum
fr in pace manet
Sponte sub
esse nolo
Sponte
subicitur
hic sedet in paupertate sed cum hilaritate.
Claustralis

# 7 The Wheel of True and False Religion

**MS 107; Hugo de Folieto, *De claustro animae* and *De rota verae et falsae religionis***
England, a Cistercian house (later owned by Buildwas Abbey);
second half of the twelfth century
Latin; vellum; 316 x 220 mm; ff. ii + 94
Illustrated: (*opposite*) f. 84v, the wheel of true religion;
(*right; detail*) f. 57r, decorated initial C

The works of Hugh of Fouilloy (*c.*1100–73), also known as Hugo de Folieto, Augustinian canon and prior of St-Laurent-au-Bois, near Amiens, were widely read in the Middle Ages, particularly by the Cistercians. His *De claustro animae*, datable after 1153, and *De rota verae et falsae religionis*, composed sometime between 1132 and 1150 (Gobry 1995), are both found in this twelfth-century volume from the Cistercian abbey of Buildwas, Shropshire. Scribal use of the *punctus flexus* (a punctuation mark resembling a 'U' above a point, used like a comma) indicates Cistercian origin, but how Buildwas acquired the manuscript is unknown. The *ex libris* ('Liber Sancte Marie De Bildewas', f. ii) from the end of the century shows that the volume was already at Buildwas by this date and bears witness to the rapid diffusion of Hugh's writings.

Whereas red and green initials with stylised foliage alternate to indicate divisions in *De claustro* (ff. 1–83v), two full-page coloured drawings (ff. 84v and 89r) illustrate *De rota* (ff. 83v–93v). These expressive and harmonious drawings demonstrate English artists' particular flair for the technique. They form an essential part of the text and derive from Hugh himself. De Clercq (1963) was unaware of Lambeth MS 107 when he proposed that the twelfth-century manuscript HS 226 in the Heiligenkreuz Stiftsbibliothek best represented the original diagrams.

Deploying the metaphor of the wheel of fortune, Hugh of Fouilloy uses the wheels to contrast the true and false religious life. Inscriptions in their rings and spokes quote the text, while those in the outer frames explain the figures. The monk seated at the foot of the wheel of virtuous religion rises unwillingly on the left to become prior, and, as abbot, rules with dignity and charity, before renouncing his position out of humility. While the good monk in the first drawing is portrayed as a scribe, with a quill in his right hand and penknife in his left, writing the opening of Psalm 1, 'Beatus vir …', the bad monk in the second drawing sits idly, with furrowed brow,

at the foot of the wheel of false religion. He becomes Prior through bribery, and, as abbot, rules with pride, and is deposed because of negligence. It is interesting to note that the figure of the good abbot was the model for an image of St Bernard in an early thirteenth-century copy of his sermons written and decorated at Buildwas, Balliol College, Oxford, MS 150, f. 2v (Sheppard 1997).

*Pamela Robinson*
*Institute of English Studies, University of London*

C. De Clercq (ed.), 'Le "Liber de Rota Verae Religionis" d'Hugues de Fouilloy', *Archivum Latinitatis Medii Aevi* 29 (1959), pp. 219–28, 30 (1960), pp. 15–37
C. De Clercq, 'Hugues de Fouilloy, imagier de ses propres œuvres?', *Révue du Nord* 45 (1963), pp. 31–42
C. Dereine, 'Hugues de Fouilloy', *Dictionnaire d'histoire et de géographie ecclésiastique* 17 (1971), cols 1271–78
I. Gobry, *Le De Claustro Animae d'Hugues de Fouilloy* (Amiens, 1995)
J. M. Sheppard, *The Buildwas Books: Book Production, Acquisition and Use at an English Cistercian Monastery, 1165–c.1400* (Oxford, 1997)

# 8 Llanthony Priory Manuscripts

**MS 239; Clement of Llanthony, *In Epistolas Catholicas***
Llanthony Priory; late twelfth century
Latin; vellum; 270 x 200 mm, ff. 280
Illustrated: (*below; detail*) folio preceding 1r, initial 'C', for Clement

**MS 119; John of Llanthony, *In Apocalipsim***
Llanthony Priory; late twelfth century
Latin; vellum; 315 x 230 mm, ff. 213
Illustrated: (*opposite*) f. 72r

Lambeth Palace Library holds approximately 120 manuscript books from Llanthony Priory. Overall, approximately 180 manuscripts (and two printed books) from Llanthony are extant, the largest corpus from any Augustinian religious community in England and Wales. Ranging in date from the ninth to the sixteenth century and from attractive copies of theological works to untidy students' textbooks, they reveal that the Augustinian canons obtained books by manufacturing them in-house, by buying them and by donation and that individual impetus significantly shaped the collection.

Llanthony began life around 1100 as a hermitage in the remote Welsh Black Mountains. Finding themselves on the front line of hostilities along the English–Welsh border, the canons were forced to flee in 1136. Their refuge on the outskirts of Gloucester grew into a daughter-house that soon eclipsed the original foundation in size and wealth. No longer cloistered from the world, Llanthony began a half-century of vigorous efforts to acquire essential texts. Among approximately 65 surviving volumes of *c.*1150–*c.*1200, several contain the work of Llanthony's in-house scholars. Always of high rank within the community, these scholars are likely to have been the very individuals who attempted to build up a wider book collection there.

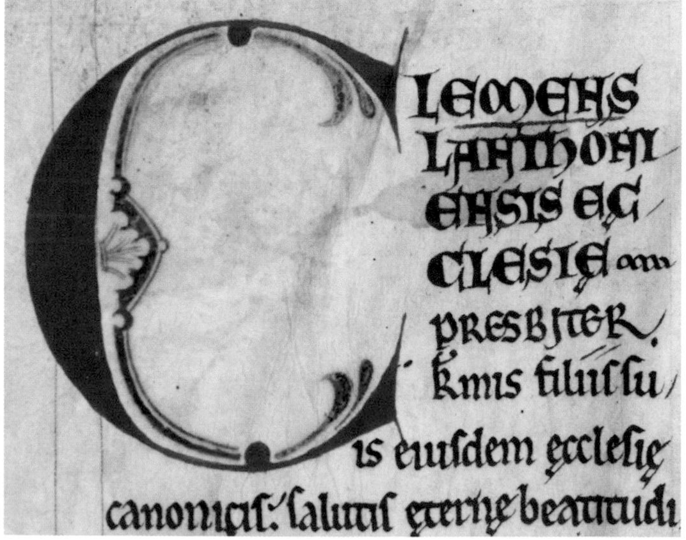

Some, such as Clement of Llanthony (Prior from *c.*1150 to post-1169), whose commentary on the Catholic Epistles survives solely in Lambeth MS 239, achieved a measure of repute. By contrast, John of Llanthony is known only from MS 119. Inscribed *Johannes supprior super Apocalipsim*, this late-twelfth-century book is the unique copy of his commentary on the Apocalypse. It consists of salient passages from esteemed authors, interwoven and identified by marginal notes – the page illustrated here demonstrates John's knowledge of Augustine and Jerome. Other annotations, erasures and insertions in the text indicate its revision and suggest that MS 119 was John's own copy. Folio 72r opens the second *visio* of John's commentary, which is heralded by the finest initial in the volume. Its design of delicate internal fringing and open circles is related to one found otherwise only in a group of books produced at Llanthony a generation earlier.

After 1250 Llanthony never again acquired books in such numbers or in such an organised manner. Nonetheless, the efforts of the early canons had borne fruit: a cataloguer of *c.*1350 recorded around 500 volumes in the Priory's library. As with so many medieval collections, the precise whereabouts of Llanthony's books between its Dissolution in 1538 and the early 1600s is unclear. Some were acquired by local collectors, through whom they reached Oxford colleges, but the bulk probably passed from Llanthony's last prior via his kinsman and executor Thomas Theyer to Archbishop Bancroft. Many Llanthony volumes (including MS 119) are listed in the 1612 inventory of the books that Bancroft bequeathed to Lambeth.

*Kirsty Bennett*
*Independent Scholar*


N. R. Ker (ed.), *Medieval Libraries of Great Britain, A List of Surviving Books*, 2nd edn (London, 1964) and N. R. Ker and A. G. Watson (eds), *Medieval Libraries of Great Britain: Supplement to the Second Edition* (London, 1987)
T. Webber and A. Watson (eds), *The Libraries of the Augustinian Canons*, Corpus of British Medieval Library Catalogues 6 (London, 1998), lists A16 and A17
K. Bennett, 'The Book Collections of Llanthony Priory from Foundation until Dissolution (*c.*1100–1538)', Ph.D thesis (University of Kent, 2006)

VIS II

molatione agni. qui non sine carne
liber primo aperitur et per ea .vii. signacula
ei solvitur. Primum enim ea que veteris te-
stamento prefigurabantur aperienda erant.
deinde que per .vii. status ecclesie clausa
tenebantur manifestanda. Incipiens
ergo a primo adventu Christi et a prima predica-
tione baptismatis in apertione primi
sigilli peregit revelationem misterio-
rum usque ad secundum adventum per angelum
habentem signum dei vivi. quod ostendit
in fine apertionis sexti sigilli. et in apertione septimi sigilli factum est silenti-
um in celo .i. in ecclesia quasi dimidia
hora quia initium beate vite et eterne
quietis. His perlibatis veniamus
ad expositionem secunde visionis.

Visio secunda de revelatione miste-
riorum per apertionem libri veteris
testamenti et novi et .vii. sigillorum.

POST HEC VIDI ET ECCE HOSTIUM APERTUM IN CELO. Et vox prima quam audivi tamquam tube loquentis mecum dicens. Ascende huc et ostendam que oportet fieri cito post hec. Augustinus super apo-
calipsim sermone tertio.

Ostium apertum Christum dicit
quia ianua est. Celum ecclesiam
dicit ubi celestia geruntur.
sicut apostolus dicit instaurata
re omnia que in celis et que in terra sunt.
Celum intellige primitivam ecclesiam de
iudeis. terram vero ex gentibus. Quod autem
dicit post hec in adversitatem temporis re-

ferendum est. secundum ordinem visionum. Vidit enim hec in corporeo intuitu secundum istius sic
sed dictum est: dominica die. post ea scilicet que
supra vidit: vidit et ista que sequuntur.
Primasius sup
hunc locum sic ait. Ostium apertum
Christum dicit natum et passum. ac suscitatum.
quia ianua ipso dicente. ego sum hostium.
Celum ecclesiam dicit quod sit habitaculum
dei ubi celestia geruntur. Hoc est quod sic
in celo voluntatem dei fieri postulamus
in terra. Aliqui autem celum et terram ecclesiam dicunt. quia terra que celum consistit.
Sive cum infideles rectis fidelium
predicationibus adquiruntur. sive cum
caro spiritui subditur. sive cum terrena cele-
stibus reconciliata iunguntur. Ieronimus. Ostium apertum in celo no-
vi testamenti predicator. Vidit iohannes. et dicit
ei ascende huc. Quando apertum osten-
ditur clausum fuisse hominibus manife-
stum est. Satis autem et plene satis patefactum
est. quando Christus in corpore in celis ad pa-
trem ascendit. Et vox prima quam audivi
divit tamquam tube loquentis mecum
dicens. Ascende huc et ostendam
que oportet fieri cito post hec. Ieronimus super apocalipsim. Vox autem prior
quam audierat cum dicit illum secum
locutum. sine contradictione arguuntur
qui alium in propheta, illum in evangelio dicunt fuisse locutum. cum magis ipse qui
venit ipse in prophetis locutus est. Iohannes
enim ex circumcisione erat. et omnis ille
populus veteris testamenti qui ei predica-
tionem audierat. illa voce edificatur.
Illa eademque vox inquit quam audieram
illa me dicit ascende huc. idem scilicet ipse quem
paulo ante filium hominis inter can-
delabra aurea ambulantem se vidisse

Ieronimus

clausum

Ieronimus

# 9 The Lambeth Apocalypse

**MS 209; Apocalypse (Book of Revelation) with commentary by Berengaudus**
London?; *c.*1260–67
Latin; vellum; 272 x 200 mm; ff. ii + 54
Illustrated: (*right; detail*) f.48r Eleanor de Quincy, patroness of the book; (*opposite*) f. 1r, John on Patmos woken by the Angel (Rev. 1: 9–11); (*overleaf*) f. 7v, the Four Angels holding the Winds; the Angel with the Sign of the Living God (Rev. 7: 1–3); f. 8r, the Multitude adore God and the Lamb; the Ancient explains to John (Rev. 7: 9–17)

From the mid-thirteenth century to *c.*1275 there was great interest in England in illustrated Apocalypses, of which this is one of the finest. The text of St John's Book of Revelation, composed at the end of the first century, is accompanied by extracts from an eleventh-century theological commentary by Berengaudus explicating its complex allegories and symbols, accompanied by 78 pictures.

St John's visions on Patmos narrate events leading to the Last Judgement and the establishment of the New Jerusalem and are mainly concerned with a struggle between the forces of Good and Evil, with the eventual triumph of the righteous and destruction of the wicked. After the first visions, in which Christ appears to John among seven candlesticks with a sword in his mouth, John is instructed to write to the seven churches of Asia. His letters warn of the tribulations these churches are suffering, and encourage them to prevail against them.

The reasons for the popularity of illustrated Apocalypses in mid-thirteenth-century England are various. The book was interpreted in its commentary as referring to a reign of Antichrist which would lead to the end of the world and Second Coming, heralding a new heaven and earth as described in the final two chapters, ending with the contemplation of the throne of God and the Lamb. This interest in the last things, although often prevalent in the Middle Ages, was particularly pronounced during the mid-thirteenth-century in England. Prophecies circulated forecasting the end of the world: events surrounding Emperor Frederick II led to him being identified as the Antichrist; the Tartar invasion of eastern Europe in 1241 was equated by some with the tribes of Gog and Magog, who join Satan to attack the holy city.

In the 1250s and 1260s, at the time when the artist of the Lambeth Apocalypse was working, English painters came under the influence of contemporary painting in French 'court style'. A centre of French influence in the period was Westminster Abbey, and it is possible that the Lambeth Apocalypse was made in London.

At the end of the book there is a picture of Eleanor de Quincy, Countess of Winchester, kneeling before the Virgin and Child. The book was probably made for her after the death of her husband, Roger de Quincy, in 1264, and before her marriage to Roger de Leybourne in 1267.

*Nigel J. Morgan*
*Corpus Christi College, Cambridge*

G. Henderson, 'Studies in English Manuscript Illumination I, II, III', *Journal of the Warburg and Courtauld Institutes*, 30 (1967), pp. 71–104, 104–37; 31 (1968), pp. 103–47
N. J. Morgan, *Early Gothic Manuscripts* [II] *1250–1285. A Survey of Manuscripts Illuminated in the British Isles*, vol. 4 Part 2 (London, 1988), no. 126, pp. 101–06, ills. 133–141; colour pl. on p. 17; fig. 10
N. J. Morgan and M. P. Brown, *The Lambeth Apocalypse, Manuscript 209 in Lambeth Palace Library* (London, 1990)
S. Lewis, *Reading Images. Narrative Discourse and Reception in the Thirteenth-Century Illuminated Apocalypse* (Cambridge, 1995)

I.

Incipit plogus apocalipsis iohannis apostoli.
Apocalipsis iohannis tot habet sacramenta:
quot uerba. Parum dictum est: et pro
merito uoluminis. laus omnis inferior est.
In uerbis singulis: multiplices latent intelli-
gentie. Explicit plogus. Incipit apoc. ioh.
Apocalypsis ihu xpi
quam dedit illi deus
palam facere seruis
suis. que oportet fieri cito. et significauit mit-
tens per angelum suum
seruo suo iohi: qui te-
stimonium perhibuit
uerbo dei: et testimonium ihu quecumque uidit.
Beati qui legunt et qui audiunt uerba prophetie huius.
et seruant ea que in ea scripta sunt. Tempus enim prope
est. Iohannes septem ecclesiis que sunt in asya.
gratia uobis et pax ab eo qui est. et qui erat. et qui
uenturus est: et a septem spiritibus qui in conspectu throni eius sunt: et ab ihu xpo qui est
testis fidelis. primogenitus mortuorum et princeps regum
terre. Qui dilexit nos et lauit nos a peccatis nostris in
sanguine suo. et fecit nos regnum et sacerdotes
deo et patri suo. ipsi gloria et imperium in secula seculorum
amen. Ecce uenit cum nubibus. et uidebit eum
omnis oculus: et qui eum pupugerunt. et plan-
gent se super eum omnes tribus terre: etiam amen.
Ego sum A. et ω. principium et finis dicit
dominus deus. qui est. et qui erat. et qui uenturus est
omnipotens. Ego iohannes frater uester et particeps
in tribulatione. et regno. et patientia. in ihu:
fui in insula que appellatur pathmos. propter
uerbum domini et testimonium ihu. Fui in
spiritu in dominica die: et audiui post me uocem
magnam tamquam tube dicentis. Quod uides
scribe in libro. et mitte septem ecclesiis. ephesum.
et smirnam. et pergamum. et thyathyram.
et sardis. et phyladelphyam. et laodici-
am. Et conuersus sum ut uiderem uocem
que loquebatur mecum. Expositio
Apocalypsis: reuelatio interpretatur.

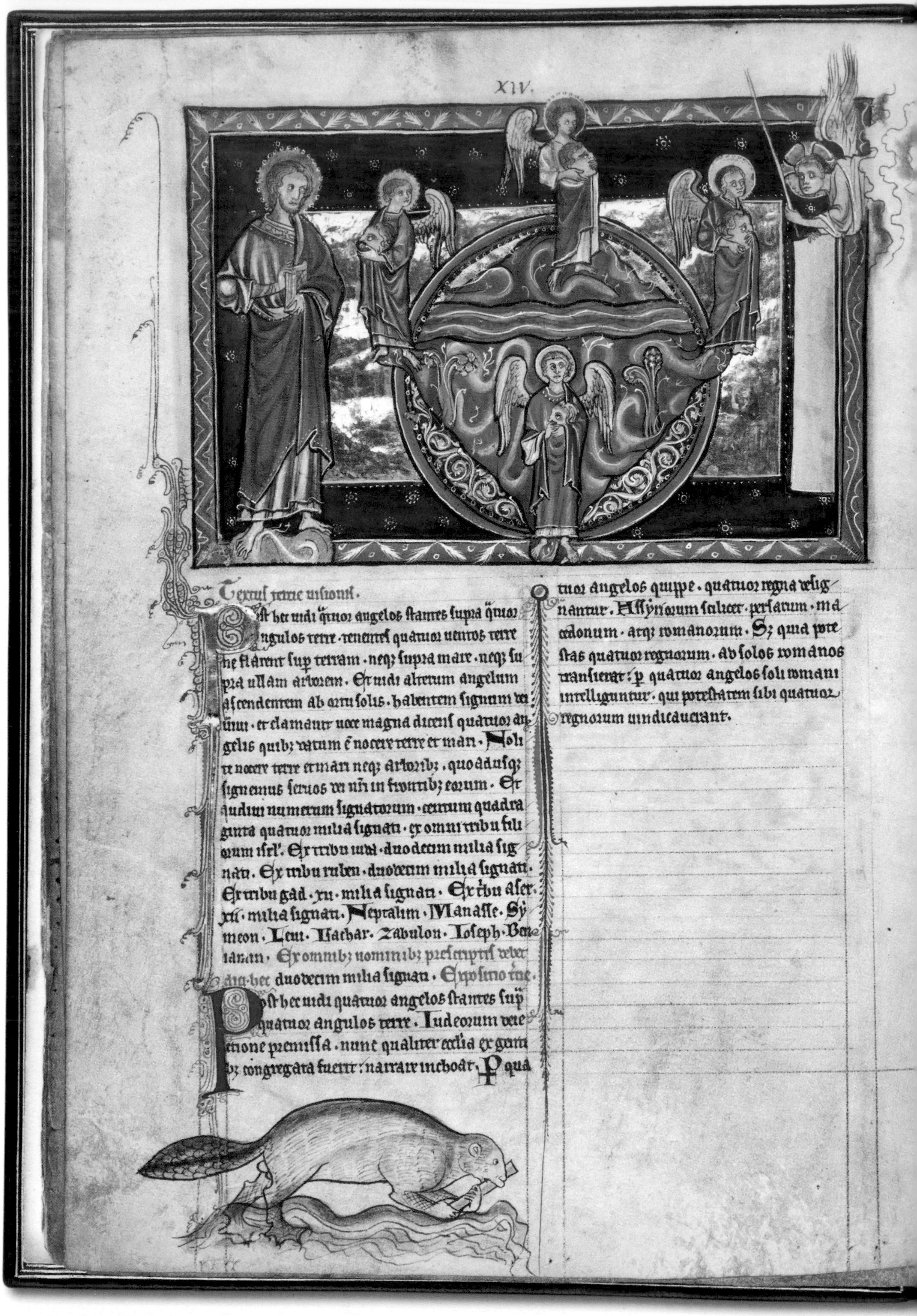

xiv.

Textus tercie visionis.

Post hec vidi quatuor angelos stantes supra quatuor angulos terre, tenentes quatuor uentos terre ne flarent sup terram, neq supra mare, neq supra ullam arborem. Et vidi alterum angelum ascendentem ab ortu solis, habentem signum dei uiui, et clamauit uoce magna dicens quatuor angelis quibus datum est nocere terre et mari. Nolite nocere terre et mari neq arboribus, quousq signemus seruos dei nostri in frontibus eorum. Et audiui numerum signatorum, centum quadraginta quatuor milia signati, ex omni tribu filiorum israel. Ex tribu iuda duodecim milia signati. Ex tribu ruben duodecim milia signati. Ex tribu gad xii milia signati. Ex tribu aser xii milia signati. Neptalim. Manasse. Symeon. Leui. Ysachar. Zabulon. Ioseph. Beniamin. Ex omnibus nominibus prescriptis debet dici hec duodecim milia signati. Exposicio eius.

Post hec vidi quatuor angelos stantes sup quatuor angulos terre. Iudeorum uocatione premissa, nunc qualiter ecclesia ex gentibus congregata fuerit narrare inchoat. Per quatuor angelos quippe quatuor regna designantur. Assyriorum scilicet, persarum, macedonum, atque romanorum. Set quia potestas quatuor regnorum ad solos romanos transierat, per quatuor angelos soli romani intelliguntur, qui potestatem sibi quatuor regnorum uindicauerant.

XV.

Textus tercie visionis.

Post hec vidi turbam magnam quam dinu-
merare nemo poterat ex omnibus gentibus
et tribubus et populis et linguis stantes ante
thronum et in conspectu agni amicti stolis albis et palme in manibus eorum. et clamabant voce magna dicentes. Salus deo nostro qui sedet super thronum et agno. Et omnes angeli sta-
bant in circuitu throni et seniorum et quatuor
animalium. Et ceciderunt in conspectu throni in facies suas. et adoraverunt deum dicentes amen. Benedictio et claritas et sapientia
et gratiarum actio. honor et virtus et fortitudo deo
nostro in secula seculorum amen. Et respon-
dens dixit michi. Hii qui amicti sunt stolis
albis. qui sunt et unde venerunt. Et dixi illi.
Domine mi tu scis. Hii sunt qui venerunt
de tribulatione magna. et laverunt stolas suas et dealbaverunt eas in sanguine agni.
ideo sunt ante thronum dei. et serviunt ei
in templo eius die ac nocte. et qui sedet in thro-
no habitat super illos. Non esurient neque
sitient amplius. neque cadet super illos sol neque
ullus estus. quoniam agnus qui in medio
throni est. reget illos et educet eos ad vite fontes
aquarum. et absterget deus omnem lacrimam
ab oculis eorum.

Exposicio tercie visionis.

Et qui sedet super thronum habitat super illos.
Thronum dei: sancti dei sunt sicut superius
diximus. Qui ergo designantur per thronum dei.
ipsi sunt super quos habitat deus. cum eos suo
lumine illuminat.

MATHEVS
IOHANNES
MARCVS
LVCAS

# 10 The Vaux–Bardolf Psalter

**MS 233; Psalter**
England; *c.*1310–*c.*1320
Anglo-Norman and Latin; vellum; 313 x 228 mm; ff. 242
Illustrated: (*opposite*) f. 14v, Christ in Majesty; (*right; detail*) f. 189v, initial depicting the owner at prayer; (*overleaf*) ff. 100v–101r, initial depicting Christ with orb, blessing, above Jonah and the Whale

Impressively large in dimensions, size of script and scale of illustrations, the manuscript takes its name from arms represented on a shield, heraldic banners and line-fillers. Heraldry was used in fourteenth-century illumination to identify owners, their ancestors and families with whom they wished to be associated. In this manuscript, the arms of one of the branches of the Vaux family are often linked to those of the Bardolf family of Wormegay, Norfolk, and Shelford, Nottinghamshire. On the banners above the initial for Psalm 68 they are in the male position, perhaps referring to an unrecorded marriage between a male Vaux and female Bardolf. It was indeed a married woman for whom the manuscript was made. Accompanied by her dog, she is represented at prayer in the initial for Psalm 119 (Vulgate), which opens with the words, 'In my trouble I cried to the Lord: and he heard me'.

The pictorial programme opens with a full-page Christ in Majesty, unique as the frontispiece of fourteenth-century English psalters, but, in subject and position, recalling earlier English manuscripts such as the Amesbury Psalter (All Souls College, Oxford, MS 6, *c.*1250–55). Next is a series of historiated initials at the main-text divisions. Varied in theme, the first, a Tree of Jesse for Psalm 1, visually traces the ancestry of Christ from Jesse, father of David. Others (Psalms 26, 38, 51, 52, 80, 101) also represent David, author of the Psalms, while still others (Psalms 68 and 97) show subjects elicited by the opening words of the Psalms. Foliated marginal extensions from the historiated initials frame the text. These are associated with marginalia, some of them figures bearing heraldic banners, some animal chases and some hybrid fantasies.

Several artists were responsible for the illustrations, all working from the design and drawing of a single hand. The figure style of the main painter – characterised by shaded drapery contrasting with black-outlined faces and hair – is found in a number of other manuscripts from various sources, including portions of the Tickhill Psalter, made for John Tickhill, Prior of Worksop Priory, Nottinghamshire, between 1303 and 1314, and the Pabenham–Clifford Hours (Fitzwilliam Museum, Cambridge, MS 242), probably made for the marriage of John Pabenham of Favenham, Bedfordshire, and Joan Clifford of Frampton, Gloucestershire, which took place around 1314. It would be reasonable to conclude then that the Vaux–Bardolf Psalter dates from early in the second decade of the fourteenth century.

Where the manuscript was executed is no more certain than the identity of its owner. The calendar, with entries in Anglo-Norman, is the type used by Augustinian Friars, who often served as confessors to laypeople, and its English saints point towards the Midlands. The litany suggests the diocese of York, which includes Nottinghamshire, where the Bardolfs had a seat. Consequently, it is possible that the book was produced at a centre in the region in which it was intended to be used.

*Lucy Freeman Sandler*
*Helen Gould Sheppard Professor Emerita of Art History,*
*New York University*

E. G. Millar, *Les Principaux Manuscrits à Peintures du Lambeth Palace à Londres*, Bulletin de la Société Française de Reproduction des Manuscrits à Peintures (Paris, 1924–25), pp. 5–11

D. D. Egbert, *The Tickhill Psalter and Related Manuscripts* (New York, 1940), pp. 90–94, 175–81

L. F. Sandler, *Gothic Manuscripts 1285–1385. A Survey of Manuscripts Illuminated in the British Isles*, 5, 2 vols (London, 1986), vol. I, ills. 74 and 76, vol. II, no. 30, pp. 35–36

ferent reges munera.
Increpa feras arundinis congre
gatio taurorum in uaccis populorum:
ut excludant eos qui probati sunt
argento.
Dissipa gentes que bella uolunt ue
nient legati ex egypto: ethiopia
preueniet manus eius deo.
Regna terre cantate deo: psallite do
mino.
Psallite deo: qui ascendit super celum
celi ad orientem.
Ecce dabit uoci sue uocem uirtutis: da
te gloriam deo super israel magni
ficentia eius ⁊ uirtus eius in nubibus:
Mirabilis deus in sanctis suis: deus
israel ipse uirtutem ⁊ fortitudinem

plebi sue benedictus deus.
SALVUM ME FAC DEUS
quoniam intraverunt aque:
usque ad animam meam.
Infixus sum in limo profundi: et
non est substantia.
Veni in altitudine maris: et tem

# 11 The Prohibited English Bible

**MS 25; 'Wycliffite' Bible**
London?; *c.*1400
Vellum; 395 x 255 mm; ff. i (strip pasted on replacement leaf) + 369
Illustrated: (*below; detail*) f. 255r, decorated initial A; (*opposite*) f. 159r, opening of Tobit, with 'a glos'

MS 25 is one of the earliest surviving copies of the Wycliffite Bible. In this copy, which was in Essex in the 1540s and may have been owned by Edmund Bonner, Bishop of London, the books of the Pentateuch (Genesis through Deuteronomy) are in the 'Earlier Version' of the Wycliffite Bible, a closely literal translation of the Latin. Work on this version, probably instigated by John Wyclif, after whom this Bible is named, began in the early 1370s in Queen's College, Oxford. The remainder is in the 'Later Version', completed around 1390. During the revision process the translators did their best to establish an authoritative text of the Latin Bible, with the help of the commentary by Nicholas of Lyra, and the Later Version of the Wycliffite Bible is consequently more accurate than the Earlier Version, as well as more idiomatic. The gloss in the margin of f. 159r follows Lyra in asserting that the events of the Book of Tobit took place in the sixth year of King Hezekiah.

Only 20 complete Wycliffite Bibles survive. The scribes who wrote them were clearly professionals, and MS 25 closely resembles the late-medieval Latin Bible in format, decoration and content. Among Wycliffite Bibles at Lambeth, MS 1033 and Sion College Arc.L 40.2/E.1 both contain Old Testament books only, but may originally have been part of two- or three-volume sets: the first leaf of Matthew in MS 25 is worn, suggesting that the New Testament of this Bible once had a separate existence. However, complete Bibles were beyond the means of most would-be owners, and most surviving manuscripts of the Wycliffite Bible – including, at Lambeth, MSS 369, 532, 547, 1150, 1151, 1366 and Sion College Arc.L.40.2/E.2 – contain books of the New Testament only.

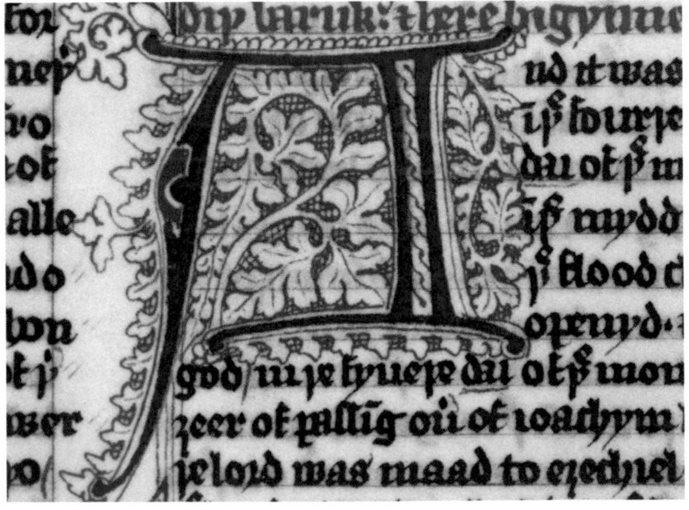

As one advocate of Scripture in English argued around 1400: 'Christ says in the gospel that the word that he has spoken shall judge us at the last day (John 12: 48), and if we are to be judged by Christ's word it is necessary to learn his word and know it.' The Wycliffite Bible made Holy Writ accessible for the first time to readers literate in English but not Latin. It also enabled English readers as a whole to read the Bible in their native tongue in a translation commanding respect as a literal and meaningful rendering of a carefully edited original. 'Let the Church of England approve th[is] accurate and complete translation', says the writer of the Prologue to the Wycliffite Bible.

It was unfortunate that clerical antagonism towards the Bible associated with Wyclif culminated in the constitutions against heresy issued by Archbishop Arundel at the Council of Oxford in 1407. These prohibited any public or private use or dissemination of the English Bible. Possession of Scripture in English was grounds for suspicion of heresy, and a trial could result in imprisonment, excommunication and even death by burning. Nevertheless, the desire for Scripture in English was so great that the prohibition failed. More than 250 manuscripts of the Wycliffite Bible, or parts of it, survive – considerably more than of any other text in Middle English.

*The late Mary Dove*
*Professor of English Studies, University of Sussex*

J. Forshall and F. Madden (eds), *The Holy Bible … in the Earliest English Versions Made from the Latin Vulgate by John Wycliffe and his Followers*, 4 vols (Oxford, 1850)
C. de Hamel, *The Book: A History of the Bible* (London, 2001)
M. Dove, *The First English Bible: The Text and Context of the Wycliffite Versions* (Cambridge, 2007)
R. Marsden, 'The Bible in English', in R. Marsden and E. Ann Matter (eds), *The New Cambridge History of the Bible. Vol. 2: c.600–1450* (Cambridge, 2010)

… porters. & þe firste fruytis of þe preestis:
… for hem. forsoþe in alle þese þingis I was
… for in þe ii. & xxx. ȝeer of artaxerses king
… I cam to þe king. & in þe ende of daies I
… & I cam in to ierusalem. & I vndirstood þe yuel
… hadde do to tobie. to make to him a
… of goddis hous. & to me it he…
… & I castide forþ þe vessels of þe hous
… of þe tresorie. & I comaundide: & þei
… & I brouȝte aȝen þere þe vessels of
… sacrifice & encense. & I knew þat þe partis
… weren not ȝouun. & þat ech man of þe deke…
… syngers & of hem þat mynystriden: hadden
… cuntrey. & I dide þe cause aȝens magis…
… whi forsake ȝe þe hous of god:
… hem to gidere. þat is dekenes & mynystris
… go awei: & I made to stonde in her sto…
… iuda brouȝte þe tiþe of whete. of wyn
… bernes. selemye þe preest & sadoch þe
… of þe dekenes: & bisidis hem. a
… of zaccur. þe sone of mathanye. for
… feiþful men: & þe partis of her briþeren
… to hem. my god haue mynde of me for þis
… awei my merciful doingis. whiche I dide
… god. & in his cerymonyes. Capitulum xiii.
… I siȝ in iuda men tredinge pressours in þe
… bringynge heepis. & chargynge on as…
… & figis & al birþun. & bringynge in to
… of sabat. & I witnesside to hem: þat þei schulden
… which it was leueful to sille. & men of tire
… & brouȝten in fischis & alle þingis set to sale
… sabatis: to þe sones of iuda & of ierusalem
… þe principal men of iuda: & I seide to hem
… yuel þing which ȝe doen: & maken vn…
… þe sabat. wher oure fadris diden not
… oure god brouȝte on vs al þis yuel.
… & ȝe encreessen wraþþfulnesse on
… þe sabat. forsoþe it was don. whanne
… hadden restid in þe dai of sabat: I seide
… ȝatis. & þei schittiden þe ȝatis. & I comaundide
… not opene þo ȝatis: til after þe sabat.
… I ordeynede nouþris on þe ȝatis: þat
… bringe in birþun: in þe dai of sabat. & mar…
… sillinge alle þingis set to sale: dwelliden
… ones & twies. & I areside hem: & I seide
… ȝe euene aȝens þe wal. if ȝe don þis
… I schal sette hond on ȝou. þerfor fro þat ty…
… not in þe sabat. also I seide to dekenes. þat
… clensid. & þat þei schulden come to kepe þe ȝatis:
… dai of sabat. & þerfor for þis þing my god
… me: & spare me bi þe mychilnesse of
… þingis. but also in þo daies I siȝ iewis wed…
… wymmen of azotus. & wymmen of amony…
… of moabitis. & her children spaken half p…
… azotus. & kouden not speke bi þe speche
… spaken bi þe langage of puple. & of pu…
… hem: & I curside. & I beet þe men of hem:

& I made hem swerid. & I made hem to swere bi þe lord: þat
þei schulden not ȝyue her douȝtris to þe sones of þo
aliens. & þat þei schulden not take of þe douȝtris of þo
aliens to her sones & to hem silf. & I seide. wher salomon
þe king of israel: synnede not in such a þing: & certis in many
folkis. was no king lik him: & he was loued of his god
& god settide him king: on al israel. & þerfor alien wymmen
brouȝten him to synne. wher also we vnobedient. schul
den do al þis grete yuel: þat we trespasse aȝens oure
lord god. & wedde alien wyues. forsoþe sanaballath
horonyte hadde weddid a douȝter of þe sones of ioiada
sone of eliasib þe grete preest: which sanaballath I
droof awei fro me. my lord god haue mynde aȝens
hem þat defoulen preesthod: & þe riȝt of preestis & of dekenes.
þerfor I clensid hem fro alle aliens. & I ordeynede ordris of hem
preestis & of dekenes. ech man in his seruyce: & in þe offringe.
þat is. dressinge of trees in tymes ordeyned. & in þe firste
fruytis. my god haue mynde of me: in to good. here
endiþ þe secounde book of esdre: & here bigynneþ
þe book of tobie. Capitulum i.

Tobie was of þe lynage & citee of
neptalym: which is in þe hiȝere partis
of galilee aboue naason. bihynde þe
weie þat ledeþ to þe west: & hath in þe
left side þe citee of sapheth. whanne he
was takun in þe daies of salmanasar king of assiriens:
neþeles he set in caitifte. ȝhe takun prisoner. forsook not
þe weie of treuþe. so þat he departide ech dai alle þingis
whiche he myȝte haue: with caitif briþeren þat weren of his
kyn. & whanne he was ȝongere þan alle in þe lynage of
neptalym: neþeles he dide no childische þing in werk.
forsoþe whanne alle ȝeden to þe golden calues
whiche ierobaum þe king of israel made: þis tobie
aloone fledde þe cumpenyes of alle men. & he ȝede to ie
rusalem to þe temple of þe lord: & þere he worschipide þe lord
god of israel. & he offride feiþfulli alle hise firste fruy
tis & hise tiþis. so þat in þe iii. ȝeer he mynystride al
þe tiþe: to conuersis & comelingis. þe ȝonge man kepte
þese þingis. & þingis lik þese: bi þe lawe of god of heue
ne. soþli whanne he was maad a man: he took a wif
anne of his lynage. & he gendride of hir a sone: & put
tide his owne name to him. whom he tauȝte fro ȝong
childhod for to drede god: & for to absteyne fro alle
synne. þerfor whanne bi caitifte he was comun with his
wif & sone. in to þe citee nynyue. with al his lynage.
& alle men eeten of þe metis of heþene men: þis
tobie kepte his soule. & was neuere defoulid in þe
metis of hem. & for he was myndeful of þe lord in al his
herte: god ȝaf grace to him in þe siȝt of salmanasar
þe king. & he ȝaf to tobie power to go whidur euer he
wolde: & he hadde fredom to do what euer þingis he wolde.
þerfor he ȝede bi alle men þat weren in caitifte: & ȝaf to hem
þe heelþis of helþe. soþli whanne he was comun in to ra
ges a citee of medeis: & hadde x. talentis of siluer of
þese þingis bi whiche he was onourid of þe king. &
he siȝ gabelus nedi þat was of his lynage. with mede
… of his kyn: tobie ȝaf to him vndir an obliga

a glos

This storie bifelde in þe vii. ȝeer of king ezechie.

# 12 The Chichele Breviary

**MS 69; breviary with calendar**
London; before 1416 (*c.*1408–14)
Latin; vellum; 335 x 228 mm; ff. i + 418
Illustrated: (*below; detail*) f. 1r, initial depicting Bishop Chichele; (*opposite*) f. 209r, with initial portraying the anointing of King David

This is the most beautiful breviary made in England during the fifteenth century – splendid in the artistry of its historiated initials and the elegance of its borders, flourished initials, calligraphic initials and broad margins. It is also of considerable importance because this is the masterpiece of Herman Scheerre, a pre-eminent illustrator of the period. He is thought to have come to England from Cologne around 1405, and to have worked in London for at least ten years with English border artists and flourishers. Scheerre directed three other artists in illustrating the Breviary's 29 initials, and was responsible for the opening initial depicting the commissioner, Henry Chichele (*c.*1364–1443), Bishop of St David's from 1408 to 1414. Chichele points to a book as he instructs a group of kneeling clerics. Later Archbishop of Canterbury from 1414 to 1443, Chichele founded All Souls College, Oxford, and this image emphasises his interest in books and the education of clerical scholars.

Another painter, the Carmelite-Lapworth Master, worked on nine initials and his assistant made five initials for the Psalms – their iconography repeated in the famous Bedford Hours and Psalter (British Library, Add. MS 42131). This assistant was apparently the first to reintroduce traditional 'life of David' scenes, such as the anointing by Samuel, instead of contemporary English iconography. MS 69 also contains a scene unique in English book art, the Vision of the Sacristan of St Peter's, as the illustration for All Saints. Another unusual feature is a corrector's mark on nearly every quire from f. 88v, demonstrating the care with which the book was made.

This was the first manuscript in which the name 'Hermann' was found in 1908; his full name was subsequently found in British Library, Add. MS 16998, a book of offices. Further unsigned work has been identified on stylistic grounds in a substantial number of other manuscripts. A newly located manuscript with an initial by Scheerre of King David harping is British Library, Harley MS 1798, a breviary, and a new identification of border work by one of the collaborators in MS 69 is British Library, Add. MS 36683, a primer and psalter.

Of the large number of surviving fifteenth-century English breviaries, no other contains the number and quality of illustrations as in the Chichele Breviary.

*Kathleen L. Scott*
*Independent Scholar*

E. F. Jacob, *Archbishop Henry Chichele* (London, 1967)
C. P. Christianson, *A Directory of London Stationers and Book Artisans 1300–1500*, (New York, 1990), pp. 157–58
K. L. Scott, *Later Gothic Manuscripts 1390–1490. A Survey of Manuscripts Illuminated in the British Isles* 6, 2 vols (London, 1996), vol. I, ills. 127–33 and pl. 5, vol. II, no. 30, pp. 112–14

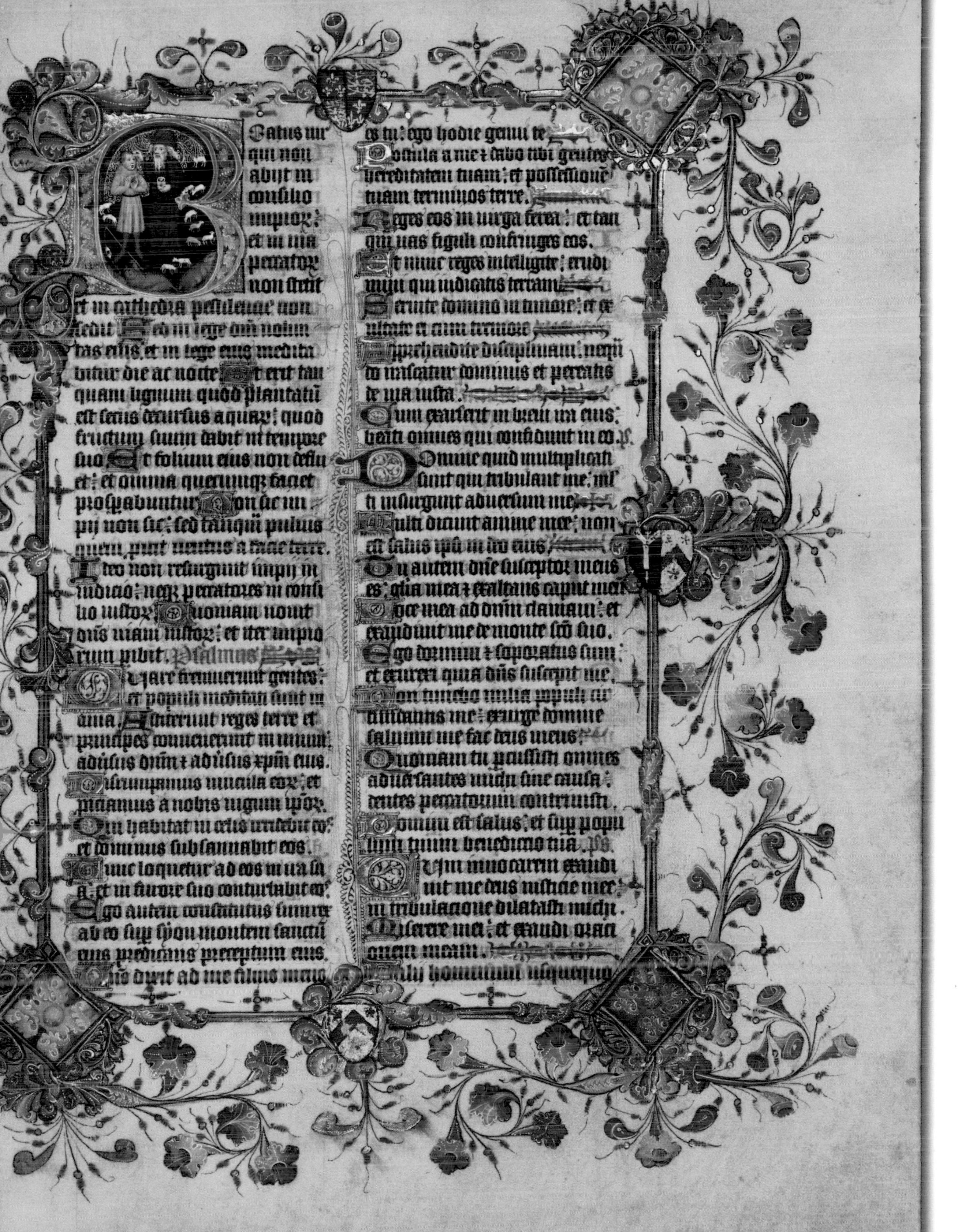

# 13 The Pilgrimage of the Soul

**MS 326; Jean Galopes, *Liber peregrinationis animae*;**
**Latin translation of Guillaume de Digulleville's *Pèlerinage de l'âme***
Paris?; *c.*1427
Latin; parchment; 270 x 210 mm; ff. 145
Illustrated: (*opposite*) f. 1r, Galopes presents his book to John, Duke of Bedford; (*overleaf and detail below*) ff. 4v–5r, the author dreams of his work

Jean Galopes dedicated his Latin prose translation of Guillaume Digulleville's *Pèlerinage de l'âme* (Pilgrimage of the Soul) (ff. 1–82) to John, Duke of Bedford (1389–1435), brother of Henry V and Regent of France for King Henry VI. Bedford loved books. He bought the great Louvre library of over 800 manuscripts. Other manuscripts were specially written and decorated for him in England and France, some by members of his household. Galopes, who was Dean of the collegiate church of Saint-Louis de Saussay (diocese of Evreux), described himself as Bedford's chaplain, and may have served in the Regent's household chapel. By 1427 Galopes was a canon of Rouen Cathedral; he represented the chapter at the council of Basle, where he died in 1435.

Bedford's perception of his duties and burdens as Regent is revealed by a specially composed prayer in his small Book of Hours (British Library, Add. MS 74754). These themes are echoed in the Latin dedication of the *Pèlerinage de l'âme*: Bedford's need for God's guidance and his accountability before his Maker. Other copies of the dedication are known in both Latin and French.

Remarkably, a payment to Jean Thomas, a scribe of Paris, for writing this text has survived. It is dated 1427 and is authorised by Galopes himself (British Library, Add. Ch. 104). Thomas was paid for twelve quires (gatherings) of parchment, each costing 16 sous of Paris. Only the first 82 folios of MS 326 contain the *Pèlerinage de l'âme.*

In the dedication miniature (f. 1r) Galopes kneels to present his translation to the Regent, who turns to discuss it with a councillor. A sergeant with a mace holds back the next suitor, a tonsured cleric. This has been attributed to the so-called 'Hannibal Master', who worked for King Henry V and other Englishmen in France. Puzzlingly, some details of the heraldry are incorrect, but this is very probably the presentation copy. The roots and boughs decorating the wall-hanging are the badges of the Regent and his first wife, Anne of Burgundy.

The author, Digulleville, a monk, drafted this work, the second part of his devotional verse trilogy, around 1332. He is depicted lying on a bed asleep, dreaming of the subject of his book, the soul's pilgrimage separated from the decaying body (f. 4v). The chair and desk where he will write are visible in the background.

*Jenny Stratford*
*Institute of Historical Research, University of London*

E. G. Millar, 'Les principaux manuscrits à peintures du Lambeth Palace Library à Londres', *Bulletin de la Société française de Reproduction de Manuscrits à Peintures*, ix (1924–25), pp. 13–15 and pls xlii, xliii

J. Stratford, 'The Manuscripts of John, Duke of Bedford: Library and Chapel', in *England in the Fifteenth century. Proceedings of the 1986 Harlaxton Symposium*, ed. D. Williams (Woodbridge, 1987), p. 348 and note 67

J. Stratford, *The Bedford Inventories. The Worldly Goods of John, Duke of Bedford, Regent of France (1389–1435)* (London, 1993), p. 123

R. H. and M. A. Rouse, *Illiterati et Uxorati. Manuscripts and their Makers. Commercial Book Producers in Medieval Paris, 1200–1500*, 2 vols (London, 2000), vol. 2, p. 87

*Paris 1400. Les Arts sous Charles VI*, ed. E. Taburet-Delahaye (Paris, 2004), no. 222 and p. 346

J. Stratford and C. Reynolds, 'The Foyle Breviary and Hours of John, Duke of Bedford, in the British Library', in *Tributes to Lucy Freeman Sandler. Studies in Illuminated Manuscripts*, ed. K. A. Smith and C. H. Krinsky (London and Turnhout, 2007), pp. 358–62

Prohemium actoris in libro peregrinationis anime
Illustrissimo et potenti principi ac domino pre
cipuo. Johanni filio Patruo que Regis Regenti
Regnorum francie et Duci bedfordie. Johannes ita
Ropes dictus le galope Decanus ecclesie collegi
BIBLIOTHECA
LAMBETHANA

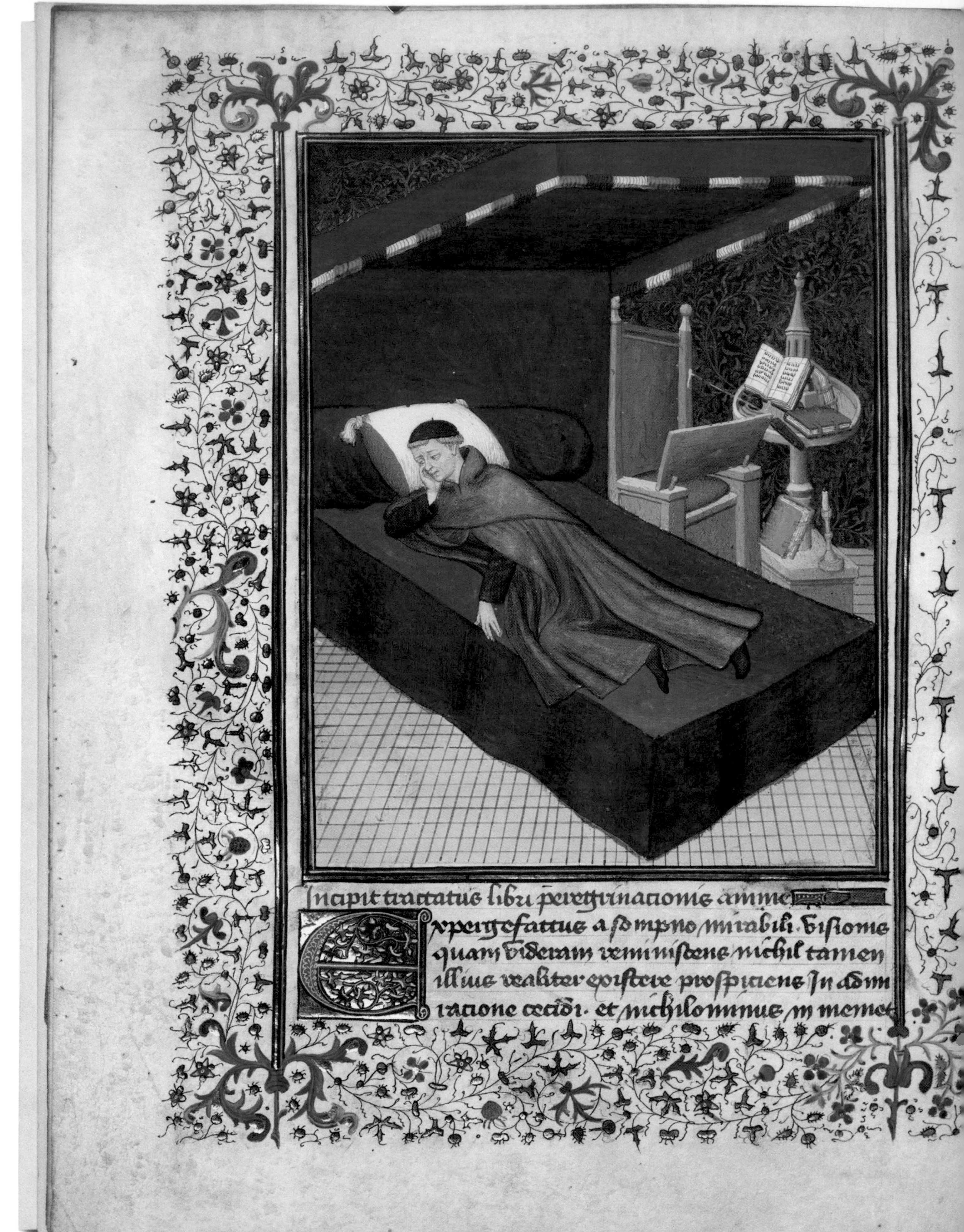
Incipit tractatus libri peregrinationis anime
Expergefactus a sompno mirabili visione
quam videram reminiscens nichil tamen
illius realiter existere prospiciens in admi
ratione cecidi. et nichilominus in memet

ipso cogitare cepi / quod insana fructuosa quia spica si bene
perquiratur granum bonum reperitur / Et in tali cogita
tione suspensus consideraui vitam hominis / multis in
mundo subiacere periculis / quinymo iuxta doctrinam Job
capitulo decimo quarto. sic dicentis. homo quasi flos
egreditur et conteritur velut vmbra. hominem iudicaui
similem fore flori ad flatum venti in terram cadenti / et
tali prostratione arefacto qui post eius casum a pede con
culcatur / et pro nichilo reputatur / cum humana natura
tam diuinis dotata quam ab illis denudata ab ortu eius nun
quam in eodem statu permanet. fugit quia velut vmbra
luce solis propinquante. Hec et alia premeditando
Iterato obdormiui / et raptus in sompnis / infirmitate
ad mortem me percussum credidi / Ac tali morbo animam
subito a corpore separari. In aerem quia leuari hic in terra
corpus iacet / anima iacens sursum stante. Ipsum quia vermibus expost
Postea ad terram conspiciens tum contemplante
in ea iacere prostratum et morti traditum / sine
vllo motu corpus meum fetidum / et quasi sterquilinio com
peratum / percepi. Animam quia meam ipsum inhabitasse
nunquam credidissem / nisi sic decenti ab illo exiuisset
prope quos astare vidi / misericordiam ipsum dimittis
alligantem / et intro terram inhumantem a quibus
non longe stabat oratio / cuius vox polum tangebat
Requestam deo faciens vt michi indulgere dignaretur
veniam quia michi prestaret. Et pro certo hac valde in
digebam propter sathan subito me rapere volentem qui
tunc sic me allocutus est. O misera anima dies
tuos / male complesti tempus autem excubiarum mearum
pro perditione tua non perdidi / cum exitu tuo in peccatis
moriebaris / Etenim sic te decepi. vt pro demeritis tuis
ad infernum mecum descenderes / quapropter mecum nunc

# 14 The Gutenberg Bible

**MS 15; Bible (New Testament only)**
Germany, Mainz; Gutenberg; *c.*1455
Latin; vellum; 430 x 325 mm, ff. 128
Illustrated: (*right; detail*) f. 96r, decorated initial P (Acts chapter 1); (*opposite*) f. 77r, St Paul's letter to the Galatians

On 12 March 1455 Enea Silvio Piccolomini, later Pope Pius II, wrote a business letter to the Cardinal for whom he worked. In passing he mentioned that, in Frankfurt, a marvellous man had been promoting his Bibles. This is our earliest reference to the first book to emerge from a printing press. Piccolomini explained that the lettering was so clear that the Cardinal could read it without glasses. He reported that either 150 or 180 copies were produced and that all had already been sold.

The Bible may seem an obvious choice for Johann Gutenberg to print but, as a book, it did not play the same role in church as in later times. Biblical passages were read in church every day and these readings were organised in Missals, for the performance of the Mass, according to the different days of the liturgical year. However, being different from diocese to diocese, Missals could not provide a large customer base. Gutenberg had to aim at a wider geographical market. Bibles were also different from region to region. The selection of texts contained in the Gutenberg Bible is based on a tradition current in fifteenth-century Rhineland and differs in many ways from the selection of texts of the standard Latin Bible now known as the Vulgate, which was not to become established until the late sixteenth century. However, this diversity was not of liturgical importance and there may have been little awareness of it until the international distribution of commercially produced printed Bibles made buyers aware of the different forms of the Bible.

Despite these differences, a Bible had potential to sell all over western Europe and the Lambeth copy of the Gutenberg Bible, which comprises the New Testament only, lacking the Old Testament, documents this potential. A scribbled note in English, which cannot be much later than 1500, indicates that the book arrived in this country at a very early stage. More importantly, the extensive hand-painted decoration of this copy is the work of a fifteenth-century English artist and was probably added not long after 1455. This may therefore be the first printed book ever to reach this country. Many copies are not illuminated at all and most of those which are have illumination on only a few pages. The Lambeth copy has a painted initial and decoration at the beginning of every significant text, and is printed on vellum rather than paper. Its owner must have been very wealthy, whether he purchased it for his own use or as a gift. Churches or religious houses rarely bought books for themselves; an analysis of surviving copies of Bibles printed in the fifteenth century indicates that they were bought by individuals who gave them to religious houses in return for prayer.

Although we know from a legal dispute in 1455 that it was Gutenberg who printed the first Bible, for a long time it was uncertain which edition it was. By 1789 the matter was settled and bibliophiles began a hunt for copies all over Europe. Yet the copy that had long been at Lambeth, catalogued among the manuscripts, remained unidentified until 1873.

*Kristian Jensen*
*British Library, London*


S. W. Kershaw, *Art Treasures of the Lambeth Library* (London, 1873), no. 15

E. König, 'A Leaf from a Gutenberg Bible Illuminated in England', *British Library Journal* (1983), pp. 32–50

G. Bechtel, *Gutenberg et l'Invention de l'Imprimerie: Une Enquete* (Paris, 1992)

K. L. Scott, *Dated and Datable English Manuscript Borders, c.1395–1499* (London, 2002), pp. 80–1

K. Jensen, 'Printing the Bible in the Fifteenth Century: Devotion, Philology and Commerce', in *Incunabula and their Readers*, ed. K. Jensen (London, 2003), pp. 115–38

dissensiones detractiones susurratio
nes inflationes seditiones sint inter
vos. Ne iterū cū venero humiliet me
deus apud vos: ⁊ lugeā multos ex hijs
qui ante peccaverūt et nō egerūt peni
tentiā sup immūdicia et fornicatione
et impudicicia quā gesserunt.
Ecce tercio hoc venio ad vos. In
ore duoꝝ vel trium testiū stabit
omne verbū. Predixi eni et predico ut
presens vobis ⁊ nūc absens hijs qui
ante peccaverūt ⁊ ceteris omībꝫ: qm̄ si
venero iterū nō parcā. An experimētū
queritis eius qui in me loquit̄ cristus?
Qui in vobis non infirmatur sed po
tens est in vobis. Nam ⁊ si crucifixus
est ex infirmitate: sed vivit ex virtute
dei. Nam et nos infirmi sumus in il
lo: sed vivimus cum eo ex virtute dei
in vobis. Vosmetipsos temptate: si
estis in fide ipsi vos probate. An nō
cognoscitis vosmetipsos: quia cristus
ihesus in vobis est? Nisi forte repro
bi estis. Spero autem quod cognosce
tis: quia nos non sumus reprobi. O
ramus autem deum ut nichil mali fa
ciatis non ut nos probati appareamus
sed ut vos quod bonum est faciatis.
Nos aūt ut reprobi simus. Non enī
possumus aliquid adversus veritatem:
sed pro veritate. Gaudemus enī quoniā
nos infirmi sumus: vos aūt potentes
estis. Hoc et oramus: vestrā ɔsūmatio
nem. Ideo hec absens scribo: ut nō pre
sens durius agā scd̄m potestatē quā
dn̄s dedit michi in edificationē et nō
in destructionē. De cetero fratres gau
dete: perfecti estote: exhortamini: idipm̄
sapite. Pacē habete: et deus pacis et
dilectionis erit vobiscū. Salutate in
vicem in osculo sancto. Salutāt vos
omēs sancti. Gratia dn̄i nostri ihesu
cristi et caritas dei ⁊ communicatio san
cti spiritus sit cū omībꝫ vobis amē. Ex
plicit epl̄a scd̄a ad corinthios. Incipit
prologus in epistolam ad galathas.
Galathe sunt greci. Hij ver
bū veritatis primū ab a
postolo acceperūt: sed post
discessū eius temptati sūt a fal
sis apl̄is: ut i legē ⁊ circūcisionē ne ver
terent̄. Hos apl̄us revocat ad fidē veri
tatis: scribēs eis ab epheso. Explicit
prologus. Incipit epl̄a ad galathas.
Paulus apostolus
nō ab hominibꝫ ne
qꝫ per hominē sed p
ihesum cristū et deū
patrē qui suscitavit
eū a mortuis: et qui
mecū sunt omnes fratres: ecclesijs ga
lathie. Gratia vobis ⁊ pax a deo patre
nr̄o et dn̄o ihesu cristo: qui dedit semet
ipm̄ pro peccatis nr̄is ut eriperet nos
de presenti seculo neqꝫ scd̄m volūtatē
dei et pr̄is nr̄i: cui est gloria in secula se
culoꝝ amen. Miror qꝫ sic tā cito trans
feremini ab eo qui vos vocavit i gra
tiā cristi in aliud evangeliū qd̄ nō est
aliud: nisi sint aliqui qui vos contur
bāt: et volūt ɔvertere evangeliū cristi.
Sed licet nos aut angelus de celo eu
angelizet vobis preterqꝫ quod euāge
lizavimus vobis: anathema sit. Sicut
prediximus ⁊ nūc iterū dico: si quis vo
bis evangelizaverit preter id quod ac
cepistis: anathema sit. Modo enī ho
minibꝫ suadeo: an deo? An quero ho
minibꝫ placere? Si adhuc hominibꝫ
placerē: cristi servus nō essem. Notū enī
vobis facio fratres evangeliū qd̄ euā
gelizatū est a me: quia nō est scd̄m ho
minē. Neqꝫ enī ego ab homine accepi
illud neqꝫ didici: sed per revelationem

Gloriare
Tu es firmus in fide
Coronã meruisti
Exalta te ipsum
In paciẽcia pseuerasti

# 15 How To Die Well

***Ars moriendi***
Lower Rhine or Netherlands; *c.*1465
Blockbook; Latin; 275 x 200 mm; 12 surviving leaves [of 24]
Illustrated: (*opposite*) woodcut, temptation from the devil to spiritual pride; (*overleaf*) woodcut and text, the angel inspires faith

Blockbook printing was invented in the 1440s or 1450s to facilitate the reproduction of books with text and pictures, or for which, as with certain schoolbooks, it was desirable to print short runs on demand. The earliest examples, the Dutch *Pater noster* (most likely 1440s), the Latin *Apocalypsis Johannis* (Netherlandish, *c.*1450–52), and the German *Antichrist* (Central Bavaria, *c.*1449–52) are contemporary with the first experiments with movable type that culminated in the printing of the Gutenberg Bible around 1455.

The term 'blockbook' is generally employed to designate books with text and/or pictures printed on double leaves, often on one side of the paper and with water-based ink rather than printer's ink, so that, when placed in sequence, the two-leaf units could be bound as a book. In some early examples the text was added by hand. Blockbook printing made use of the methods developed for the printing of single leaves (broadsides) from incised wood blocks, a procedure first reliably attested shortly after 1420.

One of the most successful texts printed by this technique was the *Ars moriendi* (How to Die Well), which is known from some 20 Latin, German and French blockbook editions, dating from *c.*1465 to the 1490s. It was printed in two versions. The first consists of a small-format booklet, with seven pairs of scenes, in which a dying man is challenged by devils who have prompted him to commit a deadly sin and encouraged by the counterarguments of a guardian angel. These are accompanied on the text pages by prayers. This version has survived only in later copies, but there is some evidence that booklets of this type might already have been printed as early as the mid-century or 1450s.

The second type, as in the Lambeth copy, is a handsome folio version. Here pictures of the devils challenging the dying man are matched by illustrations of the guardian angel coming to his defence. The text consists of rhetorical speeches in which the devils try to bring the dying man to despair, whereas the angels offer him their fulsome support. This version seems to have been designed in the mid-1460s, in the region of the Lower Rhine or eastern Netherlands. It brought together a skilled writer and a woodcut artist of exceptional talent.

The Lambeth copy is significant in that it preserves a large fragment, 12 of originally 24 leaves, printed from the plates of the earliest known edition. The 'prancing unicorn' watermarks, identifying the paper stock as the same as that used in some other early blockbooks, suggest that it may be a slightly earlier impression than the only surviving complete copy, which is in the British Library. The Lambeth copy forms part of an incunable 'Sammelband' (a volume containing a miscellany of works printed before 1501 and bound together), along with books printed in Utrecht and Heidelberg in 1474 and 1488. Its binding is identifiable as the work of a Cambridge binder, W. G., working from 1494 to 1534, and provides evidence that it was in England at a very early date.

*Nigel F. Palmer*
*St Edmund Hall, Oxford*

N. F. Palmer, 'Ars Moriendi und Totentanz', in *Tod im Mittelalter. Konstanzer Kolloquium 1990*, ed. A. Patschovsky (Konstanz, 1993), pp. 313–34
*Ars Vivendi. Ars Moriendi. Katalogbuch zur Ausstellung im Erzbischöflichen Diözesanmuseum Koln*, ed. J. M. Plotzek et al. (Munich, 2001)
D. Akerboom, '"Only the Image of Christ in us" – Continuity and Discontinuity between the Late Medieval *Ars moriendi* and Luther's *Sermon von der Bereitung zum Sterben*', in *Spirituality Renewed*, ed. H. Blommestijn et al. (Leuven, 2003), pp. 209–72
N. F. Palmer, 'Blockbooks: Texts and Illustrations Printed from Wood Blocks', *Journal of the Printing Historical Society*, new series, vol. 11 (2008), pp. 5–23

Sis firmus fide
Fugiamus
Victi sumus
Frustra laboravimus

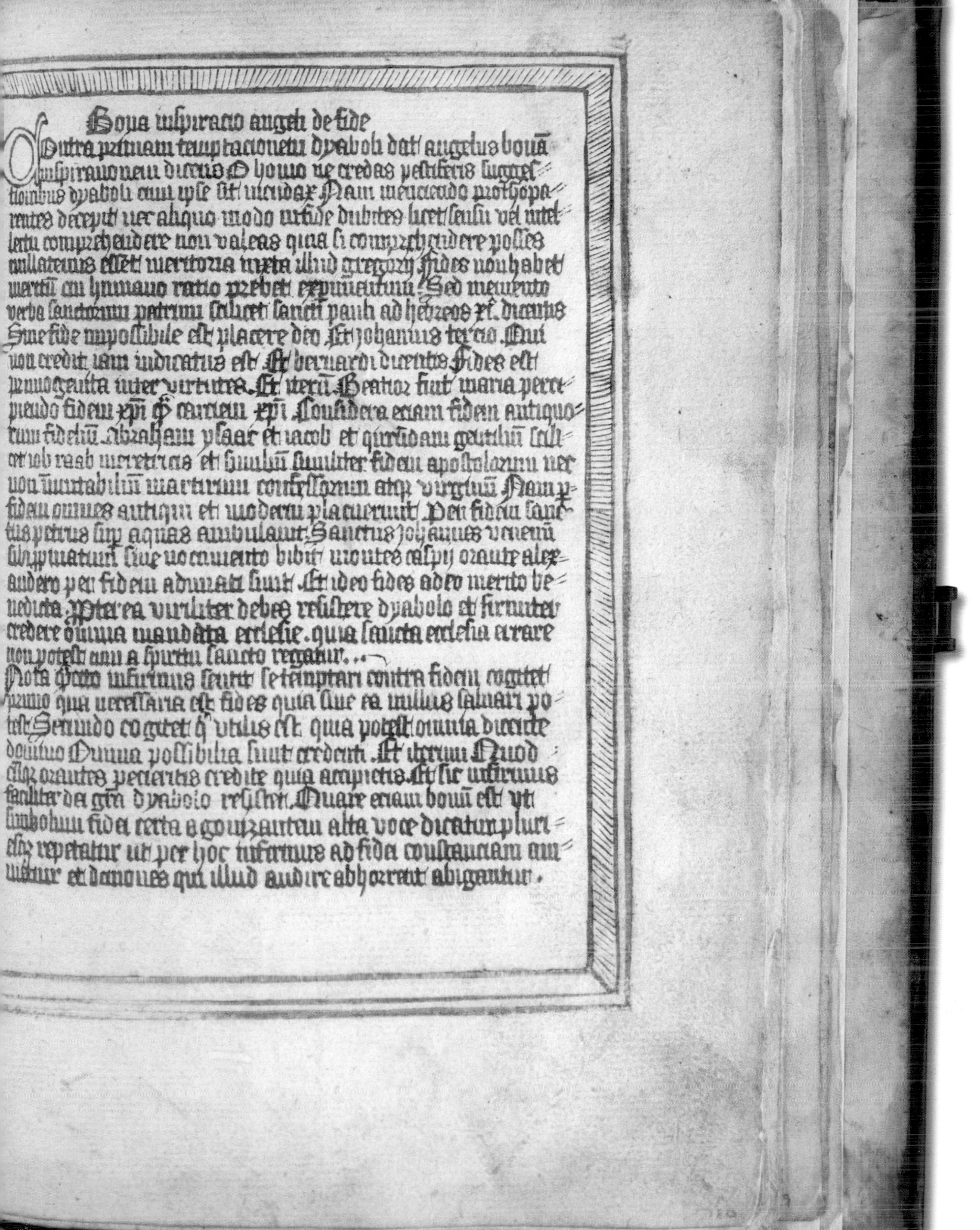

Bona inspiracio angeli de fide

Contra primam temptacionem dyaboli dat angelus bonā
inspiracionem dicens. O homo ne credas pestiferis sugges-
tionibus dyaboli cum ipse sit mendax. Nam mentiendo prothopa-
rentes decepit. nec aliquo modo in fide dubites licet sensu vel intel-
lectu comprehendere non valeas quia si comprehendere posses
nullatenus esset meritoria iuxta illud gregorii. Fides non habet
meritū cui humana ratio prebet experimentum. Sed memento
verba sanctorum patrum scilicet sancti pauli ad hebreos xi. dicentis
Sine fide impossibile est placere deo. Et johannis tercio. Qui
non credit iam iudicatus est. Et bernardi dicentis. Fides est
primogenita inter virtutes. Et iterū. Beatior fuit maria perci-
piendo fidem xpi q̄ carnem xpi. Considera eciam fidem antiquo-
rum fideliū. abraham ysaac et iacob et quorūdam gentiliū scilicet iob raab meretricis et similiū. Similiter fidem apostolorum nec
non innumerabiliū martirum confessorum atque virginū. Nam per
fidem omnes antiqui et moderni placuerunt. Per fidem sanctus petrus super aquas ambulavit. Sanctus johannes venenū
sibi propinatum sine nocumento bibit. montes caspij orante alex-
andro per fidem adiuncti sunt. Et ideo fides adeo merito be-
nedicta. Propterea viriliter debes resistere dyabolo et firmiter
credere omnia mandata ecclesie. quia sancta ecclesia errare
non potest cum a spiritu sancto regatur..
Nota quando infirmus sentit se temptari contra fidem cogitet
primo quia necessaria est fides quia sine ea nullus salvari potest. Secundo cogitet q̄ utilis est quia potest omnia dicente
domino Omnia possibilia sunt credenti. Et iterum Quod-
cumque orantes petieritis credite quia accipietis. Et sic infirmus
faciliter dei gracia dyabolo resistet. Quare eciam bonū est ut
simbolum fidei circa agonizantem alta voce dicatur pluri-
esque repetatur ut per hoc infirmus ad fidei constanciam ani-
metur et demones qui illud audire abhorrent abigantur.

This boke late translate here in sight

# 16 Copying Caxton

**MS 265; manuscript copy of William Caxton's printed edition of *Dictes and Sayings of the Philosophers*; English translation by Anthony Woodville, Earl Rivers, from the French of Guillaume de Tignonville**
Westminster; 24 December 1477
Middle English; vellum; 279 x 202 mm; ff. ii + 107
Illustrated: (*opposite; detail*) f. vi verso, Earl Rivers presenting the volume to Edward IV and family; (*right; detail*) f. 63v, initial A with humanist vine-scroll ornament

The *Dictes and Sayings of the Philosophers* was one of the first books printed in England by William Caxton (*c.*1422–92) and was evidently a best-seller as he published it twice in 1477 (*Short-Title Catalogue* [STC] 6826, 6827), again in 1480 (STC 6828) and finally in 1489 (STC 6829). Not all readers, however, chose this new-fangled form, preferring manuscript copies. Lambeth MS 265, British Library, Add. MS 22718, the Newberry Library, Chicago, MS f. 36 (Ry 20), and Columbia University Library, New York, Plimpton MS 259, were all copied from Caxton and excerpts also occur in British Library, Add. MS 60577 (the 'Winchester Anthology').

This copy is the handsomest, beautifully written with major text divisions signalled by vine-stem initials in the latest humanist fashion and blue and gold paraphs indicating minor divisions. An inserted leaf bearing a miniature and dedicatory verse (f. vi verso) establishes that this was the presentation copy of the text, a translation from the French of Guillaume de Tignonville by Anthony Woodville, Earl Rivers. His title, Rivers, has been erased in the verse, possibly after his execution in 1483. He is depicted, in armour and a surcoat bearing his arms, kneeling and presenting this actual manuscript (the gilt-edged leaves depicted remain, but the binding has been replaced) to Edward IV. Queen Elizabeth (Woodville's sister) and the Prince of Wales (later Edward V – one of the 'Princes in the Tower') look on. The portrait of the future Edward V has been hailed in the recent exhibition on Tudor royal portraiture, 'Lost Faces', as the only contemporary painted likeness of the prince. Another figure wearing ermine may be the future Richard III.

The tonsured figure in black may be the scribe, Hayward, who signed the book (f. 106r) at St James in the Fields, a hospital near Westminster Abbey, where Caxton set up his press. Scott suggests that this figure is the original author, but Tignonville was a layman and would not have been tonsured.

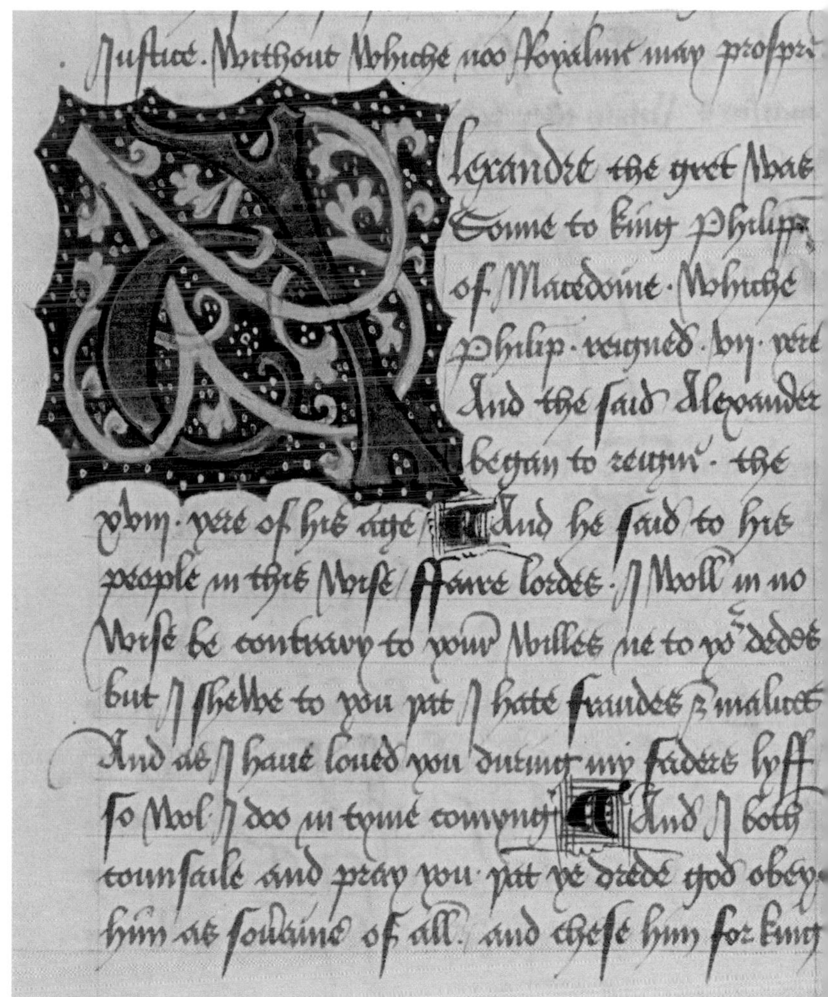

The manuscript, copied from Caxton's first edition, is dated 24 December 1477. STC 6827 is dated 18 November 1477. Could the manuscript have been produced so quickly? The specific date was, however, added to STC 6827, while STC 6826 is only dated 1477 (Hellinga 1982). Thus Hayward may have had longer to copy the text than first appears. That another copy, British Library, Add. MS 22718, is dated 28 November has previously gone unnoticed.

*Pamela Robinson*
*Institute of English Studies, University of London*

C. F. Bühler, 'The Verses in Lambeth Manuscript 265', *Modern Language Notes* 72 (1957), pp. 4–6
L. Hellinga, *Caxton in Focus. The Beginning of Printing in England* (London, 1982), pp. 77–86
K. L. Scott, *Later Gothic Manuscripts 1390–1490. A Survey of Manuscripts Illuminated in the British Isles* 6 (London, 1996), no. 125
*Lost Faces: Identity and Discovery in Tudor Royal Portraiture*, exh. cat. (London, 2007), pp. 18–21

# 17 A London Liturgical Psalter

**MS 186; Psalter**
Southern England, London?; *c.*1480
Latin; vellum; 289 x 197 mm, ff. 173
Illustrated: (*right and below*) f. 1r, border details; (*opposite*) f. 109r, Psalm 109 with an initial depicting the Trinity; (*back cover*) f. 1r, Psalm 1, with an initial portraying King David

In the fifteenth century, extensively illuminated Psalters like the Vaux–Bardolf Psalter (no. 10) became less common as the Book of Hours with its selection of Psalms became the laity's most popular devotional book (see no. 19). The Psalter, however, remained essential for performing the full cycle of offices for the hours of the day contained in the breviary (see no. 12). As this Psalter includes in the calendar the number of lessons for some offices, it was perhaps intended primarily to accompany a breviary.

Richly embellished pages mark the eight divisions of the Psalter, one for each day of the week starting from Sunday, with a final division, illustrated here, for the last two liturgical hours of Saturday. The opening words of Psalm 109, in the numbering of the Latin Vulgate, 'The Lord said to my Lord sit thou at my right hand', were traditionally interpreted as referring to God the Father, shown in the initial 'D' for *Dixit* (said), with an older appearance, and God the Son, distinguished by the Cross in his left hand. The Cross surmounts the world globe at their feet and their shared book embodies the Word. The Trinity is completed by the Dove of the Holy Ghost.

In the margins, specialist border illuminators animated the stylised plants with an owl, a green bird, a peacock and a nest with bagpipe-playing bear. Although flowers and drolleries could have symbolic meanings, these designs seem to be largely decorative, as they recur elsewhere. Indeed, the owl has been taken as the hallmark of this group of illuminators, centred on London, who were encouraged in their bold motifs by trends in the northern Netherlands. England was very open to foreign art and artists: the painter of the Trinity was possibly influenced by styles evolved in English-ruled Normandy earlier in the fifteenth century. He worked on several manuscripts produced between about 1465 and 1485, probably in London, among them a luxurious Book of Hours owned by 1507 by John Morton, nephew of the Archbishop of Canterbury of that name (University of California, Berkeley, MS UCB 150).

The Psalter is a luxury item, with its large script and spacious layout, apparently produced in London for someone in the southern counties. The calendar is typical of the Use of Sarum (Salisbury) except for the feast of St Elena, written in red to signal its importance, on 2 May. As St Elenaria, whose feast is on that day, was little honoured beyond St-Riquier in Picardy, it is probably Helena, finder of the True Cross, the usual red feast (a feast day whose importance is signalled by the use of red ink) for 3 May, who is meant. Helena was more popular in the Midlands and the North but was also patron of important churches in Colchester and Abingdon, which may give a clue to the original commissioner.

An early owner added guidance in English on the Psalms appropriate to moments of specific need. The recusant Robert Hare (*c.*1530–1611), who provided an index, was in Louvain in 1563, the year he obtained the Psalter, which had possibly left England with another Catholic exile. Four of Hare's manuscripts were acquired by Archbishop Bancroft, bringing the Psalter into the Library's founding collection.

*Catherine Reynolds*
*Christie's, London*

K. L. Scott, 'A mid-fifteenth-century English Illuminating Shop and its Customers', *Journal of the Warburg and Courtauld Institutes* 31 (1968), pp. 170–96
K. L. Scott, *Later Gothic Manuscripts 1390–1490. A Survey of Manuscripts Illuminated in the British Isles* 6, 2 vols (London, 1996), vol. I, ills. 204–06, vol. II, no. 52, pp. 162–64
A. G. Watson, 'Robert Hare's Books', pp. 209–32 in *The English Medieval Book, Studies in Memory of Jeremy Griffiths*, A. S. G. Edwards, V. Gillespie and R. Hanna (eds), (London, 2000); reprinted in A. G. Watson, *Medieval Manuscripts in Post-Medieval England* (Aldershot, 2004)

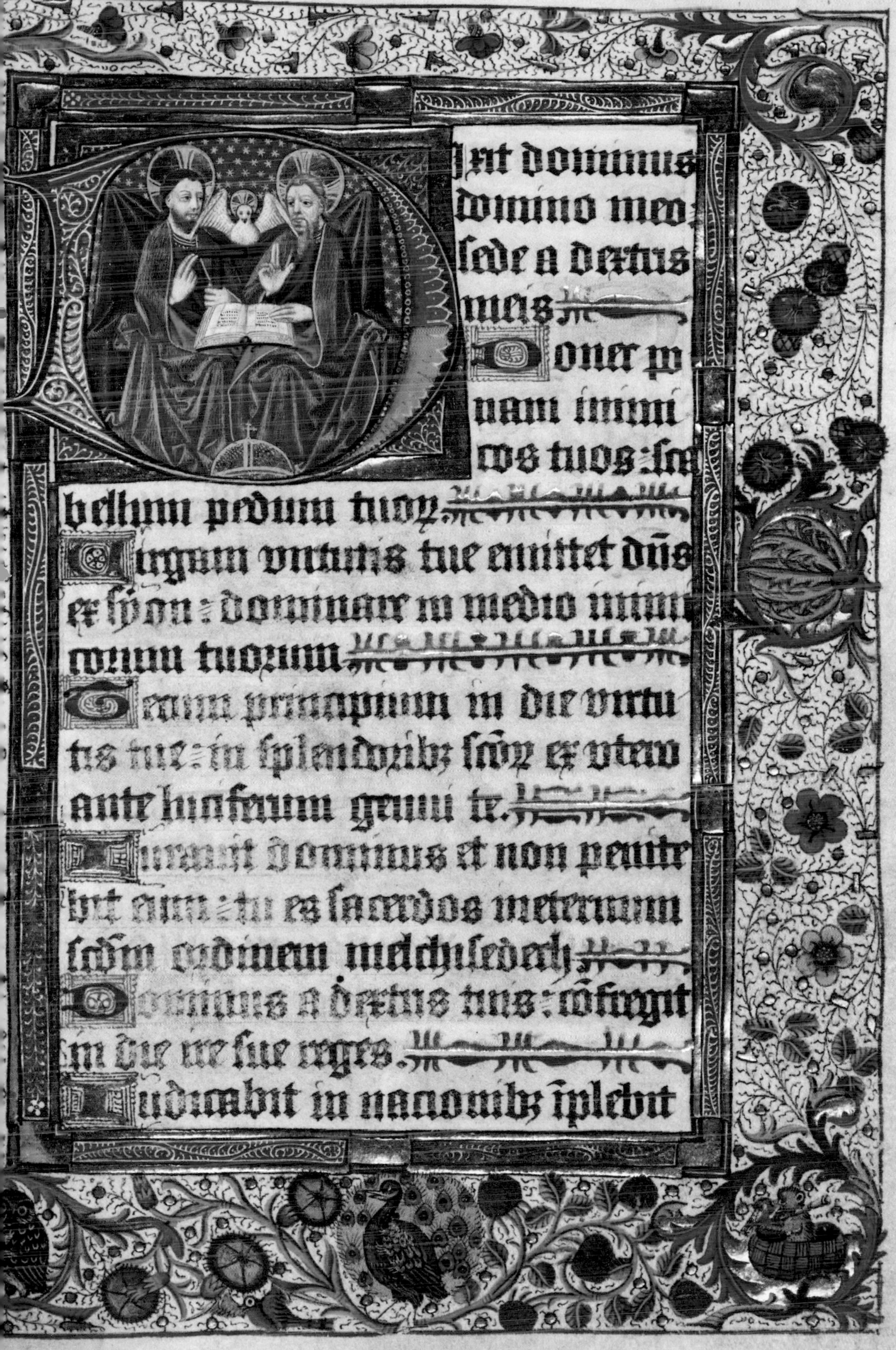

109

Dixit dominus
domino meo:
sede a dextris
meis.
Donec po
nam inimi
cos tuos: sca
bellum pedum tuorum.
Virgam virtutis tue emittet dñs
ex syon: dominare in medio inimi
corum tuorum.
Tecum principium in die virtu
tis tue: in splendoribus sanctorum ex utero
ante luciferum genui te.
Iuravit dominus et non penite
bit eum: tu es sacerdos in eternum
secundum ordinem melchisedech.
Dominus a dextris tuis: confregit
in die ire sue reges.
Iudicabit in nationibus implebit

How Julius Cesar come in to Britayn that after was clepid Angleland to kalenge þe lond & two tymes was dryuen out. And how he come ageyne the iij.de tyme and conquerd þe londe & putit to a gret tribuyt. & after went to Rome ageyne.

Aftir the deth of Lud regned his brother Cassabilan. And he made for to norish and to kepe up wele the two sones of Lud of his owne gentilnes and good wille which that were but yong and tendir of age. And what tyme they were come to age he made Androgeus the eldre brothir erle of Caerlud and of Kent. And he made Tenuance the yonger brother erle of Cornwaille. In the tyme of this kyng Cassabilan Julius cesar other wise clepid Julius gayus emperour of Rome come in to britayn wt a gret power of romeyns and calengid the land and said how that Eneas had no cosyn

nor kynne

# 18 Chronicles of England

**MS 6; Prose *Brut* to 1436, traditionally known as 'the St Albans Chronicle'**
Probably written in England and illuminated in Bruges by the Master of Edward IV, *c.*1480
Middle English and Latin; vellum; 430 x 310 mm; ff. i + 258

Illustrated: (*opposite*) f. 24v, Julius Caesar's invasion; (*overleaf left*) f. 43v, King Vortigern and Merlin watch two dragons fight (red signifying the Britons and white the Saxons); (*overleaf right and detail below*) f. 243r, Battle of Agincourt, 1415

Seventy miniatures illustrate this splendid manuscript, which contains a history of Britain from its legendary discovery by the evil queen Albina and its conquest by the Trojan hero Brutus, all the way up to the Siege of Calais in 1436. The core text is the Middle English Prose *Brut*, with interpolations from other sources. It interweaves history with legend, and it is shot through with violence, piety, heroism and villainy. Designed to stimulate English patriotism, the Prose *Brut* was one of the most popular works in English in the fifteenth century. Of the surviving Prose *Brut* manuscripts, this copy is remarkable on three counts: it is one of only two that contain the continuation of *Brut* to 1436; of all the copies of the text that survive, it is by far the most lavishly illuminated; and it was produced through an unusual collaboration between an English scribe and a talented Flemish illuminator.

This illuminator was the anonymous Bruges artist known as the Master of Edward IV. Active from the late 1470s to the 1490s, he is named after the illumination he provided for several manuscripts made around 1480 for Edward IV of England. In the Lambeth manuscript, he was assisted by two other artists, who supplied 21 illuminations. The Master was responsible for 19 of the 20 large miniatures, and 30 of its 51 small images. Instructions to the artists were written in French, suggesting that they could not read English well. Given the scribe's evident proficiency in English, it seems likely that the text was copied in England then shipped to Bruges for illumination, although the scribe could have been based in Bruges, where many English merchants operated.

The rich visual programme frequently puts a forceful pro-English spin on the narrative. In one striking example, the chronicle describes the Roman conquest, emphasising it took Julius Caesar three attempts to conquer the British. Instead of showing the climactic Roman triumph, the miniature depicts the English (identified by St George's Cross) forcing Roman soldiers back to their ships, downplaying the ultimate British defeat.

The patronage of this fine manuscript remains uncertain. It has been linked to William Purchase, mercer and Lord Mayor of London from 1497 to 1498, but the escutcheon on f. 1r differs significantly from Purchase's documented arms. Whoever commissioned this deluxe book had the vision, means and connections to have underwritten a manuscript of English history that rivals the deluxe histories in French produced for continental patrons.

*Alixe Bovey*
*School of History, University of Kent*


F. W. D. Brie (ed.), *The Brut or the Chronicles of England*, *EETS* 136 (1908), vol. 2, pp. 559–84
E. G. Millar, 'Les Principaux Manuscrits à Peintures du Lambeth Palace à Londres', *Bulletin de la Société Française de Réproductions de Manuscrits à Peintures* 9 (1925), pp. 5–81, especially pp. 15–19
C. M. Meale, 'Patrons, Buyers and Owners: Book Production and Social Status', in *Book Production and Publishing in Britain 1375–1475*, ed. J. Griffiths and D. Pearsall (Cambridge, 1989), pp. 201–38, especially pp. 226–27, note 38
L. M. Matheson, *The Prose Brut: The Development of a Middle English Chronicle* (Tempe, Arizona, 1998), pp. 298–301
T. Kren and S. McKendrick, *Illuminating the Renaissance: The Triumph of Flemish Manuscript Painting in Europe* (London and Los Angeles, 2003), no. 84

Sedente vortigirno rege super ripam exhausti stagni egressi sunt duo dracones quorum unus erat albus et alius rubeus. Cumque alter alteri appropinquasset commiserunt diram pugnam et igneum anhelitum procreabant. Prevalebat autem albus draco rubeumque usque ad extremitatem lacus fugabat. At ille cum se expulsum doluisset impetum fecit in album ipsumque retroire coegit. Ipsis ergo in hunc modum pugnantibus precepit rex ambrosio merlino dicere quid prelium draconum pretendebat. Mox ille in fletum erumpens spiritum hausit prophetie et ait. Ve rubeo draconi nam exterminacio eius festinat. Cavernas ipsius occupabit albus draco qui saxones quos invitasti significat. Rubeus

When Harflewe was beseegid be lond ⁊ be water þer were in þe towne viii C. men of werre wt oute lord ⁊ stat. And þes were the names of þe lordes Sir Jakes de Harecourt capteyn The lord Gaucourt The lord of Hakirse The lord of Flory. The lord of Bleynuyle The lord of Typtot. The lord of Combreuyle The lord of Blaunshuyle ⁊ oþer moo which shal be rehersed heraftir.

The king þen sent to Sr Jakes de Harecourt Capteyn of Harflewe ⁊ hym comaunded to delyuer þe toun And Sr Jakes ansuard ⁊ said he toke hym non to kepe nor non he shuld haue þr.

And when þis ansuar was brought unto þe king he made to say goodgrace his gret gonne ⁊ al his oþir gunnes on ich a side and comaunded his gonners to bete doune þe wales. And so þey shote on ich side ⁊ brak doun þe walles ⁊ the houses wt in þe towne. When

# 19 The Hours of Richard III

**MS 474; Book of Hours (including Memorials, Calendar, Hours of the Virgin, Hours of the Cross)**
London; *c.*1420; prayers added for Richard III, *c.*1483–85
Latin; vellum; 195 x 136 mm; ff. 186
Illustrated: (*below; detail*) f. 7v, Richard's own entry in the calendar, recording his birthday; (*opposite*) f. 15r, with initial portraying the Annunciation

King Richard III (r. 1483–85) was the first-known owner of this book, which contains an exceptionally large number of individual prayers, mostly chosen by the original commissioner, probably a cleric. It was probably made in Paternoster Row within the circle of the illuminator Herman Scheerre. The decoration is modest, with historiated initials for the Hours of the Virgin (Annunciation, f. 15r), Penitential Psalms (Christ in Judgement, now missing, f. 55r) and the Vigil of the Dead (f. 72r) and a border exhibiting Scheerre's influence in the fine modelling of the heads of SS Peter and Paul (f. 15r).

The book appears never to have been used until chosen by Richard, perhaps to replace a volume which reminded him too much of his dead wife and son; there is no indication that he used it before he was king. His birth (2 October 1452) is entered in the calendar in his own hand: *Hac die nat[us] erat Ricardus Rex Anglie iijus apud Foderingay anno domini Mcc[cclij]* (f. 7v). Devotions were added on blank pages (ff. 1, 181–84) by a professional clerk for Richard's personal use, with his name inserted. These included a collect of St Ninian, patron saint of the Western March, where Richard had ruled as Duke of Gloucester, and a mutilated text – perhaps a crusading litany.

The most important addition was the so-called 'prayer of Richard III', a version of an ancient prayer attributed to St Augustine but probably composed in Franciscan circles in the fourteenth century; its later users included the dukes of Burgundy, Frederick of Aragon and Maximilian I. It was intended to bring relief to sadness by emphasising the goodness of God. Versions vary in minor details: the word *dolor* (grief) in Richard's copy appears to be unique and is actually linked to his name in the text. The excision of the folios containing most of the prayer to St Julian the Hospitaller (part of the original book), the saint who was invoked to secure a safe journey but who was also notorious for killing his parents, and the beginning of Richard's prayer, has led ill-informed readers to connect the two texts in an ominous way.

This book would have been in Richard's tent at the Battle of Bosworth. It passed to Lady Margaret Beaufort, mother of King Henry VII. In the 1540s and 1550s it was rebound and heavily cropped in the workshop of the King Edward and Queen Mary Binder. It came to Lambeth in the collection of either Archbishop Bancroft or Archbishop Abbot.

*Anne F. Sutton,*
*Historian Emerita, Worshipful Company of Mercers, London,*
*and Livia Visser-Fuchs, Independent Scholar*

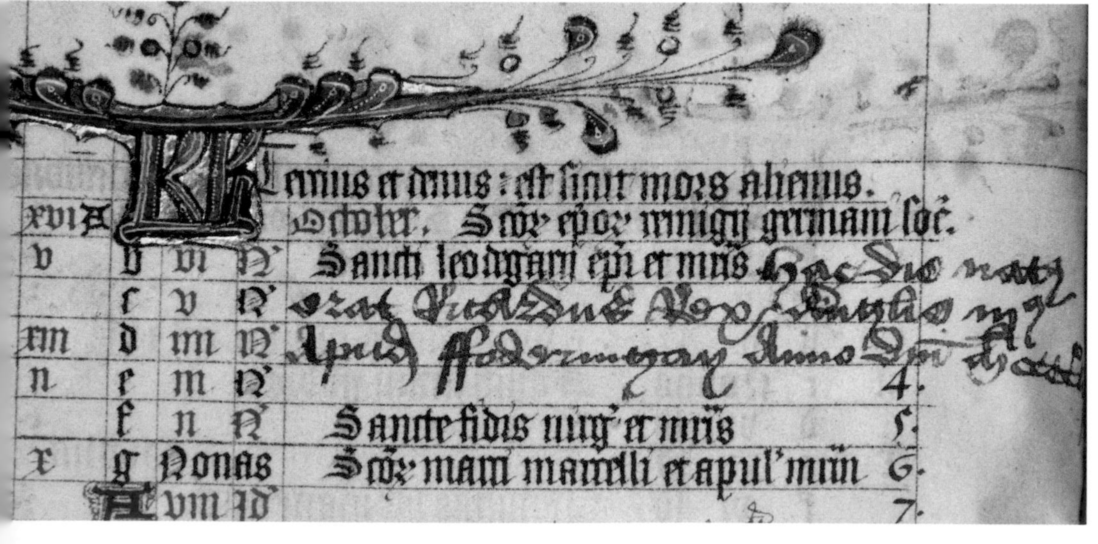

A. F. Sutton and L. Visser-Fuchs, *The Hours of Richard III*, Richard III and Yorkist History Trust (Stroud, 1990)
K. L. Scott, *Later Gothic Manuscripts 1390–1490. A Survey of Manuscripts Illuminated in the British Isles* 6, 2 vols (London, 1996), vol. I, ills. 204–06, vol. II, no. 52, pp. 162–64

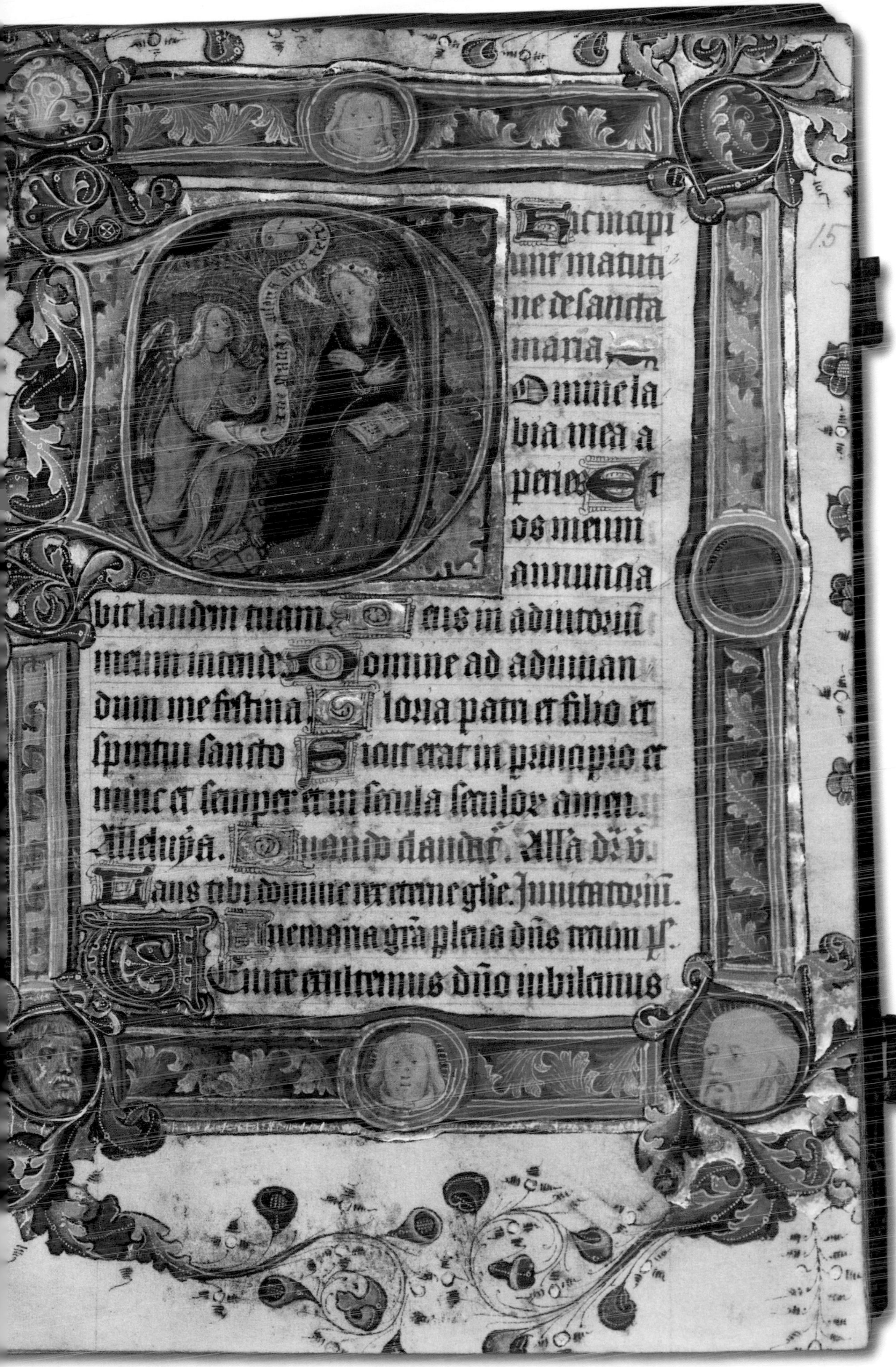
Hic incipi
unt matuti
ne de sancta
maria.
Domine la
bia mea a
peries. Et
os meum
annuncia
bit laudem tuam. Deus in adiutoriũ
meum intende. Domine ad adiuuan
dum me festina. Gloria patri et filio et
spiritui sancto. Sicut erat in principio et
nunc et semper et in secula seculorũ amen.
Alleluya. Quando dicendũ. Alla de b.
Laus tibi domine rex eterne glie. Inuitatoriũ.
Aue maria grã plena dñs tecum. ps.
Venite exultemus dño iubilemus

# 20 The Dance of Death

***Danse Macabre. Les Trois morts et les trois vifs***
Paris; Gillet Couteau [for Antoine Vérard]; after 26 June 1492
French; vellum; 290 x 205 mm; 12 ff; ISTC id00020200
Illustrated: (*right; detail*) f. 8r, Death carries off an infant;
(*opposite*) f. 2r, Death carries off a cardinal and a king

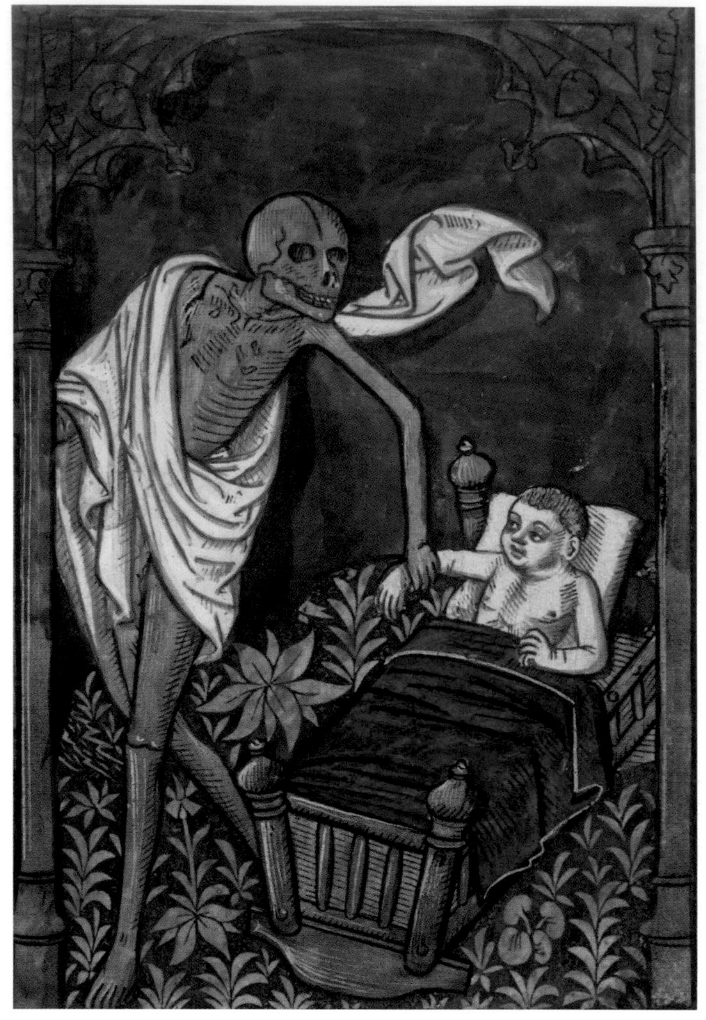

During the late Middle Ages, people were frequently encouraged to consider the inevitability of dying, and to reflect on the irrelevance of earthly things to the life everlasting, a concern perhaps reflecting the plague epidemics which afflicted Europe from the Black Death onwards. Artists seem first to have addressed this theme in wall paintings, where pairs of living, fully clothed people are contrasted vividly with grinning corpses clad in no more than a shroud. The most celebrated (and perhaps the first) of these cycles was made in 1424 at the Cimitière des Innocents in Paris, with accompanying didactic verses in the form of a dialogue between the dead and the living personages (attributed to the preacher Jean Gerson). For reasons not entirely clear these cycles became known as the *Danse macabre*. They may well have been prefigured by dramatic presentations of the subject, perhaps reflected in the way that, in the illustrations, there is a notable contrast between the static, almost rigid, portrayal of the living, and the lively appearance of the dead. The striking nature of these painted images (destroyed during the French Revolution), in a prominent part of Paris, seems to have led to similar painting cycles appearing across France as well as in Germany, Switzerland and England.

In 1485 the *Danse* was put into circulation in the form of a book by the Parisian printer Guy Marchant, with the paintings represented by woodcuts. Expanded versions of the successful original followed, and the text was soon reprinted and copied by others through the remainder of the fifteenth century and well into the sixteenth. The *Danse* has resurfaced since at those points in history when the idea has resonated with the experience of later generations.

This copy of the *Danse macabre* is from an edition prepared for the major Paris publisher Antoine Vérard, and contains the verses that accompany the wall paintings handsomely illustrated by new woodcut versions of the fifteen scenes, which in this copy have been coloured by hand. Pairs of living men drawn from a range of positions in society – from the Pope and the Emperor descending through a merchant, monk and lawyer to a friar and a child – are seen accosted, or led, by a corpse – a sign of their own future in which all ranks of society will at last be levelled. A narrator introduces the dialogues, encouraging readers to reflect on the condition of their own souls, and concludes the verses with appropriate observations. Many of these later editions add extra material, in this case the popular tale of the meeting of the Three Dead and the Three Living Men, while others extend the coverage of society by adding a *Danse des femmes*. The popularity of these books is indicated by their rarity today; their intensive use for reading and contemplation has meant that only a few survive, hidden and untouched in libraries. Of this edition of Vérard's, only one other copy is known.

*John Goldfinch*
*British Library, London*

Le mort
Vous faictes lesbahy se semble
Cardinal: sus legerement
Suiuons les autres tous ensemble
Rien ny vault esbahissement
Vous aues vescu haultement
Et en honneur a grant diuis
Prenez en gre lesbatement
En grant honneur se pert laduis

Le cardinal
Jay bien cause de mesbahir
Quant ie me voy de si pres pris
La mort mest venue assaillir
Plus ne vestiray vert ne gris
Chapeau rouge: chape de pris
Me fault laisser a grant destresse
Je ne lauoye pas apris
Toute ioye fine en tristesse

Le mort
Venez noble roy couronne
Renomme de force & prouesse
Jadis fustes enuironne
De grans pompes de grant noblesse
Mais maintenant toute haultesse
Lesseres: vous nestes pas seul
Peu aures de vostre richesse
Le plus riche na qun linceul

Le roy
Je nay point apris a danser
A danse & note si sauuaige
Las on peult bien veoir & penser
Que vault orgueil/force/lignage
Mort destruit tout cest son vsage
Aussi tost le grant que le mendre
Qui moins se prise plus est sage
En la fin fault deuenir cendre

a.ii.

# 21 King Henry VIII's Nuremberg Chronicle

**Hartmann Schedel, *Liber Cronicarum***
Nuremberg; Anton Koberger; 1493
Latin; 510 x 340 mm; [20], cclxvi,[6], cclxvii–ccxcix,[3] leaves
Illustrated: (*opposite and detail below*) f. xir, Noah's Ark, by courtesy of the Bridgeman Art Library

Known in English as the Nuremberg Chronicle, the *Liber Cronicarum* is one of the most richly illustrated examples of early printing. Among three copies at Lambeth, the most splendid has a fine blind-stamped binding and is from King Henry VIII's library at Westminster Palace, bearing the inventory number 1034. It reached Lambeth through Archbishop Bancroft, who borrowed many books from the Royal Collection.

The chronicle was produced at the instigation of, and with financial support from, Sebastian Kammermeister and his brother-in-law, Sebald Schreyer, a Nuremberg merchant and churchwarden of the city's St Sebaldus Cathedral. In 1484 they contracted to produce a sumptuous history of the world from the Creation to the year of publication. The text was compiled by Hartmann Schedel, a city doctor and a central figure of Nuremberg's humanist circle. The 1,809 woodcuts were supplied by the workshop of Nuremberg artists Michael Wolgemut and his son-in-law, Wilhelm Pleydenwurff. Latin and German editions were printed by Anton Koberger, Dürer's godfather and the greatest publisher in Europe at the time.

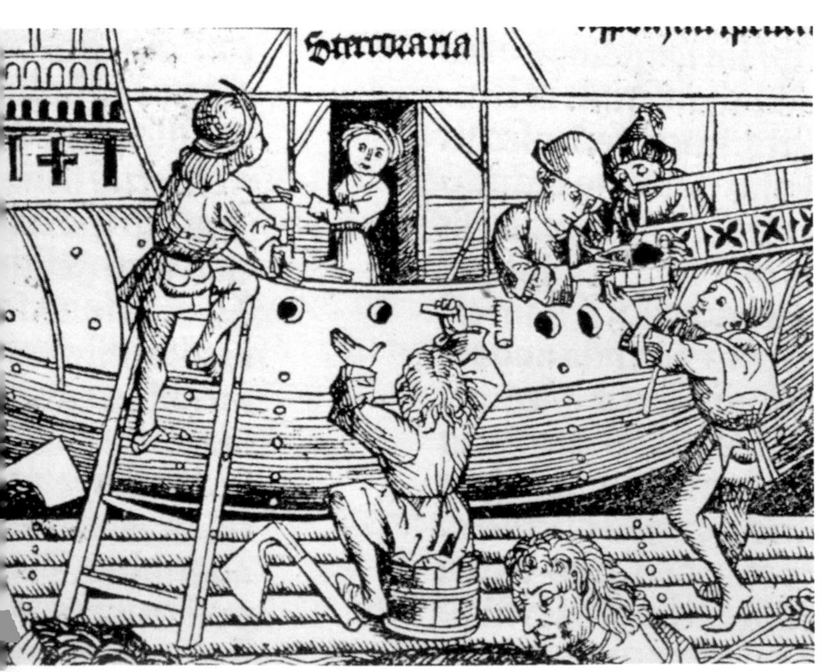

The narrative pattern of Schedel's text conforms to that of medieval universal chronicles. The history of the world is shown as a progression through six ages from the Creation to the year the book was printed, with a brief seventh age predicting the coming of the Antichrist at the end of the world and the Last Judgement. Historical events are interwoven with geographical descriptions based partly on Schedel's travels (with emphasis on the principal cities of Germany). There are digressions on natural catastrophes, Classical Antiquity, wars and curiosities. Issued seven months after Columbus landed in America, the chronicle encapsulates knowledge of the Old World on the eve of a new age.

The chronicle is a landmark in the history of book illustration because of the integration of text and painterly woodcuts. The number of illustrations used was unprecedented and there is a wide variety of formats: full-page spreads, small woodcuts placed at random in the text, genealogical tables, city panoramas, depictions of biblical sites and a Ptolemaic world map.

Work began on the woodcuts in 1487, with meticulous attention to detail. One artist was required to be on hand whenever typesetting or printing was being done to ensure that there were no defects in the blocks. The woodcuts were printed from 645 blocks and many were repeated – 96 blocks of emperors, kings and popes were used 598 times. Dürer trained at Wolgemut's workshop between 1486 and 1489 and the woodcuts of the Seventh Day of Creation and the Sun and Moon have both been tentatively attributed to him. The sheer size of the book was unparalleled. The sophisticated combination of text and illustrations made it the consummate publishing achievement of the incunable period.

*Gabriel Sewell*
*Lambeth Palace Library, London*


A. Wilson, *The Making of the Nuremberg Chronicle* (Amsterdam, 1976)
*Gothic and Renaissance Art in Nuremberg, 1300–1550* (New York and Munich, 1986)
H. Schedel, *Chronicle of the World. The Complete and Annotated Nuremberg Chronicle of 1493*, with Introduction and Appendix by Stephan Füssel (Cologne, 2001)
D. De Simone, *A Heavenly Craft. The Woodcut in Early Printed Books* (New York, 2004)

Secunda etas mūdi principiū a Noe habuit post diluuiū: qđ fuit vniuersale p totū Anno sexcētesimo vite Noe a pncipio añt mundi ſm he. Millesimosexingentesimoquinquagesimosexto. Sed ſm .lxx. interptes quos Beda et ysido. approbāt Bis mille ducenti ⁊. xlij. ⁊ durat vſq ad abrahām ſm he. 292. annis. Sed ſm .lxx. 842. annis. Ante diluuiū vo p. 100. annos Dominus apparuit Noe id ē quingentesimo anno vite Noe.

Noe diuini honoris et iusticie amator filius Lamech. ingenio mitis ⁊ integer inuenit grām coram dño. Cū cogitatio hominū pna erat ad malū. Omī tpe oēs in viam rectā reducere satagebat. Cūq instaret finis vniuerse carnis pcepit ei dñs vt faceret arcam de lignis leuigatis bituminatā intus et extra. que sit trecētoꝝ cubitoꝝ geometroꝝ longitudinis. Oro sius ⁊ post eū Augusti. ⁊ Hugo. Cubitū geometricū sex cubitos visuales facere dicūt: quā pticaꝝ noīant. Sit itaq trecētoꝝ pticaꝝ lōgitudīs: qnquaginta latitudinis ⁊ triginta altitudinis. i. a fundo vſq ad tabulatū ſb tignis. Et i cubito cōsummab illā. In q mâsiūculas cenacl'a fenestrā ⁊ ostium i latere deorsum facies. Noe igit post cētuz ⁊ xx. ānos ad arcā fabricatā. q p solatio vite erant ncēria cōportauit. Cūctoꝛūq aialiū ad bīnādū genus eoꝝ masculos ſil' ⁊ feminas pīter introduxit. Ipe deniq ⁊ filij ei⁹ vxor ⁊ vxores filioꝝ primo die meñ aprił ingressus ē. Facto diluuio cuz dñs oēm carnē deleuit. Noe cū suis saluat⁹ ē. Stetitq arca sup altissimos mōtes armenie. Qui loc⁹ egressoꝝ vocat. Egressi deo grās egerūt. Et altare facto: deo sacrificabant.

Hoc signū federis qđ do inter me et vos ⁊ ad omnē animā. Gñ. ix.

Arcus pluuialis siue Iris licet dicatur hře sex vel quatuor colores. tm duos colores pncipaliter habet. q duo iudicia repñtant. aqūs diluuiuz pteritū figurat ne ampli⁹ timeat. igneus futurū iudiciū signat per ignem vt certitudinaliter expectet.

Illo diluuij Anno prima seculi etas termiata ē ab Adā vſq ad diluuiū inclusiue. Etas scḋa incepit q ⁊ ad abrahe natiuitatē vſq perdurat.

Noe vna cū filijs ⁊ vxore ac filioꝝ vxorib⁹ ex archa egresso: ɔfestim altare edificato de cūctis pecorib⁹ volatilibusq mūdis holocausta dño obtulit. Et ei⁹ odorē suauitatis odorat⁹ est dñs. Propter qđ eidem dñs benedixit ac filijs suis dicens.

# 22 The Sarum Rite

***Missale Secundum Usum Insignis Ecclesie Sarum***
Westminster; Julian Notary and Richard Barbier for Wynkyn de Worde; 20 December 1498; STC 16172
Latin; 268 x 200 mm; ff. x, 268
Illustrated: (*opposite*) f. 1r, Mass for the first Sunday in Advent

***Processionale ... ad Usum Insignis ... Ecclesie Sarum***
London; Richard Pynson; 1501; STC 16232.6
Latin; 220 x 155 mm; not foliated
Illustrated: (*below*) procession for Ascension Day

The elaborate late-medieval liturgical practices of Salisbury Cathedral had become the norm (theoretically, anyhow) for formal worship in most of the Province of Canterbury by the end of the fifteenth century. The earliest printed edition of a missal – the celebrant's basic Massbook – of Sarum Use (Salisbury Cathedral's form of liturgical observance) was made in Paris in 1487 for William Caxton; a sole surviving copy is held by the National Trust at Lyme Park, Cheshire. Four other editions were printed in either Rouen or Venice by 1497. The Lambeth Palace folio copy dates from the following year and represents the first printing in England of the Sarum Missal. It was the product of the flourishing business of Wynkyn de Worde (d. 1534), Caxton's successor at Westminster, and clearly represents a desire to enter a profitable field.

Although the text is largely uniform with that of other Sarum Missals, both manuscript and printed, of the late fifteenth century, a desire to seem wholly up to date is discernible. Not only are all the new feasts present that became popular and/or mandated in that period, but also there are five or six masses of a votive sort for occasions which seemed on the point of becoming regularly observed feasts – Barbara, for example, who is assigned a day (16 December) that shows almost wishful thinking. Haste to publish the missal may account for the fact that no musical notes have been supplied, though four-line staves have been printed for the Proper Prefaces and at other customary places. This suggests that the edition may have been rushed onto the market (a copy in Edinburgh shares the peculiarity of having no notes); as it stands, it could be used only for a Low Mass, with no singing.

The collection of Sarum liturgical books at Lambeth contains many other treasures, including the only known copy of the first edition of the Sarum processional, printed in London by Richard Pynson in 1501. It was edited by Richard Foxe, Bishop of Winchester, and opens with his device of the pelican in her piety.

This book contains everything necessary for the conduct of the numerous processions, before High Mass on Sundays and other important occasions, that characterised the later Sarum Use. Included are texts, chant-notation, rubrics (produced properly, in red), and – the distinctive feature of printed Sarum processionals – a dozen or more diagrams indicating the relative positions of the important players. These innovative diagrams were first introduced in this edition. The participants are shown carrying holy water stoups, banners (like the great Lion and Dragon banners shown in the illustration), crosses, thuribles, candles, wands and sometimes the Reserved Host. What look like doughnuts are the tonsured heads of the participants.

*Richard W. Pfaff, Professor Emeritus of History, University of North Carolina, Chapel Hill*

Missale ad vsum chori ecclesie
Sarũ anglicane feliciter incipit.
Dñica prima aduẽtus domini.
Ad missam Introitus.
AD te leuaui animã me
am deus meus in te cõfi
do non erubescam: ne
q irrideant me inimi
ci mei etenim vniuer
si qui te expectant non confundentur.
Ps. Vias tuas domine demonstra mi
chi: ⁊ semitas tuas edoce me. Repetat
offm̃ ⁊ postea dicat. Gloria patri. Si
cut erat. tertio repetat offm̃ et sic
fiat p totũ ãnũ tã i dñicis q̃ i festis
scõꝝ cũ regimie chori ⁊ ioibꝫ mis
sis de scã maria: nisi i dñica passi
onis dñi: ⁊ abhic vsq ad cenã dñi
ad missã de tpali tm̃: tũc post ps̃m
repetat offm̃ sic. Gloria patri. Se
quat kyrie. nõ dr̃ Gl'ia in excl. p to
tũ aduẽtũ de q̃cũq dr̃ missa: nec a
septuagesia vsq ad vigil' pasche
His pactis facto q signaculo cruci
i facie sua ꝓstat se sacerdos ad ppl'ꝫ
eleuatisq aliq̃ptulũ brachiis iũcte
q manibꝫ dicat hoc mõ. Dñs vo
biscũ. Et chor⁹ respõdeat. Et cũ
spũtuo. sub eodẽ tono. Et iterũ
reuertat se sacerdos ad altare ⁊ di
cat. Oremus. Quotienscũq dr̃.
Dñs vobiscũ ad missã sp sub eod

a i

F. H. Dickinson (ed.), *Missale ad usum … Sarum* (Burntisland, 1861–83)
W. G. Henderson (ed.), *Processionale ad usum Sarum* (Leeds, 1882)
C. Wordsworth, *Ceremonies and Processions of the Cathedral Church of Salisbury* (Cambridge, 1901)
R. W. Pfaff, *New Liturgical Feasts in Later Medieval England* (Oxford, 1970)
T. Bailey, *The Processions of Sarum and the Western Church* (Toronto, 1971)
R. W. Pfaff, *The Liturgy in Medieval England: A History* (Cambridge, 2009)

¶ The fyrste chapytre of the .iii. party / sheweth of ẏ proffyte of temptacyons / and how euery soule in ẏ last ende of his lyfe shall tast and fele by knowynge or he fully pas / what peyne or ioye he shall haue after he is passed.

¶ The .iii. boke.

¶ Also how ẏ fende catcheth soules vnder the coloure of some goodnes / also this boke maketh mencyon of a vysyō that this blyssed vyrgyn had with dyuers and many maters / as it is rehersed before i the kalender. Ca. i.

The fende a mynystre ordeyned of my ryghtwysenesse to tourment soules / whiche greuously offende me. ¶ And I ordeyned theym in this lyfe / that they sholde tempte and do greate greuaunce to my creatures. ¶ Not for my creatures shol

# 23 A Bridge to Heaven

***The Orcharde of Syon***
London; Wynkyn de Worde; 1519; STC 4815
284 x 205 mm
Illustrated: (*opposite*) third part, opening of chapter 1, St Catherine prays as souls cross a bridge to heaven, escaping the assaults of devils; (*right; detail*) reverse of title page, St Catherine with twelve nuns

Syon Abbey was founded by King Henry V in 1415 on the bank of the Thames near Twickenham. It belonged to the Bridgettine Order, founded by St Bridget, and was an offshoot of her monastery of Vadstena in Sweden. Syon was a double monastery of women and a smaller number of men, most of them learned and educated at universities. The nuns were highly literate, but in English rather than in Latin. Several monks made translations from Latin for them and from the 1490s texts originating at Syon began to be more widely disseminated in print, first by William Caxton, but especially by his successor in Westminster, Wynkyn de Worde, who worked later in London. De Worde was attracted to mystical literature, and printed more devotional texts than his contemporaries.

Many of the printed books associated with Syon are modest in appearance, in line with the Order's vow of poverty, and suitable for intimate devotional reading. *The Orcharde of Syon* stands out in this sequence as a book that shows off the printer's skills. There is a great deal of red printing, and the pages are enlivened with fine initials and other typographical decoration. Eight exceptionally fine woodcuts, closely related to the text, were commissioned for this edition.

*The Orcharde of Syon* is the English version of St Catherine of Siena's mystical vision of a dialogue with God, which she experienced in October 1378, and dictated at once to her secretaries in her native Tuscan. The original *Dialogo* was widely circulated in Latin versions, one of which was introduced into England. Some 50 years later the work was translated for the nuns of Syon. The translators invented an allegorical framework of paths through an orchard, along which the sisters walk as the spirit guides them. As they wander in contemplation, readers are led to St Catherine's heavenly visions.

In an epilogue the printer writes that the steward of the abbey, Sir Richard Sutton, had found the English text in a corner, apparently forgotten after almost 100 years. Sutton, the co-founder of Brasenose College, had joined the community of the Abbey in 1513. He personally commissioned the edition, in De Worde's words 'at his greate coste ... trustinge that moche fruyte shall come thereof'. Sutton evidently thought that beautiful and vivid presentation would help not only the nuns but also lay readers in sharing the mystical experience. The printer heartily agreed.

*Lotte Hellinga*
*Formerly Deputy Keeper, British Library, London*


Sister Mary Denise, 'The Orchard of Syon: An Introduction', *Traditio* 14 (1958), pp. 269–93

P. Hodgson and G. M. Liegey, *The Orchard of Syon. Edited from the Early Manuscripts*. Early English Text Society, original series 258 (London, 1966)

E. Hodnett, *English Woodcuts 1480–1535*, 2nd edn (London, 1973), nos 862–69

J. Rhodes, 'Syon Abbey's Religious Publications', *Journal of Ecclesiastical History* 44 (1993), pp. 11–25

M. W. Driver, *The Image in Print: Book Illustration in Late Medieval England and its Sources* (London, 2004), pp. 140–46

# 25 The Arundel Choirbook and Tudor Polyphony

**MS 1; Choirbook, including music by Robert Fayrfax, Nicholas Ludford, Walter Lambe and Edmund Stourton**
Sussex, Arundel; *c.*1525
Latin; vellum; 680 x 480 mm; ff. 94
Illustrated: (*right*) ff. 56v–57r, opening of *Eterne laudis lilium* by Robert Fayrfax (d. 1521); (*opposite; detail*) f. 56v

The Lambeth or Arundel Choirbook is one of two ecclesiastical English choirbooks to have survived from the reign of King Henry VIII. It is twinned with the so-called Caius Choirbook (Gonville and Caius College, Cambridge, MS 667), which shares much of the same repertory and was copied by the same scribe using similar materials. Their size is particularly noteworthy, each folio originally measuring approximately 740 x 510 mm.

The man responsible for both choirbooks was Edward Higgons, a prominent Tudor lawyer and multiple pluralist, who was a canon of St Stephen's, Westminster, where Nicholas Ludford, the principal composer in both manuscripts, was employed from the early 1520s. The Caius Choirbook was destined for St Stephen's, while Lambeth seems to have been a working manuscript for the choir of Arundel College in Sussex. Both were produced around 1525 and were almost certainly copied in Arundel after Edward Higgons retired to the mastership of the college in 1520. The scribe may well have been Edward's brother, John, who was a singing man there and known to have been active as a copyist throughout this period.

The Lambeth Choirbook contains seven Masses, four Magnificats, seven Votive Antiphons and one Respond, and, with Caius, is the most important source of early Tudor polyphony since the great Eton Choirbook (compiled *c.*1502) of the previous generation. Upon the Dissolution of Arundel College in 1544, the Lambeth Choirbook fell into the hands of Henry Fitzalan, 12th Earl of Arundel, whose own great collection of books was wholly bequeathed to his son-in-law John, Lord Lumley. Lumley seems to have given the choirbook, along with no fewer than 21 other volumes, to Richard Bancroft sometime between Arundel's death in 1580 and the making of the catalogue of his own library at Nonesuch in 1596. In 1610 Bancroft left his books to his successors at Lambeth Palace.

*David Skinner*
*Sidney Sussex College, Cambridge*

D. Skinner, *The Arundel Choirbook* (Duke of Norfolk: Roxburghe Club, 2003)
D. Skinner, *Nicholas Ludford I: Mass Inclina cor meum and Antiphons*, Early English Church Music, 44 (London, 2003)

# ארבעה

ארבעה ראשי שני' הם באחד בניסן ראש השנה למלכי' ולרגלים באחד באלול ראש השנה למעשר בהמה רבי אלעזר ורבי שמעון אומרים באחד בתשרי באחד בתשרי ראש השנה לשנים ולשמיטין וליובלו' לנטיע' ולירקו' באחד בשבט ראש השנה לאילן כדברי בית שמאי בית הלל אומרי' בחמשה עשר בו: גמ' למלכים למאי הילכתא אמר רב חסד' לשטרות דתנן שטרי חוב המוקדמין פסולי' והמאוחרין כשרין תנו רבנן מלך שעמד בעשרים ותשעה באדר כיון שהגיע אחד בניסן עלתה לו שנה ואם לא עמד אלא באחד בניסן אין מונין לו שנה עד שיגיע ניסן אחר אמר מר מלך שעמד בעשרי' ותשעה באדר כיון שהגיע אחד בניסן עלתה לו שנה הא קא

## ארבעה

ראשי שנים הם למלכים רגילים היו למנות זמן שטרותיהם לשנות המלך משנה שעמד בה המלך כדאמרינן במסכת גיטין משום שלום מלכות וקבעו חכמים אחד בניסן לתחלת שנתן ואפילו עמד בשבט או באדר כלתה שנתו משהגיע ניסן ויתחילו למנות לו שנה שנייה: ולרגלים מפרש בגמרא: למעשר בהמה שאין מעשרין מן הנולדים בשנה זו על הנולדים בחבירתה דכתיב עשר תעשר את כל תבואת זרעך היוצא השדה שנה שנה ואמר מר בבכורות בפרק מעשר בהמה בשתי מעשרות הכתוב מדבר אחד מעשר בהמה ואחד מעשר דגן: לשנים מפרש בגמרא: לשמיטין וליובלות משהגיע תשרי אסור לחרוש ולזרוע מן התורה: לנטיעה למנין שני ערלה ואפילו נטעה באב כלתה שנתה הראשונה לסוף אלול ובכולהו מפרש טעמא בגמרא: לירקות למעשר ירק שאין תורמין ומעשרין מן הנלקט לפני ר"ה השנה על של אחר ר"ה השנה: לאילן לענין מעשר שאין מעשרין פירות האילן שחנטו קודם שבט על שחנטו לאחר שבט שהאילן הולך אחר חנטה ובגמרא מפרש מאי שנא שבט: גמ' למאי הילכתא כלומר למה הוקבע יום מיוחד למנין המלכים אימא שעל כל מלך ומלך מתחיל שנתו מיום שעמד בו: לשטרות להבחין איזה שטר מוקדם למלוה ואיזה מאוחר: דתנן במסכת שביעית: שטרי חוב המוקדמין פסולין לפי שבא לטרוף לקוחות שלקחו שדה מן הלוה מזמן שבשטר ושלא כדין הוא שהרי קדמה מכירה להלואה ובשטר מעיד שהלוא' ק"מ לפיכך קנסוהו מלגבות בו ולא יטרוף אפי' מזמן המלוה ואינו אלא כמלוה על פה שאינו גובה מן המשועבדים ואם לא קבעו יום לתחילת שנות המלך אלא כל מלך ומלך לפי שעמד אין להבחין אם השטר מוקדם או מאוחר כגון אם כתוב בו לכסליו בשנה שלישית לוה פלוני מפלוני מנה והעדים אמרו בשחתמנו בו לא ראינו שהלוהו אלא הלוה אמר לנו חתמו עליו שהרי חייב לפלוני מנה כאותה ששנינו כותבין שטר ללוה אף על פי שאין מלוה עמו ואין אנו יודעין אם הלוהו קודם לכן או אחר כן אבל ראינו שהלוהו מנה בתמוז בשנה שלישית למלך פלו' ואם אין הדיינין יודעין באיזה חדש עמד המלך אין להבחין אם תמוז קודם לכסליו אם כסליו קודם לתמוז אם שנתו מתחלת בין תמוז לכסליו נמצא כסליו קודם לתמוז בכל שנותיו ושטר מוקדם הוא ואם עמד בין כסליו לתמוז שלאחריו נמצא תמוז קודם לכסליו בכל שנותיו ושטר מאוחר הוא ועכשיו שקבעו ניסן ראש השנה לעולם תמוז קודם לכסליו עלתה לו שנה כלומר כלתה לו שנתו ומעתה מונין לו שנה שניה: מאי

## ארבעה

ראשי שנים הן בכל הוסת' תני הן דראשון הכא ובפ' בתרא דשבועות ארבע שומרים הן ובפרק קמא דחולין שלשה שימות הן שלשה יבמות הן ובפרק כל הצלמים שלשה בתים הן שלשה אבנים הן שלשה אילנו' הן אבל ברים בבא קמא תנן ארבע אבות נזיקין ולא תני הן משום דקאי בתריה כלומר ארבע אבות נזיקין הללו לא ראי זה כראי זה ותדע ד' דבגמרא במתניתא דרבי חייא ורבי אושעיא תני הן: למלכים פירש בקונטרס משום שלום מלכים ואינו דהכא למלכי ישראל קמיירי ודוקא גבי גיטין אמרינן הכי פרק הזורק אמר עולא מפני מה תקנו מלכו' בגיטין משום שלום מלכות וגבי גיטין פסולין ודאי אפילו מלכו' שאינה הוגנת כמלכו' מדי ויון אבל מתניתין דהכא פירוש לשטרות ובפרק קמא דעבודה זרה אמרינן דבגולה אין מונין אלא מלכי יון בלבד ומתניתין נמי אתא דלמלכים דהכא למלכי ארץ ישראל וכן נמי אמרינן ליקמן בגמרא לא שנו אלא למלכי ישראל אבל למלכי אומות העולם מתשרי מנינן וצריך לפרש דאין צריך שלום מלכות אלא בגט אשה לפי שהוא דבר גדול ומילתא ד' דחשיבותא לפי שעל ידי גט מותרת לכל אדם וחשיב משאר שטרות: לשטרות דתנן שטרי חוב המוקדמין פירש בקונטרס שאם לא קבעו יום לתחילת שנת המלך אלא לכל מלך לפי מה שעמד פעמים שאין להבחין כגון אם כתב בו בכסליו בשנה שלישית ובאו עדים ואמרו כשחתמנו לא ראינו ש שהלוהו אלא הלוה אמר לנו חתמו כאותה ששנינו כותבין שטר ללוה אף על פי שאין המלוה עמו ואי אנו יודעין אם הלוהו קודם לכן או אחר כך אבל ראינו שהלוהו בתמוז שנת שלש למלך ואם אין הדיינין יודעין באיזה חדש עמד המלך אין להבחין אם תמוז קודם לכסליו ואם כסליו קודם לתמוז אם שנתו מתחלת בין תמוז לכסליו נמצא כסליו קודם לתמוז בכל שנותיו ואם עמד בין כסליו לתמוז נמצא תמוז קודם לכסליו בכל שנותיו ועכשיו שקבעו ניסן ראש השנה לעולם תמוז קודם לכסליו וצריך לפרש שהודו המלוה והלוה שהלואה אחת היא דאי לאו הכי מנא ידעי' והשתא משמע לפירוש הקונטרס מספק היינו חושבים אותו מוקדם אי לאו דקבעו ניסן ראש השנה שעל ידי כן אנו יודעין בו שהוא מאוחר ואי אפשר לומר כן דאין לנו לפסול שום שטר מספק כדמוכח בריש אחד דיני ממונות דקאמר שטר שזמנו כתוב באחד בניסן בשמיטה ובאו עדים ואמרו היאך אתם מעידים על שטר זה והלא באותו יום עמנו הייתם שטר כשר ועדים כשרים חיישינן שמא אחרוהו וכתבוהו הרי שאנו תולין להכשיר מספק וכן בגט בסוף דקאמר שטר שזמנו כתוב בשבת או בעשרה בתשרי כשר שאני אומר אחרוהו וכתבוהו ומיהו יכול לפרש פירוש איפכא שיפרש שכתוב בשטר בתמוז בשנת שלש והעדים החתומים אומרים שבכסליו בשנת שלש היתה המלוה והייתי מכשיר מספק ועל ידי שקבעו בניסן ראש השנה אנו יודעין שהוא מוקדם לעולם תמוז קודם לכסליו ומיהו עיקר פירושו תימה גדולה שעשו תקנה שן ישכחו כל העולם מתי עמד המלך וכן סופר שכותב כל היום שטרות היאך ישכחו ועוד ואם כן הוה מצי למימר דנפקא מינה טובא לכל שטרות שלא ידעו מה לכתוב בו ביום ראשון יודעים מתי מתחלת שנת המלך ועוד דכי האי גוונא לאו מוקדם לאביי דאמר בפרק קמא דבבא מציעא עדיו בחתומיו זכין לו ולרב אסי דפליג עליה למה הוזכרו לעשות התקנה זו הא אמרי' אין כותבין שטר ללוה אלא אם כן מלוה עמו אלא בשטרי הקנאה ונראה דנפקא מינה לשטרי חוב המוקדמין קיימ' כגון אם עמד המלך באחד בניסן כשהגיע אחד בניסן אחר ישכח הסופר וסבור דאשתקד עמד המלך בשתים בניסן דעביד איניש דטעי חד יומא ויכתוב באחד בניסן בשנה ראשונה למלך ונמצא שטר זה מוקדם שנה שלימה שהיא שנה שניה וכתוב ראשונ' ונמצאו בית דין טורפין מן הלקוחות של שנה זו שלא כדין אבל עכשיו שקבעו ניסן ראש השנה תו לא אתי לידי תקלה דאפילו עמד אשתקד בשנים בניסן כשמגיע ניסן אחר מתחילין למנות לו שנה אחרת ואם תאמר אכתי אתי לידי תקלה דאם עמד בעשרים ותשעה באדר בשנה ראשונה למלך כשהגיע עשרים ותשע' אדר יטעה הסופר ביום אחד וסבור שעומד באחד בניסן ויכתוב עכשיו בכ"ט באדר בשנה ראשונה למלך ונמצא מוקדם שנה שלמה לאו פירכא היא דכשעמד בתשעה ועשרים באדר מיד שהגיע אחד בניסן מתחיל למנות שנה שניה ויודע הסופר שכל השנה כתב בכל השטרות שנה שנייה הלכך לא טעי ויש שיטה אחרת בירושלמי בין מאן דאמר מניסן מנינן בין מאן דאמר מתשרי מנינן מה ביניהן אמר רבי יצחק שטרות יובלות ביניהן לוה באייר וכתיב ביה שנה שנייה למלכות מכר מכירה במרחשון וכתב בו שנה שנייה למלכות מאן דאמר מניסן מנינן מלוה קדמה מאן דאמר מתשרי מנינן מכירה קדמה ומילתא אחריתי היא ולא אתי לפרושי מאי טעמא קבעו ניסן ראש השנה:

שטרי חוב המוקדמין פסולין בשילהי איזהו נשך פירש בקונטרס פסולין לגבי משעבדי אבל מבני חרי גבי ולא יתכן כמו שפירש שם: אבל

# 26 The Sion College Talmud

**Babylonian Talmud**
Venice; Daniel Bomberg; *c.*1526–48
Hebrew; 12 vols, each 375 x 270 mm
Illustrated: (*opposite*) vol. 4, first page of tractate Rosh Hashanah;
(*below: detail*) vol. 1, presentation inscription, 1629

The Babylonian Talmud, in more than 60 tractates redacted orally over centuries, is the classic work of ancient rabbinic Judaism. Encompassing Jewish law, biblical exegesis, social history and folklore, the text has been the subject of innumerable commentaries. A few tractates were printed by Jews in Italy, Spain and Portugal before 1500, but it was not until 1519 that a Christian maecenas of the Hebrew book, a native of Antwerp, ventured to set in type the entire Aramaic and Hebrew text. The Talmud issued by Daniel Bomberg at Venice is one of the greatest achievements in the history of Hebrew printing, and served as a model for all subsequent editions.

Few copies of Bomberg's tractates survived in Jewish hands. In 1553 all Jewish books in Italy were consigned to the flames by papal decree. Many tractates sent before the book-burnings to Jewish communities in Ottoman lands and northern Europe were also lost in conflagrations and persecutions over the centuries. Most complete sets of the Bomberg Talmud extant today were preserved in Christian hands – in ecclesiastical or royal collections.

One such set was among the first books purchased for the library of Sion College at its foundation in 1629. George Walker, incumbent of the London parish of St John the Evangelist, raised the price of £26 from 18 of his parishioners, whose names are inscribed in the first volume. These and many other Hebrew books were bought from Henry Fetherstone, who had advertised them in his *Catalogus librorum in diversis locis Italiae emptorum* (London, 1628), the first antiquarian catalogue by an English bookseller.

Bound in 12 volumes, the Bomberg Talmud became part of Sion's chained library. In the Great Fire of 1666, the College lost its quarto and octavo Hebrew books, but the Talmud and other Hebraica in folio survived unharmed. The Talmud was recorded in the library's published catalogues of 1650 and 1724, but its existence remained unknown to Hebrew bibliography until 1991, when it was serendipitously rediscovered in the stacks. Rebound by the English master binder Bernard Middleton, who incorporated its original English leather boards, the Sion Talmud was transferred to Lambeth Palace in 1996.

The printing history of Bomberg's Talmud is complex. Over 30 years Bomberg issued at least three editions or 'states' of many of the tractates, in runs of perhaps 1,000 copies. Comprised of tractates from what is often called his second edition of *c.*1526–48, the Sion copy is one of only about a dozen known complete sets, almost all made up of tractates from two or more of the editions. It contains annotations in an Italian hand of *c.*1600, indicating that, unlike most surviving sets, this one was actually studied. The greatest of English Christian Hebraists, Lightfoot, who moved closer to London to use Sion's Hebrew books, must also have opened it. Nevertheless, all of the tractates are in pristine condition, comparable in their perfection to the Valmadonna Talmud, held for centuries at Westminster Abbey. The Bomberg Talmud now at Lambeth is one of the finest preserved copies in the world.

*Brad Sabin Hill*
*The Melvin Gelman Library, George Washington University, Washington DC*

THE PARISHONERS. of St IOHN. the Euangelists in Watlingstreet in
London gaue this Babilonian Talmud to the new Librarie in Zion College
which great and rare work consists of 12 volumes printed at Venice.
by that famous Hebrue printer Daniel Bomberge. Anno Doi. 1548.
The price of this whole worke — £26. giuen by the parishoners afforesaid :
being in number 18. vpon the motion of Mr George Walker Rector of ye parish.
The names of the contributing parishoners.

E. Pilkington, 'Rare Talmud Found at London College', *The Independent* (London, 11 August 1992), p. 2

M. McC. Gatch and B. E. Nielsen, 'The Wittenberg Copy of the Bomberg Talmud', *Gutenberg-Jahrbuch 2003* (Mainz, 2003), pp. 296–326

S. L. Mintz and G. Goldstein (eds), *Printing the Talmud: From Bomberg to Schottenstein* (New York, 2005)

J. Roberts and G. J. Toomer, 'The Fetherstone Catalogue of Hebrew Books', *The Bodleian Library Record*, vol. 19 (Oxford, 2006), pp. 47–76

# 27 Cosmography from Archbishop Cranmer's Library

**Petrus Apianus, *Cosmographicus liber***
Antwerp; Roland Bollaert; 1529
Latin; 196 x 154 mm; 55[1] ff.
Illustrated: (*below*) title page with Cranmer's ownership inscription; (*opposite above*) f. 12v, a volvelle – an altitude sundial to tell the time in any latitude; (*opposite below; detail*) f. 53r, a volvelle – a lunar clock to determine time at night

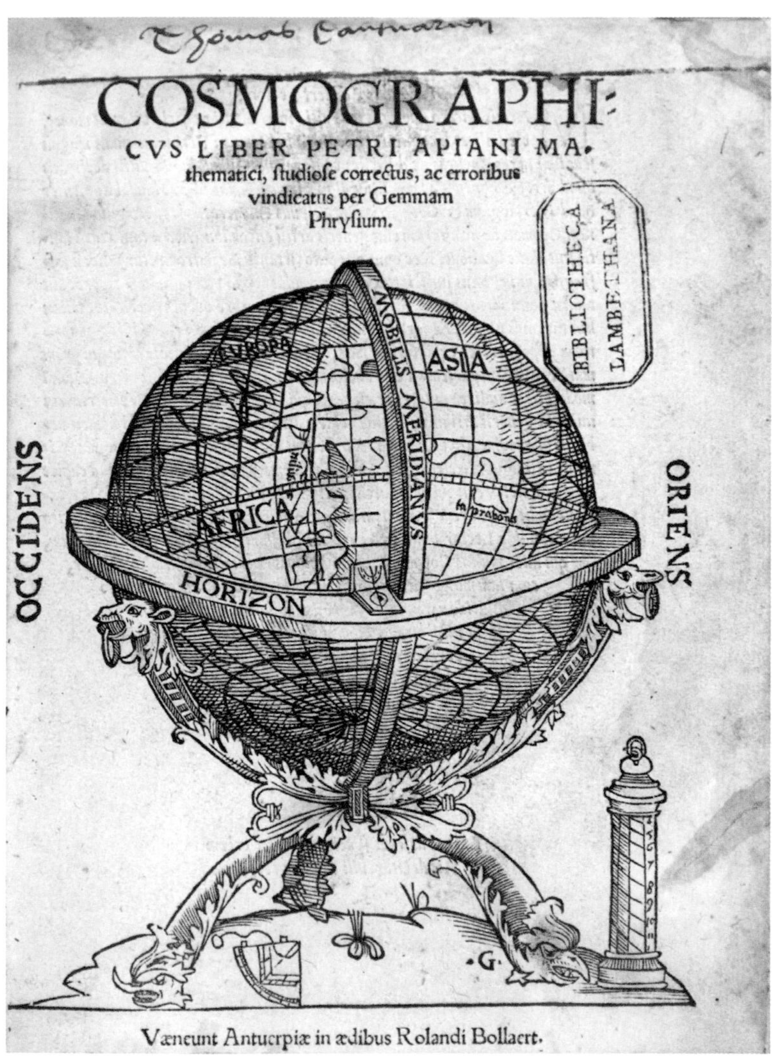


When Thomas Cranmer acquired this practical handbook it was the most up-to-date description of the known world, borrowing from Classical and medieval sources with a mixture of fact and fiction, providing the basics of astronomy, geography and navigation, and including details of newly discovered lands in the New World. It was a best-seller throughout Europe, appearing over the next century in as many as 45 editions, in 4 languages, printed in 7 cities, by at least 18 printers.

The author Petrus Apianus (1495–1552), professor of mathematics at the University of Ingolstadt, knighted by the emperor Charles V, was a pioneer in astronomical and geographical instrumentation. His *Cosmographia* was important for the imaginative use of simple mechanical devices, particularly the distinctive mobile volvelles (wheel charts with rotating parts), of which there are four in the present volume, to provide information on the position and movement of celestial bodies. This is the second edition of the original Latin text (1524), 'carefully corrected with all errors set to right' by Reiner Gemma Frisius. It is richly illustrated with woodcuts of terrestrial and celestial globes, an armillary sphere, maps of the world, wind charts, eclipses of the moon and scientific instruments for measurement.

It is tempting to imagine that Cranmer may have bought this copy of *Cosmographia*, or perhaps he was given it by the author himself, when he was sent to Germany by King Henry VIII in 1532 as ambassador to the court of Charles V. It was while still abroad that he learned of his appointment as Archbishop of Canterbury.

Cranmer owned a very significant library estimated to have numbered as many as 700 volumes, making it one of the greatest private libraries in England at the time, considerably larger than most of the college libraries at Cambridge and Oxford. Predictably the bulk of the collection was theological, although other disciplines such as history, law, medicine and science were represented. Most were printed books, but there were some manuscripts; and Latin was the predominant language. Apianus's *Cosmographia* was one of just under 20 geographical or cosmological works, among which there were several others by the same author.

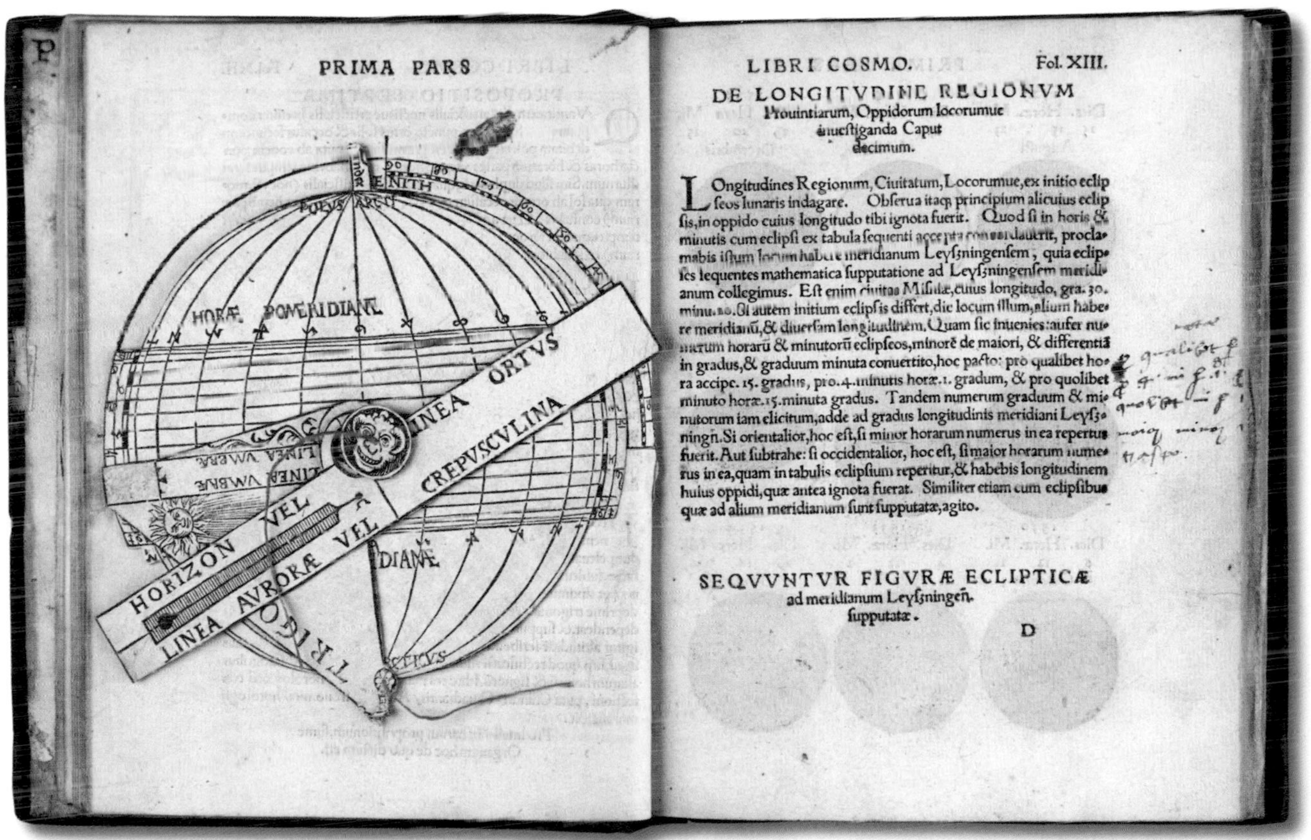

PRIMA PARS

LIBRI COSMO. Fol. XIII.

DE LONGITVDINE REGIONVM Prouintiarum, Oppidorum locorumue inuestiganda Caput decimum.

Longitudines Regionum, Ciuitatum, Locorumue, ex initio eclipseos lunaris indagare. Obserua itaq; principium alicuius eclipsis, in oppido cuius longitudo tibi ignota fuerit. Quod si in horis & minutis cum eclipsi ex tabula sequenti accepta concordauerit, proclamabis istum locum habere meridianum Leysningensem, quia eclipses sequentes mathematica supputatione ad Leysningensem meridianum collegimus. Est enim ciuitas Misnae, cuius longitudo, gra. 30. minu. 10. Si autem initium eclipsis differt, dic locum illum, alium habere meridianũ, & diuersam longitudinem. Quam sic inuenies: aufer numerum horarũ & minutorũ eclipseos, minorẽ de maiori, & differentiã in gradus, & graduum minuta conuertito, hoc pacto: pro qualibet hora accipe. 15. gradus, pro. 4. minutis horae. 1. gradum, & pro quolibet minuto horae. 15. minuta gradus. Tandem numerum graduum & minutorum iam elicitum, adde ad gradus longitudinis meridiani Leysningñ. Si orientalior, hoc est, si minor horarum numerus in ea repertus fuerit. Aut subtrahe: si occidentalior, hoc est, si maior horarum numerus in ea, quam in tabulis eclipsium reperitur, & habebis longitudinem huius oppidi, quae antea ignota fuerat. Similiter etiam cum eclipsibus quae ad alium meridianum sunt supputatae, agito.

SEQVVNTVR FIGVRAE ECLIPTICAE ad meridianum Leysningeñ. supputatae.

D



The journey of this book following Cranmer's fall from grace under Queen Mary, and his death in 1556, illustrates the fate of his great library. His possessions were seized and distributed by the Crown, the books falling to Henry Fitzalan, 12th Earl of Arundel (d. 1579). From Arundel they passed to his son-in-law John, Lord Lumley (1534–1609), and thence to Henry, Prince of Wales in 1609 (and ultimately to the British Library), but not before a number of books, many formerly Cranmer's, had been given away. The *Cosmographia* is bound, together with another thin volume, Henricus Cornelius Agrippa's *De occulta philosophia libri tres* (Antwerp, 1531), in early seventeenth-century calf with the arms of Archbishop Richard Bancroft stamped in gilt on both covers. Bancroft acquired many books from the Lumley library, and this volume was probably one of them. It was part of the foundation collection of Lambeth Palace Library, and features in the catalogue of 1612 (f. 59). At the head of the title page, written in a characteristic secretarial hand, is the inscription 'Thomas Cantuarieñ'.

*Richard Linenthal*
*London*

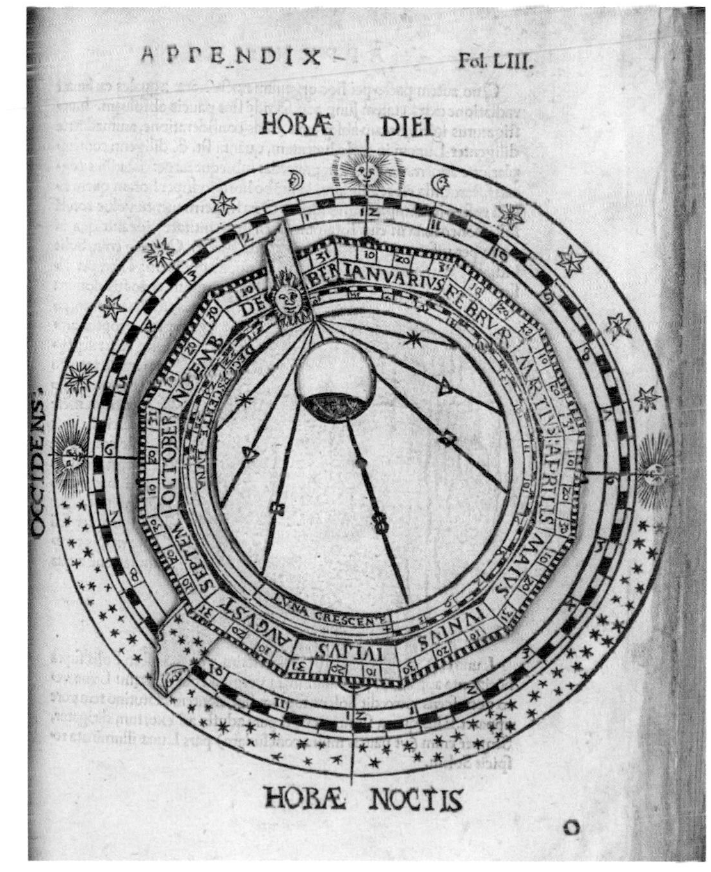

APPENDIX Fol. LIII.




Diarmaid MacCulloch, *Thomas Cranmer: A Life* (New Haven and London, 1996)
D. G. Selwyn, *The Library of Thomas Cranmer* (Oxford, 1996), no. 602

# 28 A Primer for All Seasons

***Thys prymer of Salysbury use***
Paris; Thielman Kerver; 1534; STC 15985, with extra-illustration
English and Latin; 125 x 90 mm
Illustrated: (*opposite above*) ff. 101v–102r, with added woodcut of the Pentecost; (*opposite below*) ff. 196v–197r, with added woodcut of Mary breastfeeding the Christ Child

The Book of Hours or primer, a best-seller in the later medieval period, held a central place in popular culture well into the sixteenth century. This example was printed in Paris in 1534 for the English market, which remained strong even after the Reformation was well under way. From about 1527, Paris dominated the market for English books of hours. The main printer from the late 1520s until 1538 was François Regnault, who had rearranged the contents, introduced more English material and reduced the size to create an easily accessible devotional book for popular use.

This particular edition, while printed in Paris and similar to Regnault's small-size primers in terms of content and English title page, was published by Thielman Kerver (actually by his widow, Yoland Bonhomme) and funded by the London bookseller, Johan Growte. Like Regnault's primer, this has four-line stanzas of English verse replacing the Latin versicle and response; here they appear under woodcuts in the calendar and the Gospel. This primer also follows the practice of Regnault in the prominent placing, immediately after the calendar, of three English devotions that touch on daily life: *The Dayes of the Week Moralized, The Maner to Lyue Well* (translated by Robert Copland from a French original by Jean Quentin) and Jean Gerson's *Three Verities*. Towards the end, it also includes *The Forme of Confessyon*, as found in Regnault's primers.

This edition ends with an extra gathering containing the Jesus Psalter, a popular late medieval devotion, so called because its 15 petitions, to be repeated 10 times, equal the number of Psalms. In accordance with the Act of Supremacy of 1534 and other royal proclamations, this devotion has been crossed out, as have rubrics mentioning indulgences and other forbidden practices. The name of St Thomas Becket and all mention of the Pope have also been assiduously erased throughout.

What makes this copy especially interesting as a devotional object is its chameleon-like ability to adapt to official religious changes. The addition – presumably later in the sixteenth century – of five woodcuts that are attached to existing leaves suggests Counter-Reformation devotion. The first three are pasted in: a hand-coloured woodcut of St Roche showing his wound to an angel (on the recto of a flyleaf); John the Baptist and John the Evangelist (f. 31r); and, one of the most popular images of the period, the Arma Christi portraying images of the wounds of Christ (f. 98r). The remaining two, both hand-coloured, are sewn in: the Pentecost – without the flames (f. 102r) – and the Virgin breastfeeding the Christ Child (f. 196v). Added images are not uncommon in primers of religious or lay owners, as concentrating on images, like spiritual reading, was considered to be a valid devotional practice.

Notes of births and other inscriptions suggest that this copy was in the possession of the Constable family from the East Riding of Yorkshire who followed the traditional religion.

*Ann M. Hutchison*
*Glendon College, York University, and Pontifical Institute of Mediaeval Studies, Toronto*

E. Hoskins, *Horae Beatae Mariae Virginis or Sarum and York Primers with Kindred Books and Primers of the Reformed Roman Use* (London, 1901)
P. L. Hughes, and J. F. Larkin (eds), *Tudor Royal Proclamations*, 3 vols (New Haven and London, 1964–69)
M. C. Erler, '*The Maner to Lyue Well* and the Coming of English in François Regnault's Primers of the 1520s and 1530s', *The Library*, 6th series, 6 (1984), pp. 229–43
M. C. Erler, 'Pasted-In Embellishments in English Manuscripts and Printed Books *c.*1480–1533', *The Library*, 6th series, 14 (1992), pp. 185–206
E. Duffy, *Marking the Hours: English People and Their Prayers, 1240–1570* (New Haven, 2006)

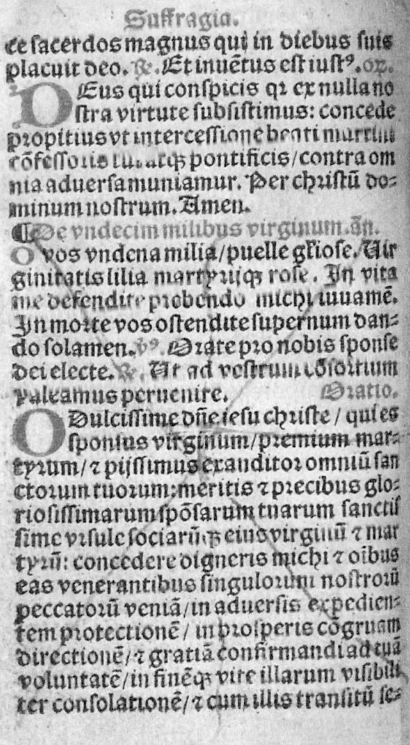

Suffragia.
ce sacerdos magnus qui in diebus suis
placuit deo. ℟. Et inuētus est iust⁹. or.
DEus qui conspicis qr ex nulla no
stra virtute subsistimus: concede
propitius vt intercessione beati martini
cōfessoris tui atq₃ pontificis / contra om
nia aduersa muniamur. Per christū dominum nostrum. Amen.
¶ De vndecim milibus virginum. an.
O vos vndena milia / puelle gl'iose. Vir
ginitatis lilia martyriiq₃ rose. In vita
me defendite probendo michi iuuamē.
In morte vos ostendite supernum dan-
do solamen. ℣. Orate pro nobis sponse
dei electe. ℟. Vt ad vestrum cōsortium
valeamus peruenire. Oratio.
O Dulcissime dn̄e iesu christe / qui es
sponsus virginum / premium mar-
tyrum / ⁊ pijssimus exauditor omniū san
ctorum tuorum: meritis ⁊ precibus glo-
riosissimarum spōsarum tuarum sanctis
sime vrsule sociarū q₃ eius virginū ⁊ mar
tyrū: concedere digneris michi ⁊ oībus
eas venerantibus singulorum nostrorū
peccatorū veniā / in aduersis expedien-
tem protectionē / in prosperis cōgruam
directionē / ⁊ gratiā confirmandi ad tuā
voluntatē / in fineq₃ vite illarum visibili
ter consolationē / ⁊ cum illis transitū se-

Suffragia. Fo. cxcvij.
ctus fructus ventris tui: quo nos dono
semper frui per hoc presens fac seculum
⁊ post mortē in eternum. Hunc virgo sa
lutis censum tue laudis gratum pēsum /
corde tuo sume pia clemens dulcis o ma
ria. Amen. Pater noster. Aue maria.
¶ Who that sayth deuoutly this hours
prayer dayly shall not depte out of this
worlde with out penaunce ⁊ admynystra
tyō of the holy sacramēt the which was
shewed by an aūgell vnto saynt bernard
AUe maria ancilla scte̅ trinitatis.
Aue maria filia sempiterni pr̄is.
Aue maria spōsa spūssancti. Aue maria
Aue maria mater dn̄i nr̄i iesu xp̄i. Aue maria soror
angelorū. Aue maria pmissio pphetar̄
Aue maria regina patriarcharū. Aue
maria magistra euangelistarū. Aue ma
ria doctrix apostolorū. Aue maria cōfor
tatrix martyrū. Aue maria fons et pul-
chritudo cōfessorum. Aue maria dec⁹ ⁊
corona virginū. Aue maria salus ⁊ con-
solatrix viuorū ⁊ mortuorū. Mecum sis
in oībus tētationibus / tribulationibus /
necessitatib⁹ / angustijs / ⁊ infirmitatib⁹
meis. Et impetra michi veniā oīm deli-
ctorū meorū. Et maxime in hora exitus
mei non desis michi o pijssima virgo ma
ria. Amen. Pater noster. Aue maria.

# 29 An Atlas for a Young Prince

**MS 463; [Battista Agnese], Atlas of 12 charts**
Venice; *c.*1543
Latin and English; vellum; binding 206 x 135 mm; charts 140 x 220 mm
Illustrated: (*below; detail*) f. 1r, the royal arms; (*opposite above*) ff. 13v–14r, oval world map, with the winds; (*opposite below; detail*) f. 14r, Europe and the Near East; (*overleaf*) ff. 6v–7r, chart of northern Europe

Sea charts were probably first created for use at sea in the twelfth century. By 1350 ambitious merchants were commissioning ornate atlases for presentation to rulers. The creator of this unsigned atlas was almost certainly the Genoese-born Battista Agnese (*fl.*1514?-*c.*1564). He was by far the most prolific sixteenth-century chartmaker, with nearly 80 atlases attributable to him or his workshop.

Though there is little that is innovative in his work, over the years Agnese's coastal outlines show steady improvement, much derived from Giacomo Gastaldi, official mapmaker to the Venetian Republic, and he had access to the best Venetian illuminators. This is one of Agnese's finest, though it does not have the flamboyant allegorical scenes that accompany his grandest atlases. It has the characteristic and elegant gold-tooled red Morocco binding with silver clasps. The content and sequence of the charts is identical to those in an atlas of 1543 originally owned by Duke Johann Ernst of Saxe-Gotha. They are skilfully drawn and the lettering is carefully handled. The royal arms of England, in the opening facing a golden-lettered dedication that has been erased, are very skilfully executed, as are the miniature female allegories of the four cardinal virtues in the four corners. These were associated with wise government.

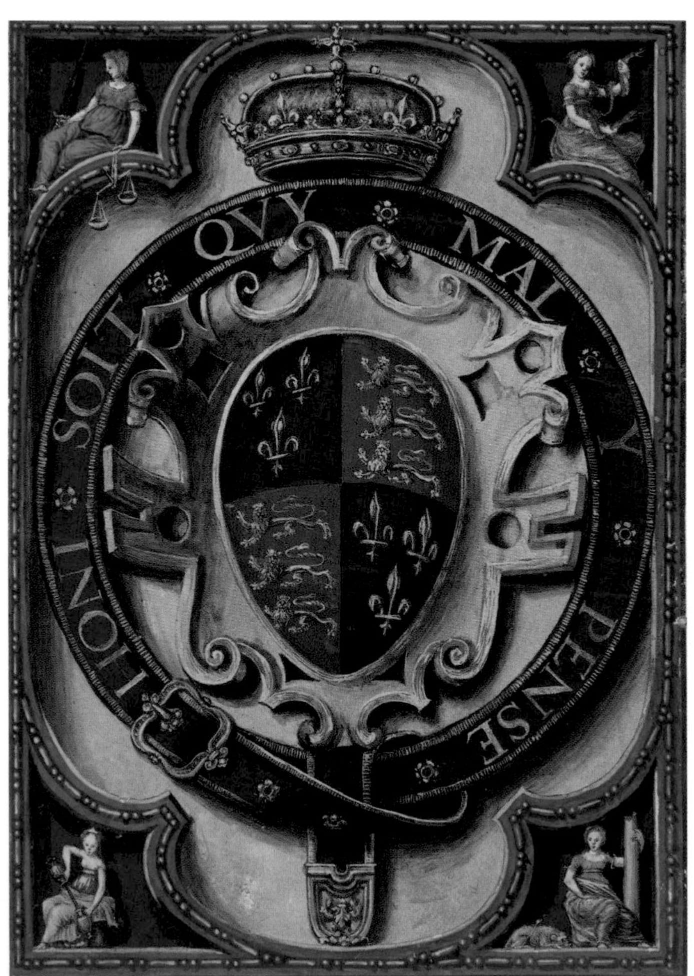


The atlas, with charts covering the whole of the then known world, including the Americas, was probably presented to King Henry VIII in 1543, perhaps by the Venetian ambassador, together with a larger atlas now in the Vatican containing 10 charts that also had the royal arms and an explicit dedication to the King. The outlines of England and Scotland in both atlases have been corrected in the same hand so that Scotland no longer appears as an island. Both have had wind directions inserted in English, again in the same hand, around the compass rose at the back of the atlas.

The Lambeth Palace atlas goes further, however. Possibly unlike any other Agnese atlas, the names of countries and provinces are inserted along the outer margins of the charts as well as on the charts themselves, as if the atlas were meant for teaching purposes. Among them is a reference to 'Britannia nunc Anglia', which would have been particularly flattering to Henry's imperial ambitions for England. Its small size suggests that the atlas may have been meant for a child – for King Edward VI while Prince of Wales rather than his father.

By 1564 the atlas was in the ownership of a recusant lawyer, Robert Hare (*c.*1530–1611), whose name and the date occur on the inside front cover. He owned at least two other books of royal provenance. It entered Lambeth Palace Library among the founding collections of Archbishops Bancroft and Abbot.

*Peter Barber*
*British Library, London*

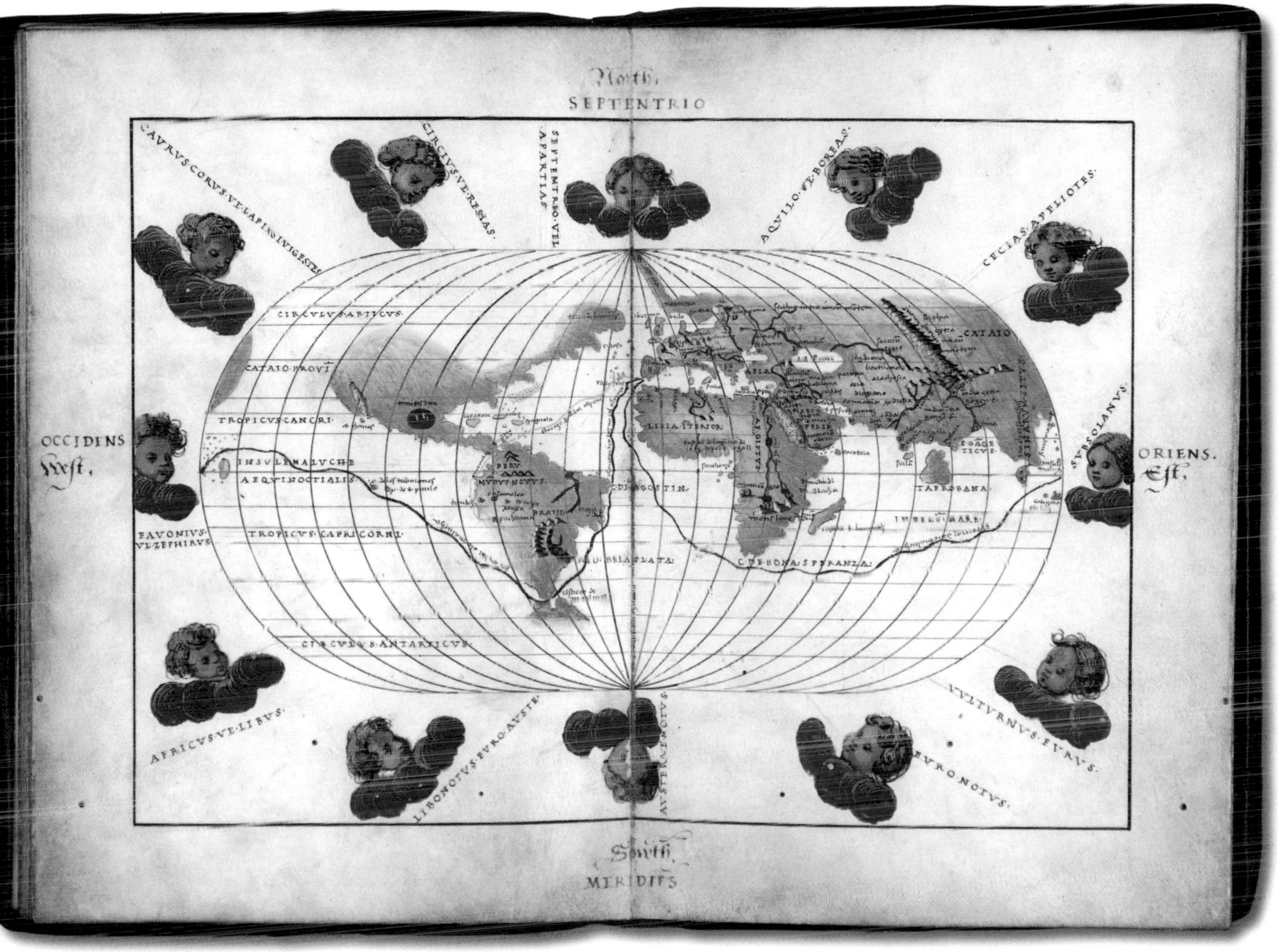

H. R. Wagner, 'The Manuscript Atlases of Battista Agnese', *Transactions of the Bibliographical Society of America* (1931)

R. Almagia, *Monumenta Cartografica Vaticana*. Vol. 1: *Planisferi, Carte Nautiche e Affini dal Secolo xiv al xvii* (Vatican, 1944), pp. 68–69; pl. xxvi

H. R. Wagner, 'Additions to the Manuscript Atlases of Battista Agnese', *Imago Mundi* 4 (1947), pp. 28–30

A. G. Watson, 'Robert Hare's Books', *The English Medieval Book. Studies in Memory of Jeremy Griffiths*, ed. A. S. G. Edwards, V. Gillespie and R. Hanna (London, 2000), pp. 209–32

C. Astengo, 'The Renaissance Chart Tradition in the Mediterranean' in *The History of Cartography*. Vol. 3: *Cartography in the European Renaissance*, ed. David Woodward (Chicago, 2007), pp. 174–262 and particularly pp. 214–15


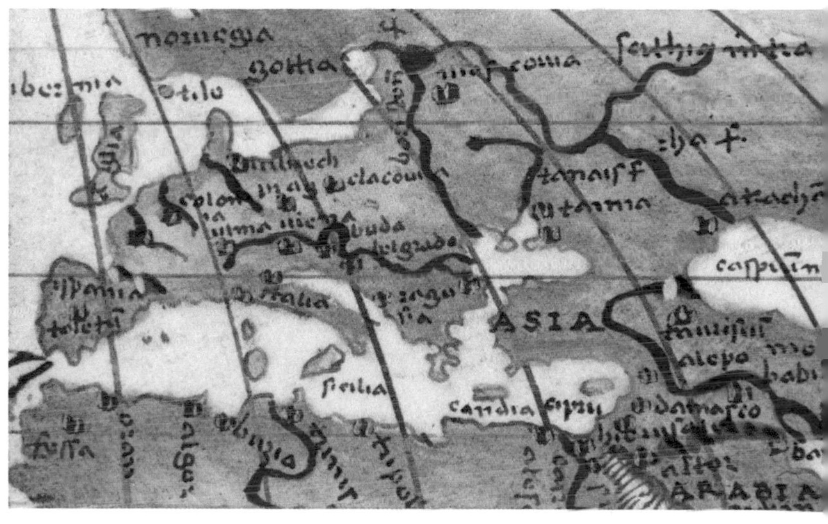

SCOTIA.
ANGLIA.
HIBERNIA,
BRITANNIA MINOR,
HISPANIÆ PARS.
SCOTIA
ANGLIA
IBERNIA
BRITANIA
ISPANIE PARS

DATIA ANTIQVITVS

CIMBRIA. MAGNA GERMANIA.

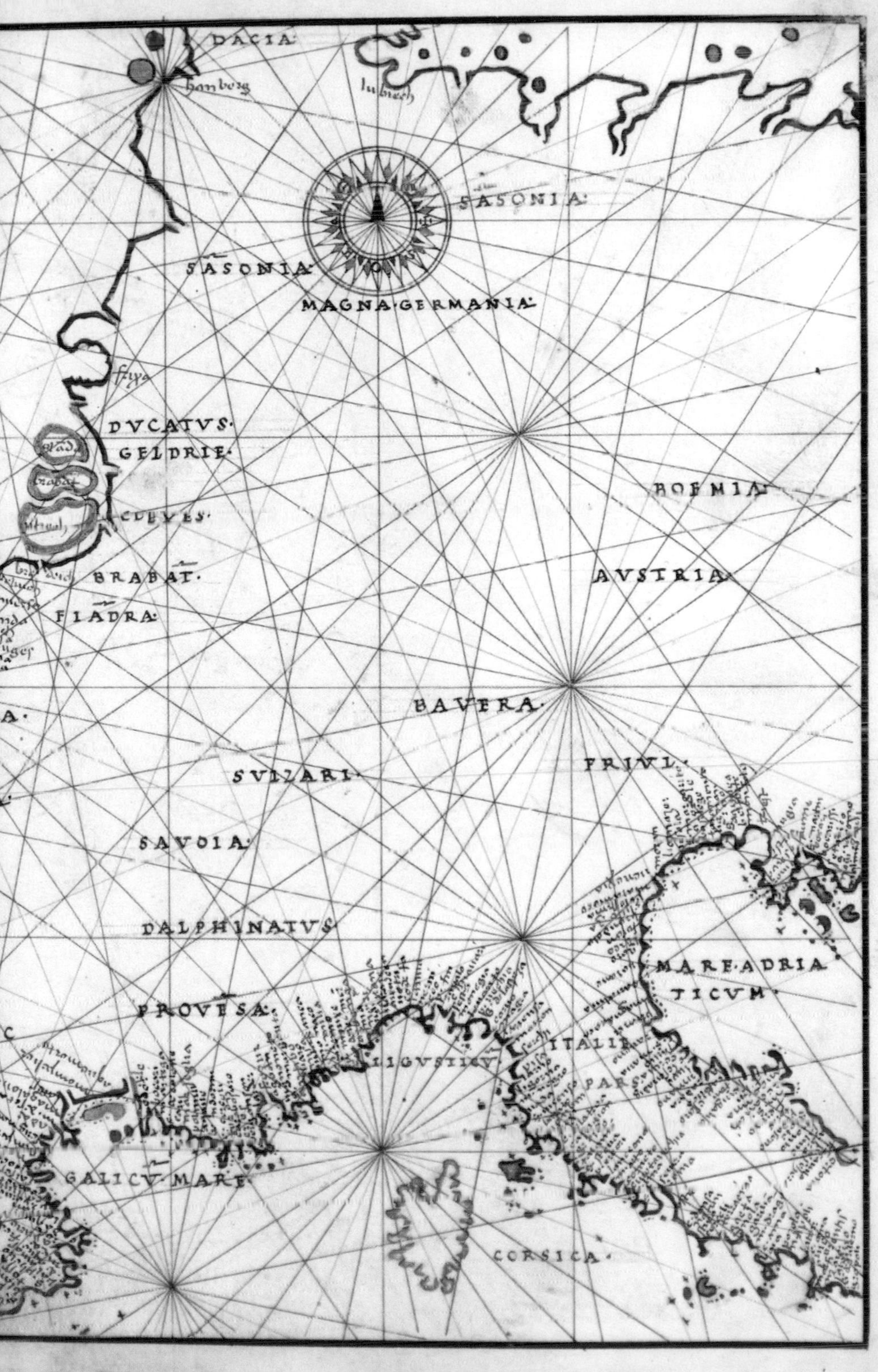


PANNONIA, AVSTRIA, VENETIÆ,

GALLIA. CORSICA. ITALIA.
INSVLA.

# 30 The Book of Common Prayer

**The Lambeth collection of Books of Common Prayer, including** ***The Booke of the Common Prayer and Administracion of the Sacramentes and other Rites and Ceremonies of the Churche: after the use of the Churche of England***
London; Edward Whitchurch; 1549; STC 16273
290 x 190 mm; [10], clvij, [1] leaves
Illustrated: (*below*) edition of 1549, title page; (*opposite left*) edition of 1632, binding for Sir Richard Browne; (*opposite right*) edition of 1680, extra-illustration of the Restoration of Charles II in 1660

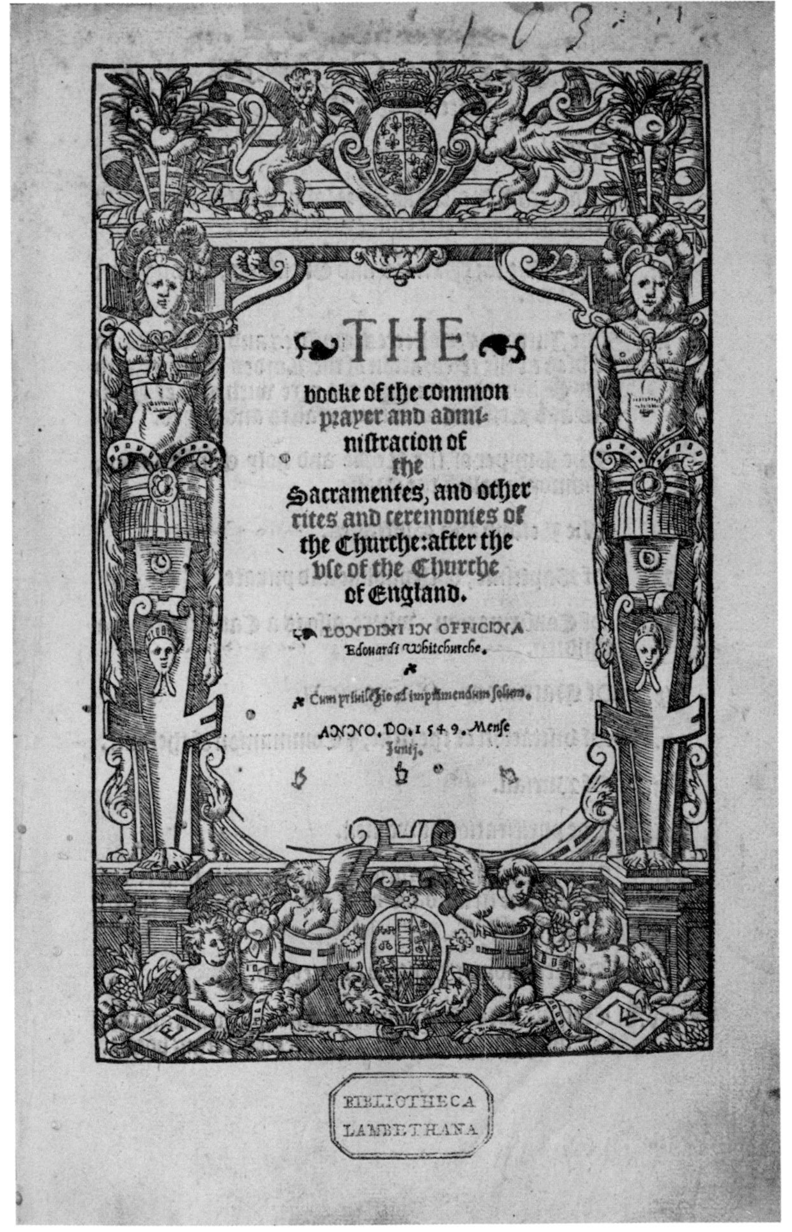


'Religion as by law established', the first *Booke of the Common Prayer* was brought into use throughout the realm of King Edward VI (r. 1547–53) on Whitsunday, 9 June 1549, an Act of Uniformity laying down penalties for those who failed to use it. It was a single service book in the English tongue, from which – according to Archbishop Cranmer's preface – the people 'should continuallye profite'. It was directed to be used by both clergy and laity, giving the laity full participation in worship and guiding them to salvation. It contained the words of the liturgical services of Holy Communion, Matins and Evensong and occasional services, including those for baptism, confirmation and marriage. It also contained the lectionary for the liturgical year and the psalter.

The book was compiled by Archbishop Cranmer and a committee of bishops and divines with the intention of reforming and simplifying the Latin services of the medieval Church. Cranmer drew on the Sarum Use, the Revised Breviary of Francis Quinones (1543), along with liturgies and books of discipline created by Protestant reformers in Europe, including Hermann von Wied's *Simplex ac pia deliberatio* (1545).

The first issue appeared on 7 March 1549, followed by 10 more issues by the end of the year. It was printed in black letter type with the title in red and black within a woodcut border. Cranmer's preface and his dignified rhetorical prose still enhance the Prayer Book today. The 1552 revision has been described as the ultimate expression of Cranmer's theological outlook. It was modified again in 1559 and 1662, but the form of the book has remained the same, described by Archbishop Ramsey as 'the bond of unity of the Anglican Communion spreading throughout the world'.

Lambeth has been associated with the Book of Common Prayer since the time of Archbishop Cranmer, and its collection is accordingly large, containing over 1,000 copies, dating from 1549 to the present day. Alongside English versions are translations into myriad languages, from Acholi to Zulu. Included is a 'sealed' copy of the edition of 1662, with the Commissioners' certification of its exact correspondence to the copy annexed to the Act of Uniformity. Also of interest are extra-illustrated copies with contemporary engraved plates and portraits (occasionally hand-coloured), inserted after

publication to create personal books of devotion. Other copies are distinguished by their provenance or binding, including those bound for Sir Richard Browne, Resident at the French court for Charles I and Charles II. During the Interregnum his chapel at the Paris Embassy became a focal point for royalists, and services there kept alive the liturgy of the Church of England.

The only legal form of worship in the Established Churches of England, Wales and Ireland until the late twentieth century, the Book of Common Prayer remains a vital element in Anglican worship today.

*Gabriel Sewell*
*Lambeth Palace Library, London*

D. MacCulloch, *Thomas Cranmer, A Life* (New Haven and London, 1996)
J. Maltby, *Prayer Book and People in Elizabethan and Early Stuart England* (Cambridge, 1998)
D. MacCulloch, *Tudor Church Militant: Edward VI and the Protestant Reformation* (London, 1999)
D. N. Griffiths, *The Bibliography of The Book of Common Prayer, 1549–1999* (London, 2002)
D. MacCulloch, *Reformation: Europe's House Divided* (London, 2003)
C. Heflung and C. Shattuck (eds), *The Oxford Guide to The Book of Common Prayer* (Oxford, 2006)

# 31 The Registers of the Archbishops of Canterbury

Archbishops' Registers, 1279–1928, including:

**Register of William Courtenay (1381–96)**
Illustrated: (*left; detail*) f. 337v, a tenant at Wingham;
(*right; detail*) f. 286r, the bells of Romney

**Register of Reginald Pole (1556–68)**
Illustrated: (*opposite left*) leaf preceding f.1r, his heraldry;
(*opposite right*) f. 1r, historiated initial R, for *Registrum*

The series of bound parchment volumes of Archbishops' registers at Lambeth runs in almost unbroken sequence from the register of John Peckham (1279–92) to that of Randall Davidson (1903–28). The registers are carefully created working documents recording the administrative activities of each Archbishop. They are not only diocesan in scope, but also record the Archbishop's administration of the province of Canterbury (England south of the Humber and the whole of Wales) and, before the Reformation, his role as papal legate.

They include episcopal appointments, administration of vacant sees, metropolitical visitations, records of the provincial council (Convocation), and major wills proved in the provincial court (including that of Dick Whittington, Lord Mayor of London). The documentation extends to royal writs, papal bulls and commissions (such as those in 1494 enquiring into the sanctity of Anselm and King Henry VI) and heresy proceedings.

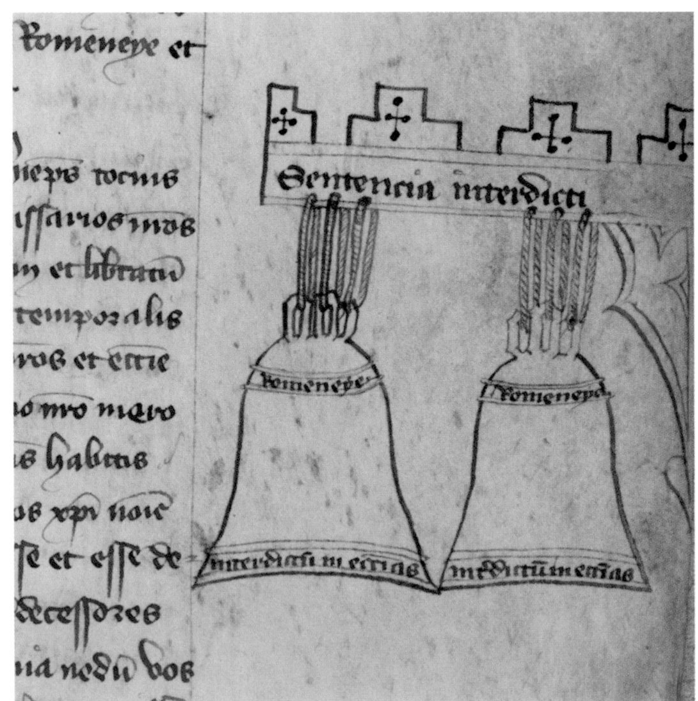

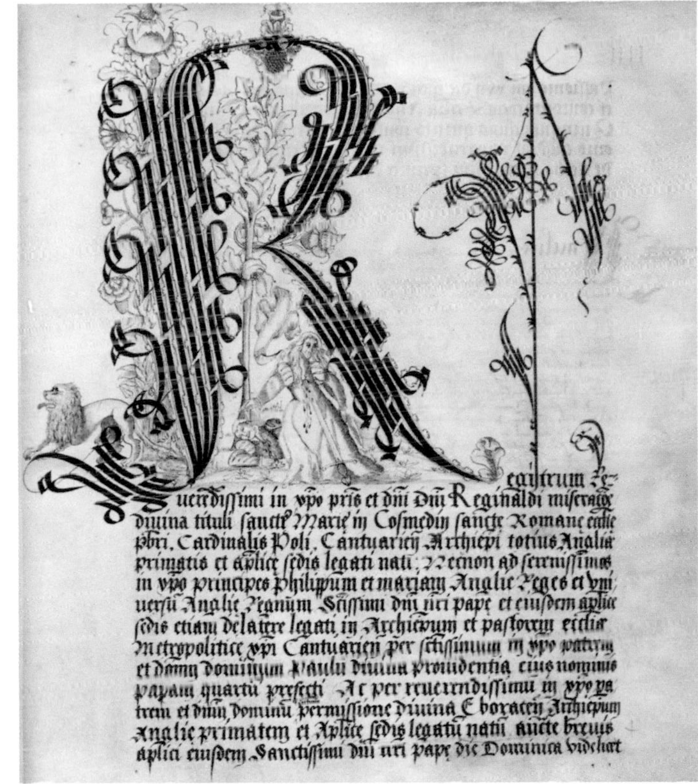

Here too may be found such items of historical interest as the passionate letters of protest against English oppression of Llywellyn ap Grufydd, the last independent Prince of Wales, and the proceedings for the annulment of King Henry VIII's marriage to Anne of Cleves, with the physicians' flattering assessment of the King's virility.

More routine entries include the institution of clergy to benefices, and the licensing of medical practitioners, but even here there can be surprises. Archbishop Parker's register records, in 1567, the earliest oath sworn by an English midwife, with such chilling promises as 'I will not distroye the childe borne of any woman nor cutte or pull of the head thereof'.

The registers are not usually illustrated or illuminated, but there are exceptions. That of William Courtenay (1381–96) contains two pen and ink sketches, both illustrating the Archbishop's determination to assert his rights as lord over his tenants in Kent, one of the centres in which the Peasants' Revolt of 1381 had started. On f. 286r the scribe sketched the bells of Romney, which summoned the inhabitants to hear the sentence of interdict pronounced against them in 1388 for disobedience. On f. 337v is an image of one of the six peasant tenants at Wingham in Kent who had failed in their duties to Courtenay and were sentenced in 1390 to undergo penance, bareheaded and barefoot, each carrying a large sack of straw.

The register of Cardinal Reginald Pole, Archbishop of Canterbury from 1556 to 1558, contains two very different illustrations. The opening leaf has an elaborate depiction of the heraldry associated with Pole. The artist, John Mulcaster, has illustrated the Archbishop's royal and noble family connections on a large shield placed below the Cardinal's hat and above a smaller shield bearing the arms of the See of Canterbury. The eight coats of arms on the large shield represent, respectively: the royal arms of England with the label of Clarence (Pole's maternal grandfather was George, Duke of Clarence, the brother of King Edward IV); Pole; Neville of Salisbury; Beauchamp, Newburgh; Montagu; Monthermer; and Despencer. The text opens with a giant initial 'R' for *Registrum*, and here the scribe-artist has portrayed the legendary deaths of the lovers Pyramus and Thisbe. Decoration of administrative records, for whatever reason, could provide pleasurable diversion for both the artist and the reader, and perhaps too for the Archbishop.

*Elizabeth Danbury*
*University College London*

W. K. Riland Bedford, *The Blazon of Episcopacy* (Oxford, 1897), pp. 1 and 5
E. E. Dorling, 'Notes on the Arms of Cardinal Pole', *The Wiltshire Natural History and Archaeological Society Magazine* 30 (1898–99), pp. 338–47
I. J. Churchill, *Canterbury Administration*, 2 vols (London, 1933)
D. M. Smith, *Guide to Bishops' Registers of England and Wales* (London, 1981)

# 32 The Dudley Binder

**Aristotle, Works, with tracts by Theophrastus, Philo and others, ed. Aldus Manutius with the assistance of Alexander Bondini**
Venice; Aldus Manutius; 1495–98; 5 vols, bound as 6
Greek; binding of brown calf over pasteboards, tooled in gold and decorated with paint by the Dudley binder for Robert Dudley, Earl of Leicester
Illustrated: vol. 6, upper cover, 307 x 207 x 45 mm

Robert Dudley, Earl of Leicester (1532–88), favourite of Queen Elizabeth, was a considerable collector of books and a patron to authors and bookbinders. Inventories made after his death mention 232 books, most kept at Leicester House in the Strand. Of these, 94, especially bound for him and showing either his coat of arms or his badge of a bear holding a ragged staff with a crescent, are now known. They are the products of more than eight binders' shops and date from *c.*1557 to the 1580s. Eight are in Lambeth Palace Library.

Perhaps the most splendid bindings made for Dudley, by the shop that bears his name, cover a set of the Aldine Aristotle. They are of brown calf over pasteboards, tooled in gold to a centre and corner design with lines and gouges, hatched tools and dots. Dudley's large badge, with the initials 'RD', is in the centre. Black and silver paint, as well as red for the crescent, provide further embellishment. The edges of the boards have been tooled in gold with lines and dashes, the edges of the leaves have been gilt, and there are traces of two pairs of fabric ties.

The badge on the Aristotle bindings was used until *c.*1563, not only by the Dudley binder but also by four other shops. Dudley probably owned the blocks and supplied them to binders when required. Nineteen volumes have survived from the Dudley bindery, fifteen of them produced for Dudley himself. The tooling is of excellent quality, and, as well as corner and centre blocks, there are elegant designs formed by gouges, often on dotted backgrounds, and a variety of hatched tools. The designs and the gouge-work, as well as the hatched tools, resemble the work of another London shop, that of the (ill-named) Morocco binder. Moreover, two pairs of tools that occur on bindings from the Dudley bindery are also found on a copy of Statutes (London, 1543), bound by the Morocco binder. As the Dudley binder probably worked until *c.*1562 and the Morocco binder started around 1563–64, it is likely that these two groups were the work of one atelier. Possibly the Dudley binder left or sold tools to the Morocco binder, the latter being his successor.

The skill in finishing the designs, the use of gouges and hatched tools that resemble those used by Jean Grolier's last binder, as well as the preponderance of smooth spines, are reminiscent of bindings produced in Paris in the 1550s and early 1560s. Despite measures to protect native craftsmen, Huguenot bookbinders continued to work in London and it is likely that the Dudley–Morocco binders came from France. As well as French binding and tool design, they brought to London the techniques of onlaying and inlaying thin pieces of leather on top of, or into, previously cut-out compartments in the covering leather. As late as 1578 native-born binders complained that they were suffering from foreign competition. However, it suited the Stationers' Company to have apprentices bound to 'such strangers … to serve with them to learne their arte', thus enhancing the skills of young binders and producing the top-quality pieces of which Dudley's Aristotle is a splendid example.

*Mirjam Foot*
*University College London*

W. E. Moss, *Bindings from the Library of Robert Dudley, Earl of Leicester* (Sonning-on-Thames, 1934)
H. M. Nixon, 'Elizabethan gold-tooled bindings', in *Essays in Honour of Victor Scholderer* (Mainz, 1970), pp. 219–70
M. M. Foot, *The Henry Davis Gift*, vol. 1: *A Collection of Bookbindings* (London, 1978), pp. 27–34
H. M. Nixon, 'Some Huguenot Bookbinders', *Proceedings of the Huguenot Society of London*, vol. 23, no. 5, 1981, pp. 319–29

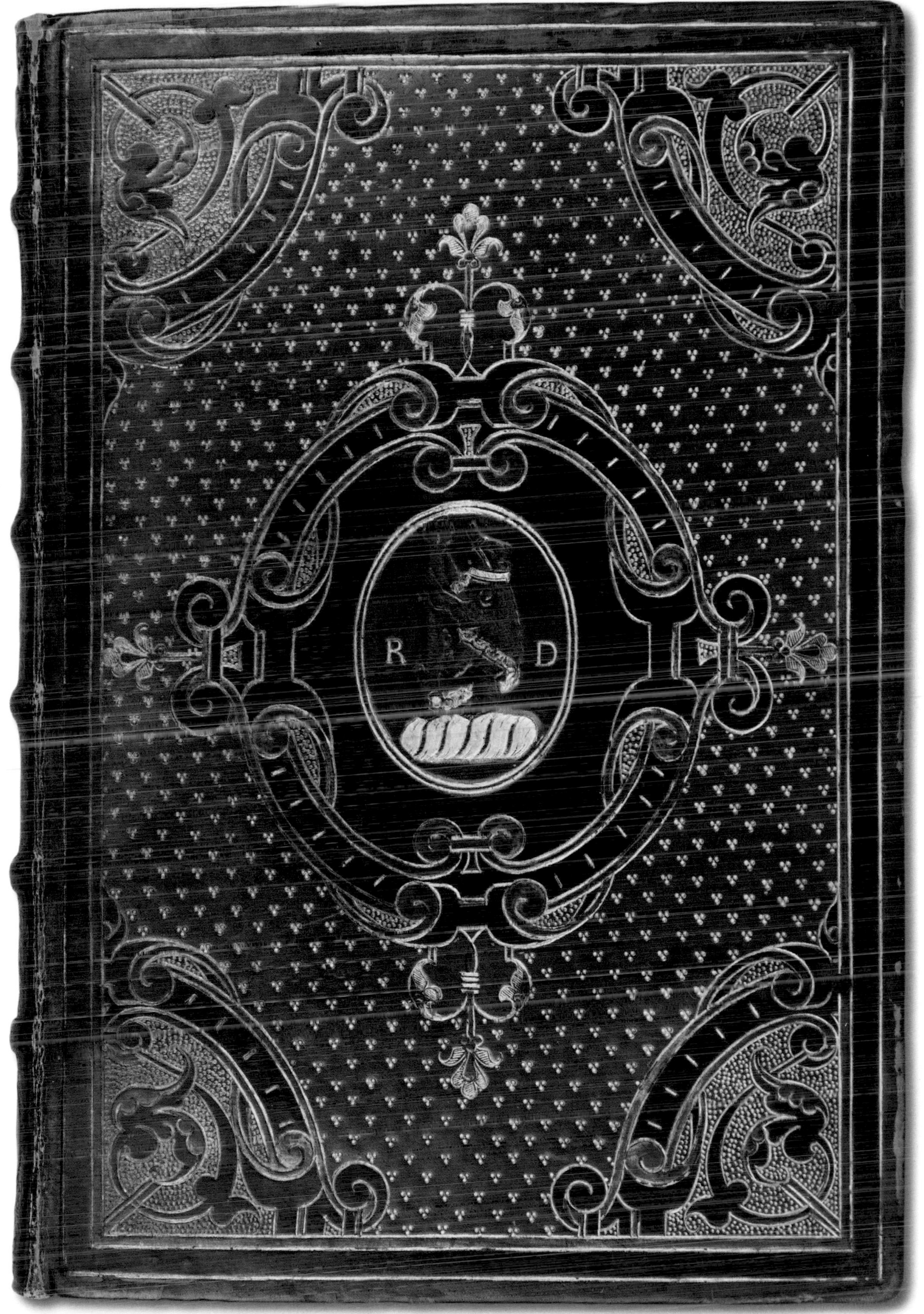
R D

# 33 Early Russian Printing

**Gospels**
Moscow; 'Anonymous Printing House'; *c.*1564
Church Slavonic; 288 x 208 mm; [10]+168+[222] = 400 ff.
Illustrated: (*opposite*) opening of the Gospel of St John

**Book of Hours, Chasovnik**
Moscow; Ivan Fedorov and Petr Timofeev Mstislavets; 1565
Church Slavonic; 175 x 123 mm; [172] ff.
Illustrated: (*below; detail*) f. 164v, Troparion of the Virgin Mary

Two of Lambeth's books, both in Church Slavonic (the language of the Orthodox Church service) and in Cyrillic types, date from the beginning of Moscow printing. Presses were founded there in the 1550s, probably at the instigation of Tsar Ivan IV (the Terrible) and Metropolitan Makarii (head of the Orthodox Church), to ensure the uniformity and wider circulation of Orthodox liturgical texts.

An undated folio edition of the Gospels *c.*1564, commonly known as the 'broad-type' Gospels, is from the first Moscow press, called the 'Anonymous Printing House', as its books have no indication of place, printer or date. After producing seven books, the printing house disappeared without trace. It is very likely that this press was the one reported by a contemporary English traveller to Moscow, Giles Fletcher, as having been set on fire 'and the press and letters quite burnt up, as was thought by the procurement of the cleargy men'. The lower clergy and the scribes were bitter opponents of the introduction of printing.

The Gospels, like other Moscow imprints of the time, was closely modelled on manuscripts, in the style of its types and beautiful interlace or foliage headpieces, and its use of decorative woodcut headings made of intertwined letters, known as *viaz'*. Of 23 surviving copies, the Lambeth copy is the only one found outside Russia and Ukraine, and is notable for its completeness. Two inscriptions, one in Cyrillic letters and one in Latin, indicate that it originally belonged to Nicholas Proctor, who was chief agent in Russia of the Russia Company from 1572 to 1573 and had also been there in 1567. It subsequently belonged to Archbishop John Whitgift. The binding has the arms of Whitgift, and incorporates leather from a sixteenth-century Russian binding. It passed from Whitgift to the Library's founder, Archbishop Richard Bancroft, who also owned a manuscript of the Acts and Epistles in Church Slavonic (now MS 108).

With the appearance of Ivan Fedorov, the 'father of Russian printing' and his assistant Petr Timofeev Mstislavets, Moscow printing reached new heights. Their imprints, beginning with the first dated Moscow book, a 1564 liturgical Gospels and Epistles, are notable for their rich ornamentation, and elegant and well-set type. In 1565 the pair produced two editions of the Book of Hours, after which they fled the country, because of (in Fedorov's words) 'great persecutions … at the hands of many powerful officials and ecclesiastical authorities and teachers, who, out of envy, tried to lay upon me many charges of heresy'.

Lambeth has one of only five surviving copies of the second edition. Books of Hours, used, along with primers and psalters, for learning to read, were often read until they fell apart in their place of origin, and owe their survival to foreign travellers, who brought them home for the purpose of studying the language, or as curiosities. The Lambeth copy has its original sixteenth-century Muscovite binding, and its inscriptions reveal that it was bought in Moscow in 1568 by a certain Thomas Lynd, probably also an early trader in Russia. It was among the books from Sion College which were transferred to Lambeth in 1996.

These works testify to the growing interest in Russia in Elizabethan England and, within the Church of England, to a heightened awareness of Russian Orthodoxy.

*Christine Thomas*
*Formerly Head of Slavonic and East European Collections, British Library, London*

---

*Cyrillic Books Printed Before 1701 in British and Irish Collections: A Union Catalogue* (London, 2000), nos 22 and 23

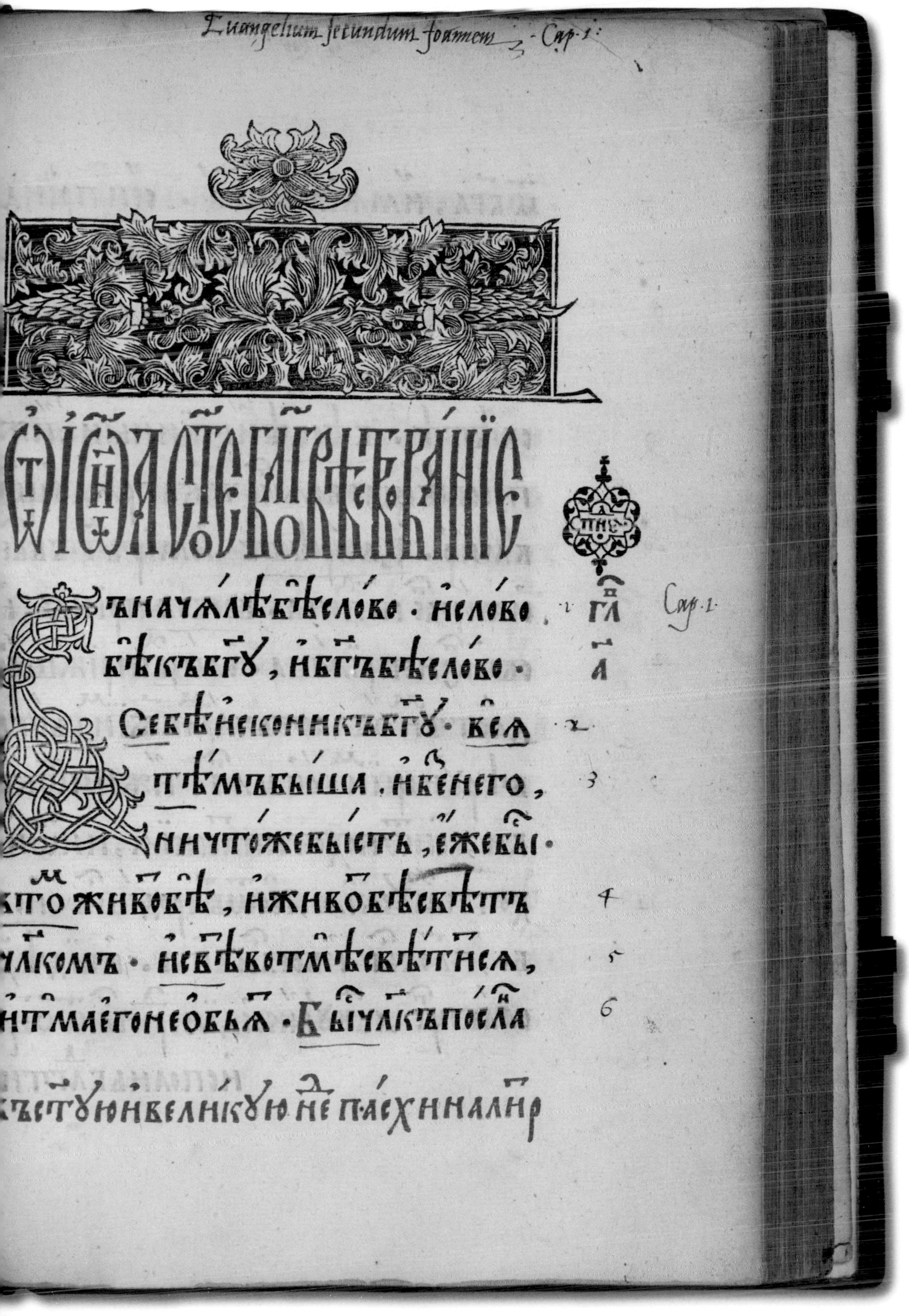
Evangelium secundum Joannem Cap. 1.

Ѿ Іѡанна свѧтое благовѣствованїе

пнѣ

ъ началѣ бѣ слово. и слово 1 глава 1 Cap. 1.
бѣ къ богꙋ, и богъ бѣ слово.
Сеи бѣ искони къ богꙋ. вса 2
тѣмъ быша. и безнего, 3
ничтоже бысть, еже бы
то животъ бѣ, и животъ бѣ свѣтъ 4
человѣкомъ. и свѣтъ во тмѣ свѣтитса, 5
и тма его не обꙗтъ. Бысть человѣкъ посла 6
въ ст҃ꙋю и великꙋю недѣлю пасхи на литꙋр

# 34 The Prayer Book of Elizabeth I

***Christian Prayers and Meditations in English, French, Italian, Spanish, Greeke, and Latine***
London; John Day; 1569; STC 6428
[344] pp.; 193 x 135 mm
Bound *c.*1670 in black Morocco, gilt, probably by Queens' Binder A [William Nott?]
Illustrated: (*below*) p2v–p3r, 'a prayer for wisedome'; (*opposite*) frontispiece, portrait of Elizabeth I

In 1569 the printer and bookseller John Day produced the most beautiful illustrated prayer book of the Elizabethan age. It was, in effect, a Protestant Book of Hours; a re-creation of a popular pre-Reformation format. Most of the prayers and meditations were extracted from a volume of *Christian Prayers and Holie Meditations* collected by Henry Bull and published in 1568, but a few compositions are original. Intriguingly, they are written in the first person, as if by the Queen. *A Prayer for wisedome to governe the*

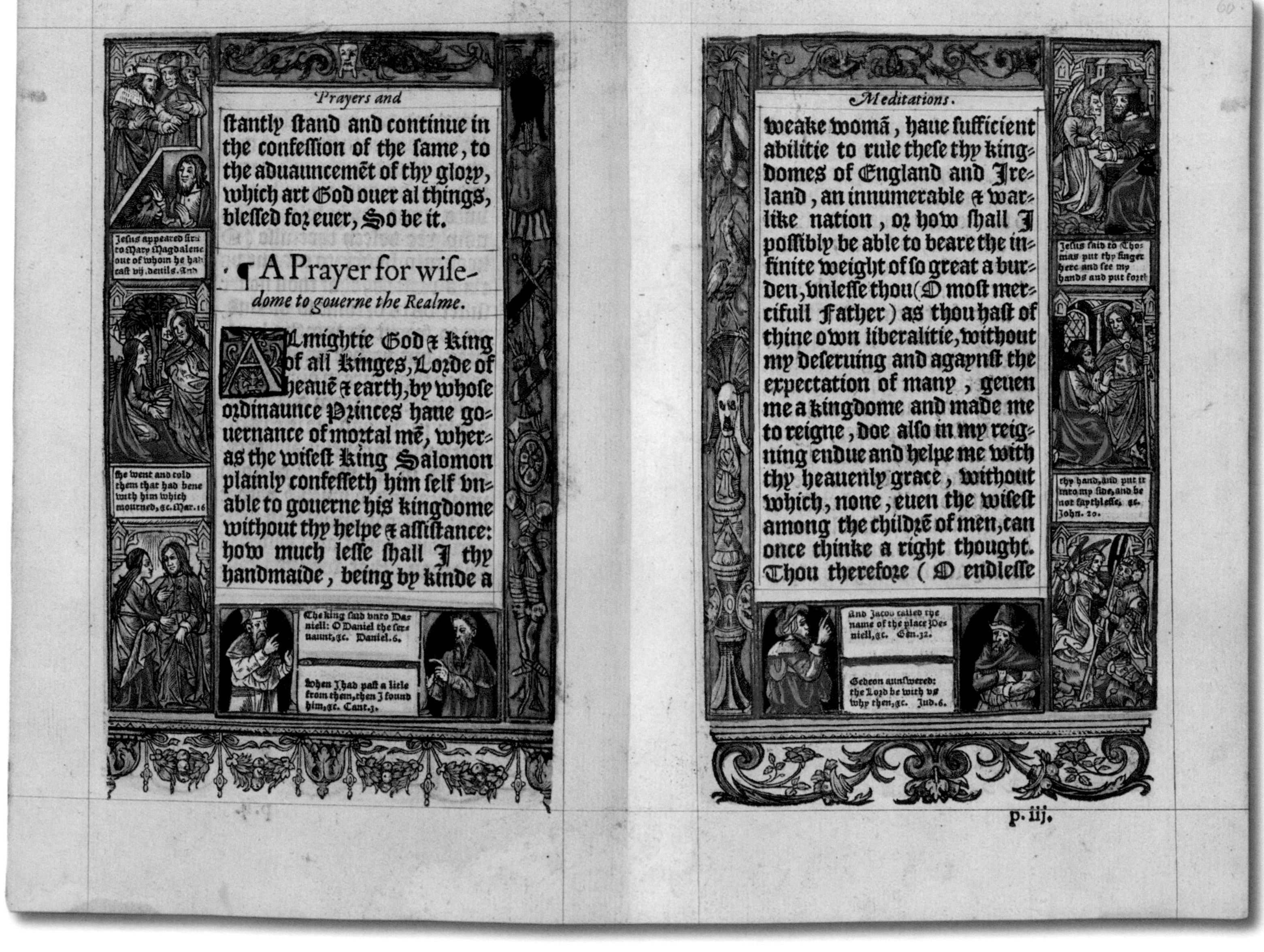

Prayers and

stantly stand and continue in the confession of the same, to the aduauncemēt of thy glory, which art God ouer al things, blessed for euer, So be it.

¶ A Prayer for wisedome to gouerne the Realme.

Almightie God & King of all Kinges, Lorde of heauē & earth, by whose ordinaunce Princes haue gouernance of mortal mē, wheras the wisest King Salomon plainly confesseth him self vnable to gouerne his kingdome without thy helpe & assistance: how much lesse shall I thy handmaide, being by kinde a

Iesus appeared first to Mary Magdalene out of whom he had cast vij. deuils.

She went and told them that had bene with him which mourned, &c. Mar.16

The king said vnto Daniel: O Daniel the seruaunt, &c. Daniel.6.

When I had past a litle from them, then I found him, &c. Cant.3.

Meditations.

weake womā, haue sufficient abilitie to rule these thy kingdomes of England and Ireland, an innumerable & warlike nation, or how shall I possibly be able to beare the infinite weight of so great a burden, vnlesse thou (O most mercifull Father) as thou hast of thine own liberalitie, without my deseruing and agaynst the expectation of many, geuen me a kingdome and made me to reigne, doe also in my reigning endue and helpe me with thy heauenly grace, without which, none, euen the wisest among the childrē of men, can once thinke a right thought. Thou therefore (O endlesse

Iesus said to Thomas put thy finger here and see my handes and put forth

thy hand, and put it into my side, and be not faythlesse, &c. Iohn. 20.

And Iacob called the name of the place Peniell, &c. Gen.32.

Gedeon aunswered: the Lord be with vs why then, &c. Jud.6.

p.iij.

*Realme* (p2v–p4v) makes a comparison to Solomon – 'how much lesse shal I thy handmaide, being by kinde a weake woma[n], have sufficient abilitie to rule these thy kingdomes of England & Ireland, an innumerable & warlike nation' – a trope to be made famous in her Armada speech referring to the 'body of a weak and feeble woman' at Tilbury in 1588. Four prayers *In time of sicknes* (i2–n2r) are also in the Queen's own voice. It had been thought that Elizabeth composed these prayers herself, but the latest view (May, p. 206) is that Elizabeth approved and used these devotions but did not write them. These prayers are followed by a selection of biblical passages relating to kingship. The final section comprises prayers in French, Italian, Latin and Greek, including a *Precatio Reginae.*

Roy Strong has suggested that the wonderful Mannerist portrait of Elizabeth kneeling at prayer may have been designed by Lavinia Teerlink. The woodcut title-page border depicts the Tree of Jesse. The remaining borders comprise two series: the first represents 43 scenes from the life of Christ with associated Old Testament scenes; the second (from kk1) is a Dance of Death. This is the only complete copy known. It has been coloured by artists in Matthew Parker's workshop at Lambeth Palace, as is evident from the distinctive palette of pinks and greens (two hands are involved; the second uses a darker palette). We know that Parker had such a workshop from a letter written in 1573 to Lord Burghley: 'I have within my house in wagis, drawers & cutters, paynters, lymners, wryters, and boke bynders'. That this copy was intended for Elizabeth herself is further demonstrated by unique press alterations in the Litany, changing references to the Queen to the first person.

Inscriptions on the flyleaves trace the descent of the volume. It had remained in the Wardrobe at Whitehall from the time of Elizabeth to that of Cromwell, when it was 'reserved' by Mr Joliffe, one of the Keepers. He later gave it to Joan Carlile or Carlell (*c.*1606–79), a painter, the wife of Lodowick Carlell (1601/2–75), a minor dramatist. She gave it to Mary, the wife of Nicholas Burwell of Gray's Inn, who had it rebound. Their daughter Elizabeth married Sir Charles Lodowick Cotterell (1654–1710), Master of the Ceremonies. A final obliterated inscription, 'The gift of Sr Charles Cottrell to Tho[?] Te..so.[?]' completes the story. This was Thomas Tenison, later Archbishop, whose gift of the volume to Lambeth Palace Library (where it was formerly MS 1049) was attested by Ducarel in 1785.

*Robert Harding*
*Maggs Bros Ltd, London*


S. C. Chew, 'The Iconography of a Book of Christian Prayers (1578) Illustrated', *Huntington Library Quarterly*, vol. 8/3 (May 1945) pp. 293–305

J. N. King, *Tudor Royal Iconography: Literature and Art in an Age of Religious Crisis* (Princeton, 1989), p. 111 ff.

R. S. Luborsky and E. M. Ingram, *A Guide to English Illustrated Books 1536–1603* (Tempe, 1998), pp. 315–19

R. Strong, *Gloriana: The Portraits of Queen Elizabeth I* (Pimlico, 2003), p. 56

S. W. May, 'Queen Elizabeth Prays for the Living and the Dead', in P. Beal and G. Ioppolo (eds), *Elizabeth I and the Culture of Writing* (London, 2007), pp. 201–11

# 35 Gloriana Unscathed

**MSS 694–710, 3192–3206; papers of the Talbot family, Earls of Shrewsbury, mainly sixteenth–seventeenth century**
Illustrated: (*right*) unknown artist, drawing in chalk of George Talbot, 6th Earl of Shrewsbury, by courtesy of the National Portrait Gallery, London (NPG 6343); (*opposite*) MS 3197, p. 41, letter from Elizabeth I to George Talbot, 6th Earl of Shrewsbury, 22 October 1572

The Talbots, Earls of Shrewsbury, were one of the greatest noble dynasties of Tudor England. From their main seat at Sheffield Castle they controlled large estates, deriving a fortune from farming and coal, iron, lead, steel and shipping interests. They were also prominent in national affairs; the 5th, 6th and 7th Earls all became Privy Councillors. The family also included Elizabeth, the termagant wife of the 6th Earl, known to posterity as 'Bess of Hardwick'.

Seventeen volumes of manuscripts (the Shrewsbury Papers) entered Lambeth Palace Library by 1715. In 1983 a further 15 volumes (the Talbot Papers) were purchased from the College of Arms, London, making Lambeth the principal custodian of the archive for the period from 1530 to 1615. The papers range from official communications involving the Privy Council and the Council in the North to private correspondence with clerics, courtiers, merchants, servants and members of the nobility and the gentry. Few Tudor notables go unmentioned. Among the signatories are Francis Bacon, William Cecil, 1st Baron Burghley, Thomas Cromwell, Fulke Greville and Francis Walsingham. There are letters from each sovereign from King Henry VIII to King James VI.

In the document illustrated here, Queen Elizabeth I (r. 1558–1603) informs Lord Shrewsbury of her recovery from a disease thought 'likely to prooue the small poxe' though some doubted that diagnosis. In a beautiful postscript in her own hand she assures the Earl that 'ther is no beholdar wold beleve that ever I had bin touched with suche a maladye'. Yet the letter is not as simple as it appears. Two figures lurk between its lines. The first is Lord Burghley, who drafted it. His draft survives, and replied to a missive from the Earl dated 16 October. The second is Mary Queen of Scots, who had been in Shrewsbury's custody since 1569. If Elizabeth were to die without producing an heir, then Mary might succeed her, a terrifying prospect for English Protestants and a decisive moment for her custodian. Hence the point of the letter to Shrewsbury (and perhaps to be seen by Mary herself), emphasising Elizabeth's renewed health and the peer's 'fidelitie, duety and love' at a critical time.

Extraneous evidence indicates that the letter alters the timeframe of the Queen's sickness. Written from Windsor, it also implies that the illness occurred there, whereas Burghley's diary suggests that it began at Hampton Court. The letter emerges as an exercise in information and misinformation, obscuring the Queen's movements and perhaps secret meetings with fugitive Huguenot leaders in the wake of the St Bartholomew's Day Massacre in France in 1572. It was a calculated component in a complex diplomatic game played for the highest stakes.

*David J. Crankshaw*
*King's College London*

*A Calendar of the Shrewsbury and Talbot Papers in Lambeth Palace Library and the College of Arms*, ed. C. Jamison, E. G. W. Bill and G. R. Batho, 2 vols (London, 1966–71)
G. W. Bernard, *The Power of the Early Tudor Nobility: A Study of the Fourth and Fifth Earls of Shrewsbury* (Brighton, 1985)
S. Doran, *Monarchy and Matrimony: The Courtships of Elizabeth I* (London and New York, 1996)

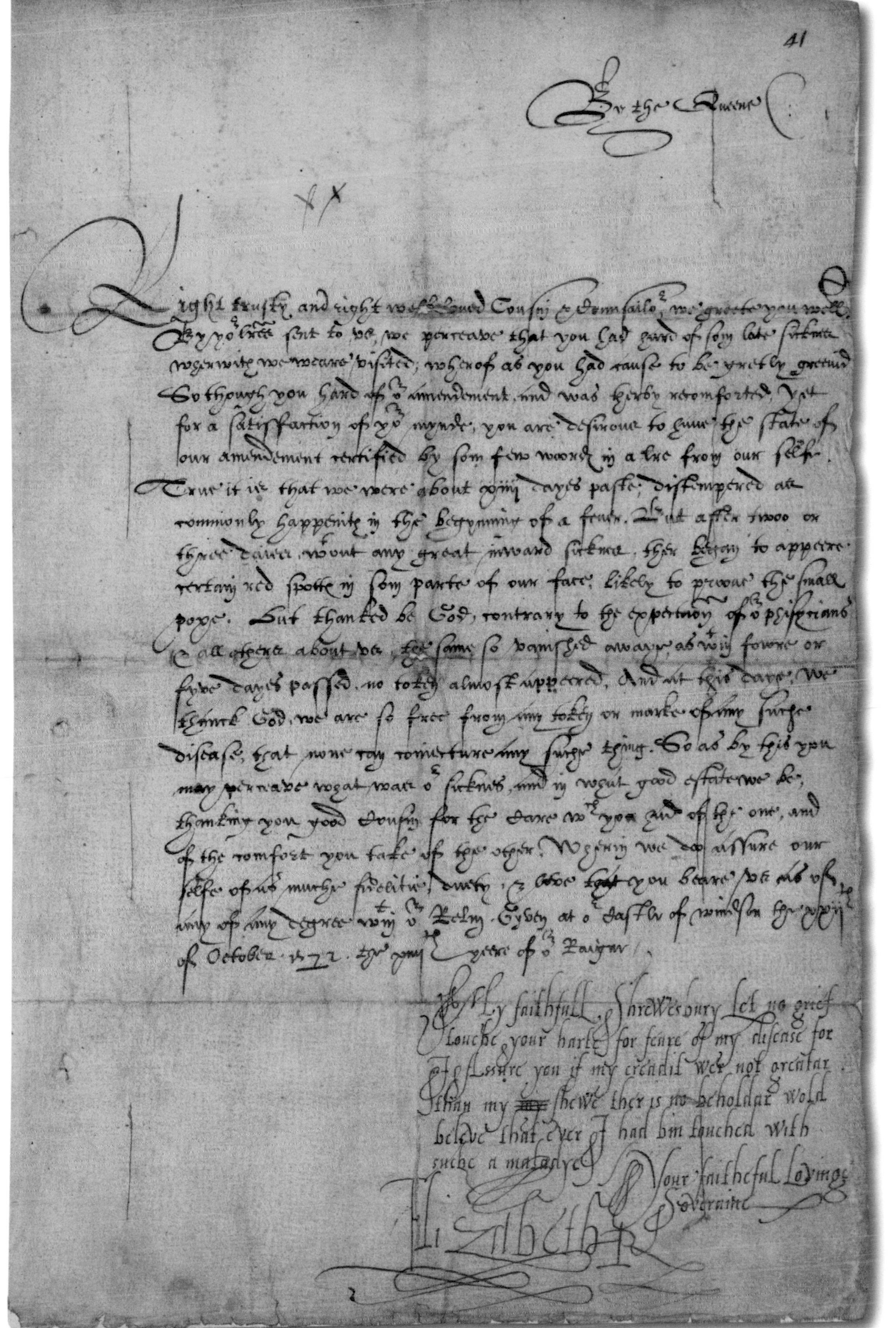

41

By the Quene

Right trusty and right welbeloved Cousin & Counsailor, we grete you well. By your lettre sent to us, we perceave that you had hard of som late sicknes wherwith we were visited; wherof as you had cause to be greatly greeved So though you hard of our amendment, and was therby recomforted, yet for a satisfaction of your mynde, you are desirous to have the state of our amendment certified by som few wordes in a lettre from our self. True it is that we were about som dayes past distempered as commonly happeneth in the begynning of a fever. But after two or three dayes without any great inward sicknes, ther began to appeare certain red spottes in som partes of our face, likely to prove the small poxe. But thanked be God, contrary to the expectation of our phisitians & all others about us, the same so vanished away, as within fowre or fyve dayes passed, no token almost appered. And at this day, we thanke God, we are so free from any token or marke of any suche disease, that none can conjecture any suche thing. So as by this you may perceave what was our sicknes, and in what good estate we be, thanking you good Cousin for the care which you had of the one, and of the comfort you take of the other. Wherin we do assure our self of as muche fidelitie, duety, & love that you beare us as of any of any degree within our Realme. Geven at our Castle of Windsor the xxij of October 1572. the xiiij yere of our Raigne.

My faithfull Shrewsbury let no grief touche your harte for feare of my disease for I assure you if my credit wer not greatar than my shewe ther is no beholdar wold beleve that ever I had bin touched with suche a maladye.

Your faithful lovinge Soveraine

Elizabeth R

# 36 Archbishop Parker's History of the English Church

**MS 959; Matthew Parker,** ***De antiquitate Britannicae ecclesiae & priuilegiis ecclesiæ Cantuariensis, archiepiscopis ejusdem 70***
London; John Day; 1572; bound in 2 vols; STC 19292, with additional documents
Latin and English; 305 x 250 mm; 395 ff.
Illustrated: (*below; detail*) f. 337r, portrait of Parker engraved by Remigius Hogenberg, 1573; (*opposite*) f. 36r, title page with manuscript additions by John Parker

On 9 May 1573, Matthew Parker, the 70th Archbishop of Canterbury, sent to Lord Burghley a copy of his history of the English Church, noting in the accompanying letter that it was a particularly rare volume: 'Which book I have not given to four men in the whole realm, and peradventure shall never come to sight abroad.... To keep it by me I yet purpose, whiles I live, to add and to amend as occasion shall serve me, or utterly to suppress it and to bren it.'

MS 959 is evidently the Archbishop's own copy, and passed to his son John after his death. It contains an archive of papers, documents and charters of relevance to the history of the archbishopric and Parker's private affairs, including personal correspondence and records, as well as a list of books published with his financial aid and measurements for new windows in Corpus Christi College, Cambridge (where Parker had been Master, and where the main part of his library is still kept).

The additions are now bound into the volume on guards, but were previously pasted in and may once have been merely interleaved. There is no apparent order or theme to these additions, and they were presumably added by Parker himself. To this John Parker made hundreds of additions of facts and transcriptions from relevant documents and chronicles, and in some areas of the book these fill almost all the blank space. It is most probably the last surviving record of a proposed extension of the text, which, like several other scholarly projects, remained unfinished on the Archbishop's death and was continued by members of his household.

In addition, this book represents a milestone in a number of fields. An inscription by John Parker in the copy presented to Lord Oxford (now Bodleian Library, Oxford, 4° Rawl. 593) states that it was printed within Lambeth Palace, giving it claim to be the first privately printed book in Britain. Very few copies were printed, and, as Parker continually added to the work or altered and reprinted existing sections, no two copies are now alike.

The present volume also contains a copy of the even scarcer portrait of the Archbishop, produced for him by the engraver Remigius Hogenberg in 1573, itself with the claim to be the first portrait known to have been engraved in Britain. There are also many academic firsts within the text, including the earliest discussion of one of the most evocative texts of the late Anglo-Saxon period, the *Sermo Lupi ad Anglos* by Archbishop Wulfstan. It is thus an important witness to the antiquarian activities of the Parkerian circle, as well as a record of the continuance of their scholarly work after the death of the Archbishop.

*Timothy Bolton*
*Sotheby's, London*

J. Martin, *A Bibliographical Catalogue of Books Privately Printed* (London, 1834), pp. 1–10
J. Bruce and T. T. Perowne (eds), *Correspondence of Matthew Parker, DD* (London, 1853), pp. 424–26

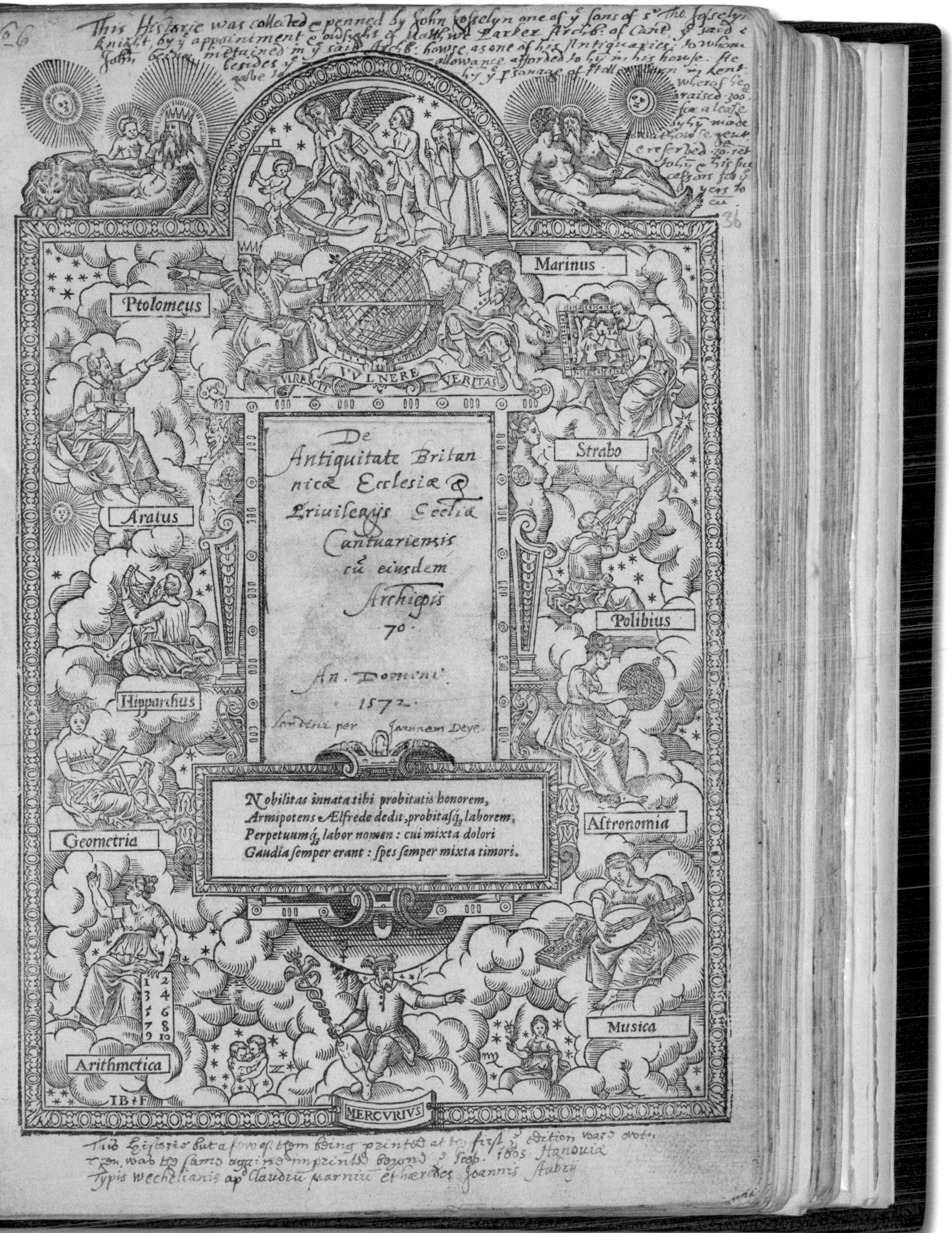
Ptolomeus
Marinus
VIRESCIT
VVLNERE
VERITAS
De Antiquitate Britannicæ Ecclesiæ & Priuilegiis Ecclīæ Cantuariensis cū eiusdem Archiepis 70.
An. Domini 1572.
Aratus
Strabo
Polibius
Hipparchus
Nobilitas innata tibi probitatis honorem,
Armipotens Ælfrede dedit, probitasq̧ laborem,
Perpetuumq̧ labor nomen: cui mixta dolori
Gaudia semper erant: spes semper mixta timori.
Geometria
Astronomia
Musica
Arithmetica
IB‧F
MERCVRIVS

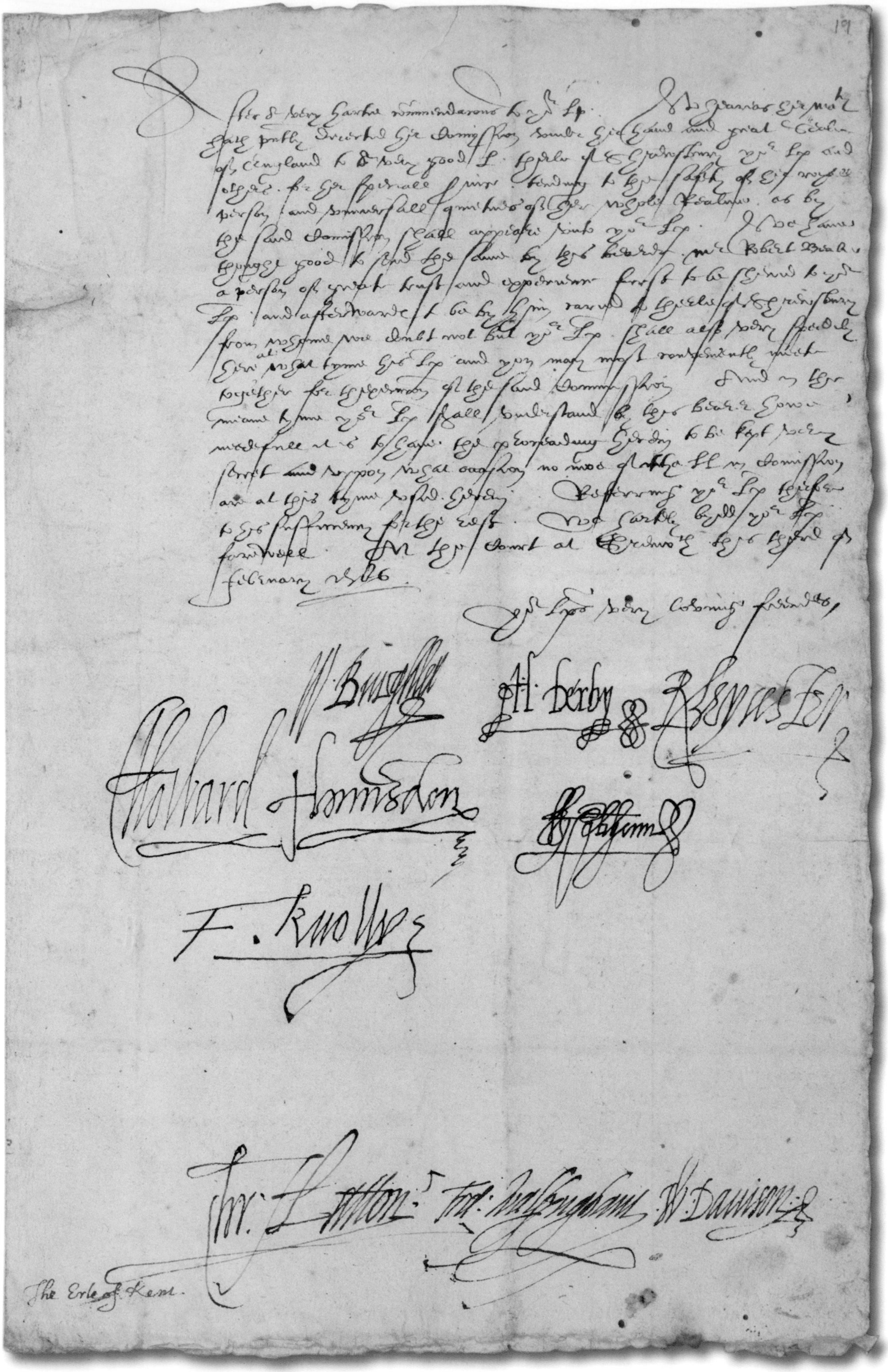

After or very hartie commendacions to yor L. Whereas her Matie hath presently directed her Comission under her hand and great Seale of England to or very good L. therle of Shrewsbury yor L. and others for the speciall service tending to the saftie of her royall person and universall quietnes of the whole Realme, as by the said Comission shall appeare unto yor L. Wee have thought good to send the same by this bearer Mr Robert Beale a person of great trust and experience first to be shewed to yor L. and afterwards to be by him caried to therle of Shrewsbury from whome wee doubt not but yor L. shall also very speedily here at what tyme his L. and you may most convenientlie meete together for the execucion of the said Comission. And in the meane tyme yor L. shall understand that this bearer hath made full [illegible] to have the proceadinge herein to be kept very secret and therefore what caution no more [illegible] Comission are at this tyme used herein. Referring yor L. therefore to this sufficiencie for the rest. Wee hartely bidd yor L. farewell. At the Court at Grenwich the third of February 1586.

Yor L. very loving frendes,

W. Burghley   Ed. Derby   R. Leycester

C. Howard   Hunsdon   Cobham

F. Knollys

Chr. Hatton   Fra. Walsyngham   W. Davison

The Erle of Kent.

# 37 The Execution of Mary Queen of Scots

**MSS 2000–2019, 3470–3533, 4267–4277, 4769; Fairhurst Papers, including documents relating to Mary Queen of Scots (MS 4267, ff. 19–34, MS 4769)**
Mainly sixteenth–seventeenth century
Illustrated: (*opposite*) MS 4267, f. 19, Privy Council letter; (*below; detail*) MS 4769, execution warrant

Between 1963 and 2008 the Library acquired the bulk of the State and ecclesiastical papers collected by James Fairhurst (d. 1999). They include records that John Selden had rescued from Archbishop Laud's study at Lambeth Palace during the Civil War, as well as documents obtained through his association with Elizabeth Grey, Countess of Kent. Her husband was the nephew of Henry Grey, 6th Earl of Kent (1541–1615), one of two officiating commissioners present at the execution of Mary Queen of Scots at Fotheringhay Castle on 8 February 1587.

The collection's jewels are the copy of the warrant for Mary's execution delivered to the 6th Earl and an accompanying letter from the Privy Council, dated 3 February 1587, instructing Kent to execute the 'Comyssion' (i.e. the warrant) for Queen Elizabeth's 'speciall s[er]vice tending to the safety of her royall person and universall quietnes of her whole Realme'. Despite Mary's involvement in the Babington Plot, Elizabeth had signed the warrant on 1 February with extreme reluctance. She had ordered her secretary, William Davison, to bring it to her only after William Cecil, Lord Burghley, her chief minister, had condoned a rumour that Spanish troops had landed in Wales.

Burghley had drafted the warrant in which he called for speedy justice against a woman who was an 'undoubted danger' to Elizabeth and the 'publyke state of this realme, as well for the cause of the gospell and the trewe religion of Christ'. But the day after signing it, Elizabeth backtracked, sending an order to Davison not to have the warrant sealed until he had spoken with her again. When they met later on 2 February, she railed against his unseemly haste, with the result that Burghley intervened, directing Davison to give the warrant (already sealed) to him, and summoning a group of Privy Councillors to a clandestine meeting in his chamber at the court in Greenwich. There, on 3 February, the Privy Councillors agreed to go ahead with the execution and not tell Elizabeth 'until it were done'.

Elizabeth had her own agenda. Although finally reconciled to the death of an anointed sister-queen, she wanted her privately assassinated. To this end, she had ordered Davison on 1 February to instruct Sir Francis Walsingham to write in his own name to Mary's keepers, encouraging a course which would have made a signed warrant superfluous. Elizabeth wanted her cousin out of the way, but without the responsibility. Wisely the gaolers refused, deeming this idea 'dishonourable and dangerous' and foreseeing that Elizabeth would soon be hunting for scapegoats.

With the original warrant almost certainly destroyed by Elizabeth's hand and the other officiating commissioner's copy now lost, the Library's copy is the most authentic relic of a momentous event. Mary's death was the first occasion in British history that regicide had been sanctioned by an act of State. It set the precedent for Charles I's execution in 1649.

*John Guy*
*Clare College, Cambridge*

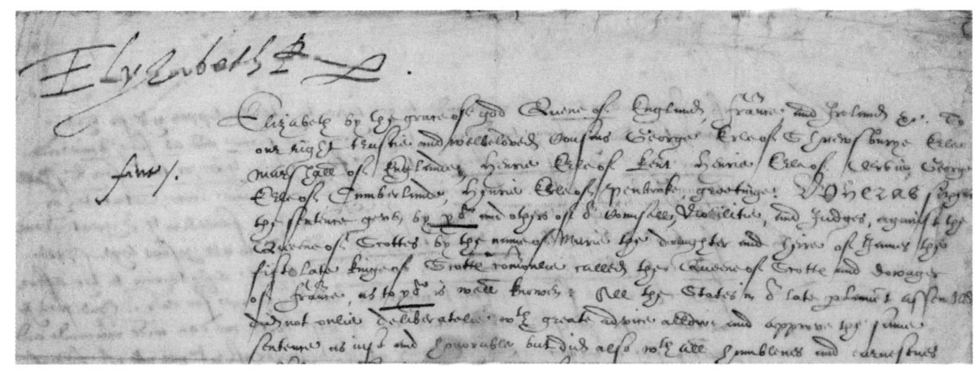


British Library, Add. MS 48027, ff. 636–658v (papers of Robert Beale)
N. H. Nicolas (ed.), *The Life of William Davison, Secretary of State and Privy Councillor to Queen Elizabeth* (London, 1823)
M. Taviner, 'Robert Beale and the Elizabethan Polity', Ph.D thesis (St Andrews University, 2000)
J. Guy, *'My Heart is My Own': The Life of Mary Queen of Scots* (London, 2004)
S. Alford, *Burghley: William Cecil at the Court of Elizabeth I* (London, 2008)

# 38 Archbishop Bancroft and Witchcraft

Witchcraft tracts from Archbishop Bancroft's collection, including:

*The Apprehension and Confession of three Notorious Witches … Executed at Chelmes-forde*
London; E. Allde [for T. Law]; 1589; STC 5114;
185 x 140 mm
Illustrated: (*below*) title page

*The Examination and Confession of Certaine Wytches at Chensford*
London; W. Powell for W. Pickering; 1566; STC 19869.5; 142 x 100 mm
Illustrated: (*opposite left*) pt 2, Aiiii, woodcut of a black dog, horned, with chain and whistle

*The most wonderfull and true storie, of a certaine witch…*
London; John Oxenbridge, 1597; STC 6170.7; 190 x 130 mm
Illustrated: (*opposite right*) title page

¶ The Apprehension and confession of three notorious Witches.
*Arreigned and by Iustice condemned and* executed at *Chelmes-forde*, in the Countye of Essex, *the 5. day of Iulye, last past.*
*1589.*
¶ With the manner of their diuelish practices and keeping of their spirits, whose fourmes are heerein truelye proportioned.



Archbishop Bancroft's collection contains a number of tracts on witchcraft, four of which are unique. One of them, *The Examination* (1566), is the earliest surviving English tract on a witchcraft trial, published four years after the statute making killing by witchcraft a capital offence. Both this work and *The Apprehension* (1589) concern Essex, and their basic facts are confirmed in the very full Assize records for that county.

The tracts were designed to educate. Both contain exhortatory introductions – that of 1566 partly in execrable verse – emphasising the malice of Satan and the damnable activities of witches. In both cases the publishers used information not available in the formal records of the Assizes; they had access to pre-trial documents, such as the testimony of witnesses and the confessions of the accused, and verbatim accounts of the court proceedings. *The Examination* records the altercation between two of the accused and a witness: did the black dog used by the former to execute their malice upon their enemies, or did it not, have the face of an ape?

Another purpose of the publishers was to sell copy. Both tracts emphasise the role of the animal agents that were an enduring aspect of East Anglian folklore. These creatures were a nuisance to the theologians, who 'read' them as 'familiar spirits' of Satanic provenance, but they did provide opportunities for compelling illustration. Law, the publisher of *The Apprehension*, used the woodcut title-page illustration in an original way in repeating details from it in the body of the text. William Pickering, a very active publisher of popular works, ballads, stories of natural disasters, almanacs and scaffold speeches, not only illustrated *The Examination*, but also allowed one of his trade collaborators, Edward White, to reuse the wood blocks in two witchcraft tracts published in 1579.

Bancroft's interest in this popular literature stemmed from his role, and that of his chaplain, Samuel Harsnett, in debates over diabolic possession, and the forms of exorcism employed by both Catholic and Puritan critics of the Church of England. In England, possession was frequently attributed to the intermediate agency of a witch. In *A Declaration of Egregious Popish Impostures*, Harsnett

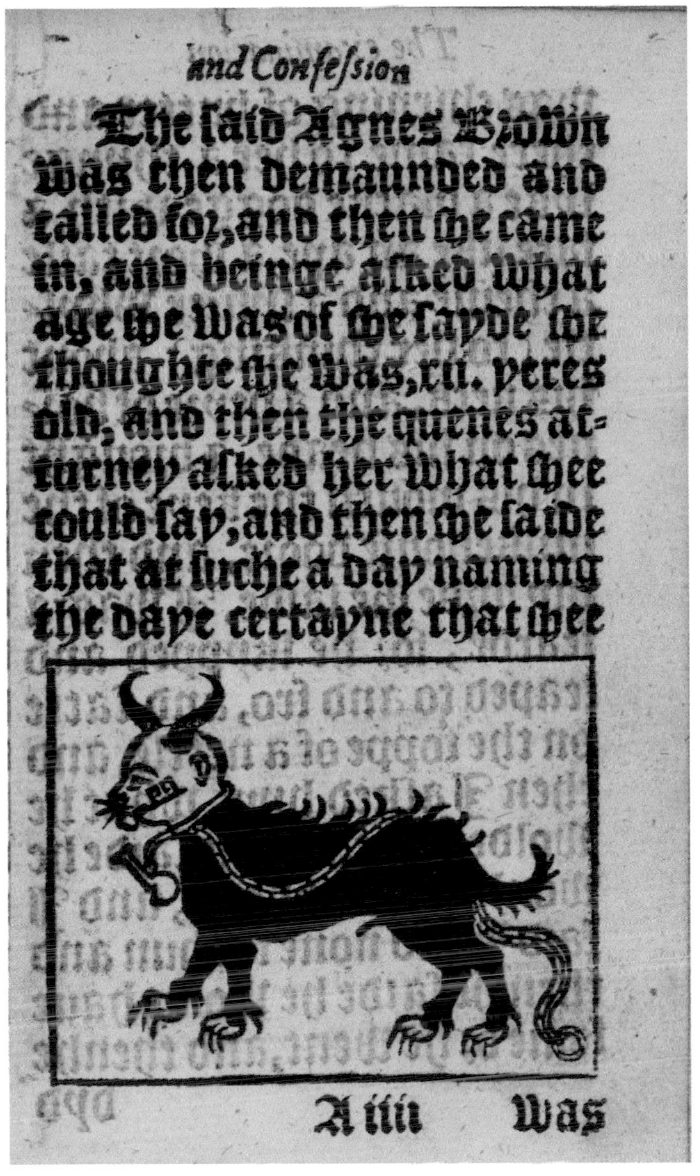
*and Confeſsion*

The ſaid Agnes Browne was then demaunded and called for, and then ſhe came in, and beinge aſked what age ſhe was of ſhe ſayde ſhe thoughte ſhe was, xii. yeres old, and then the quenes atturney aſked her what ſhee could ſay, and then ſhe ſaide that at ſuche a day naming the daye certayne that ſhee

A iiii Was

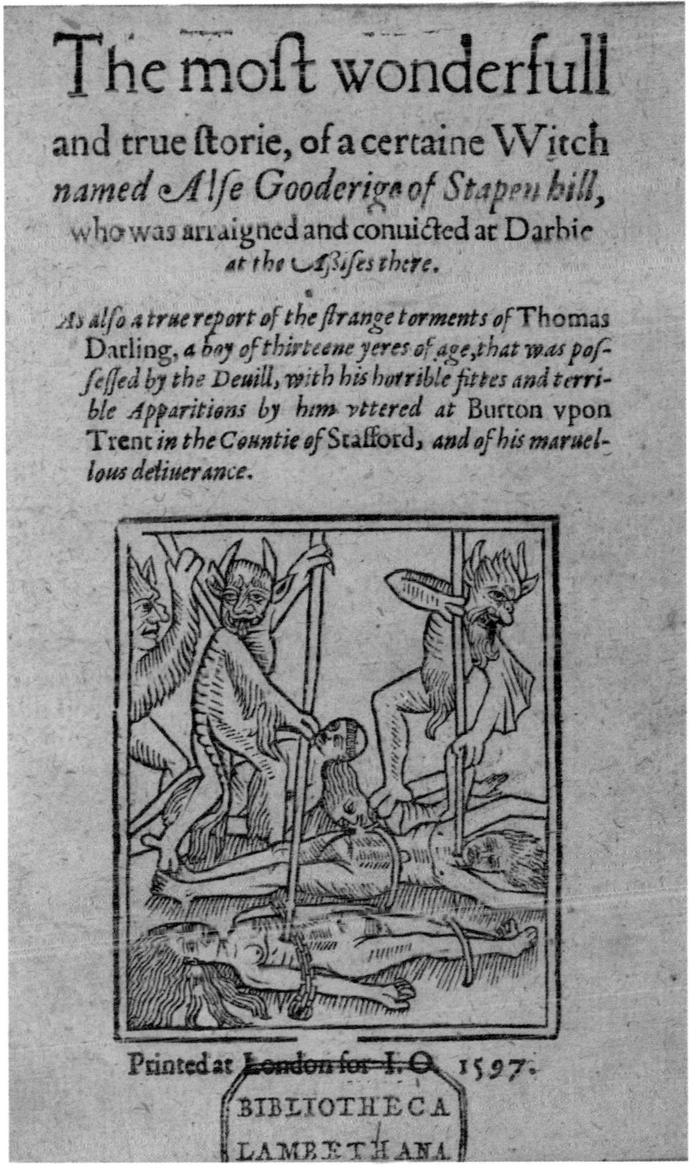
The moſt wonderfull and true ſtorie, of a certaine Witch *named Alſe Gooderige of Stapen hill,* who was arraigned and conuicted at Darbie *at the Aſſiſes there.*

*As alſo a true report of the ſtrange torments of* Thomas Darling, *a boy of thirteene yeres of age, that was poſſeſſed by the Deuill, with his horrible fittes and terrible Apparitions by him vttered at* Burton vpon Trent *in the Countie of* Stafford, *and of his maruellous deliuerance.*

Printed at ~~London for I. O.~~ 1597.



argued not only that possession was invariably fraudulent, but also went further, virtually plagiarising the language of the sceptic, Reginald Scot, whose *Discoverie of Witchcraft* insisted that the diabolic power attributed to witches was a nonsense. Bancroft, who from 1597 to 1604 was Bishop of London – a diocese which included Chelmsford – also followed this line. In 1602 he worked tirelessly to exculpate a woman accused of responsibility for the diabolic possession of a godly young woman, Mary Glover, and, upon her conviction, secured a reprieve. Harsnett and Bancroft were on dangerous ground here. The new King, James I (r. 1567–1625), had written a tract, the *Daemonologie* (1597), in which he had excoriated the 'damnable opinions' of Scot.

For Bancroft, witchcraft tracts were not just bibliophile curiosities, but documentation on an important issue which engaged his attention as a leading figure in the Church. In founding Lambeth Palace Library, he preserved these unique items for posterity.

*Clive Holmes*
*Lady Margaret Hall, Oxford*

C. Holmes, 'Popular Culture? Witches, Magistrates and Divines in Early Modern England' in S. Kaplan (ed.), *Understanding Popular Culture* (Berlin, 1984), pp. 85–111
M. MacDonald, *Witchcraft and Hysteria in Elizabethan London* (London, 1990)
M. Gibson, *Early Modern Witches* (London, 2000)
M. Gibson, *Possession, Puritanism and Print* (London, 2006)
C. Holmes, 'Witchcraft and Possession at the Accession of James I', in J. Newton and J. Bath (eds), *Witchcraft and the Act of 1604* (Leiden, 2008), pp. 69–90

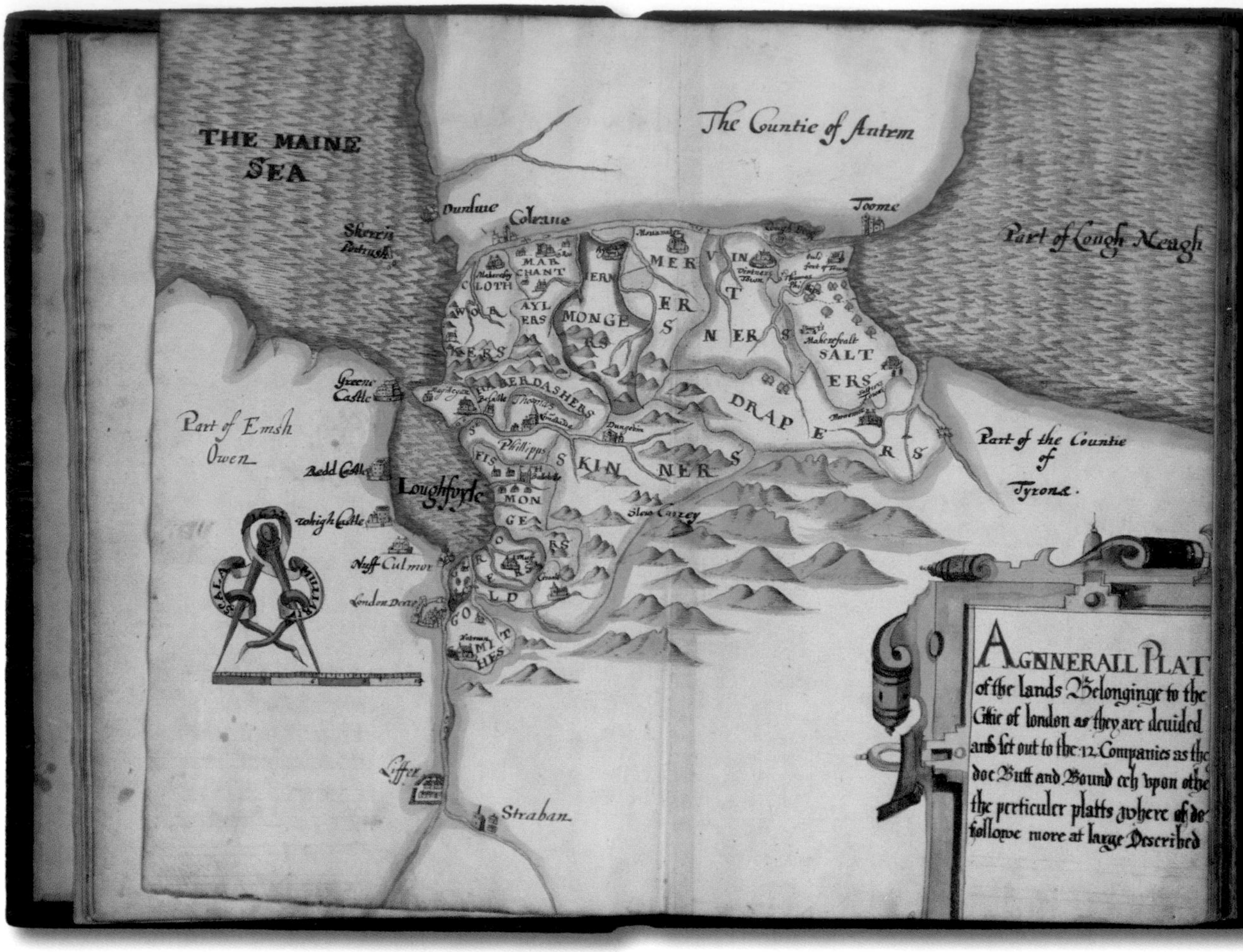

THE MAINE SEA
The Cuntie of Antrem
Part of Lough Neagh
Colrane
Toome
Greene Castle
Part of Emsh Owen
Loughfoyle
HABERDASHERS
DRAPERS
SKINNERS
SALTERS
Part of the Countie of Tyrone
Culmor
London Derre
Lifford
Straban
AGNNERALL PLAT of the lands Belonginge to the Citie of london as they are deuided and set out to the 12 Companies as the doe Butt and Bound ech vpon other the perticuler platts where of do followe more at large Described

The Church
THE FISHMONGERS' BVILDINGE AT BALLE KELLE
Ten miles from london Derrye

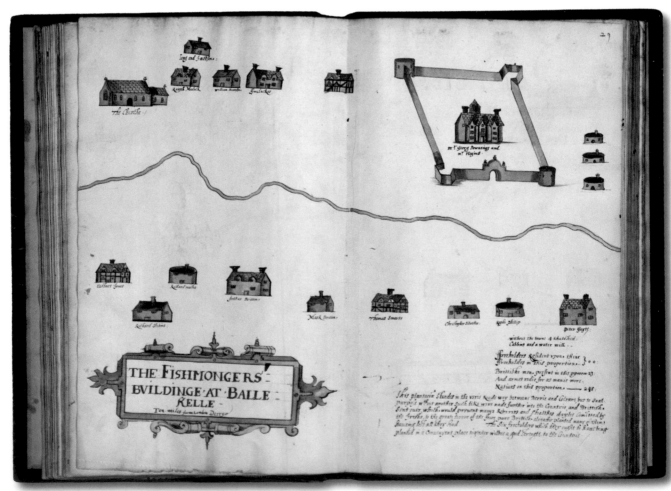

# 39 The Londonderry Plantation

**MS 634; survey of the plantation of County Londonderry by Thomas Raven for Sir Thomas Phillips and Richard Hudson**
1622, with related documents to 1624
Ink and watercolour on paper; 380 x 260 mm; ff. v, 104
Illustrated: (*opposite above*) ff.1v–2r, plan of lands assigned to livery companies; (*opposite below*) ff. 28v–29r, Fishmongers' buildings at Ballykelly; (*right; detail*) f. 4v, design for a fortification for the market place, Londonderry; (*overleaf*) ff. 7v–8r, plan of Londonderry

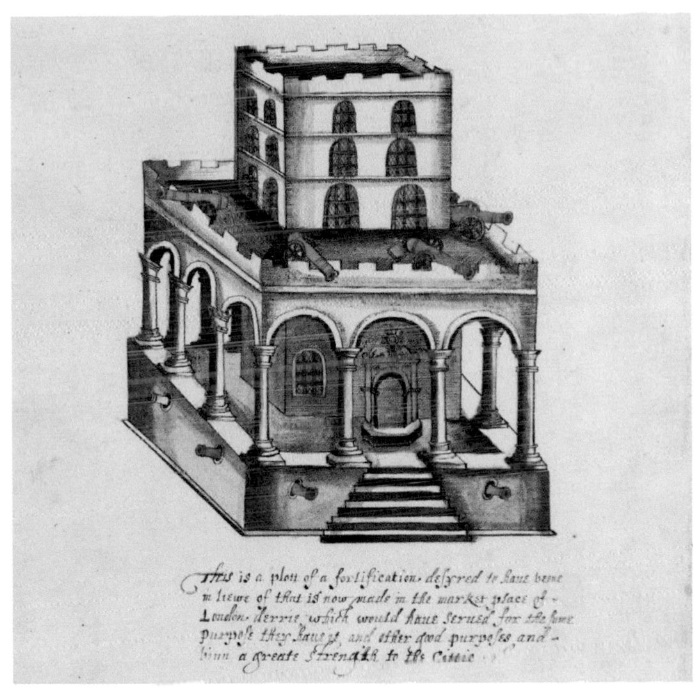


In 1610 the Privy Council reached agreement with the City of London on the Londonderry plantation, an investment scheme to pacify and exploit the commercial potential of this troubled area through fortification and settlement. Land was assigned to 12 London livery companies, an exercise which required detailed estate mapping. Estate or plantation maps were the most common form of cartographic activity in Ireland in the first half of the seventeenth century. They were essential for the identification and measurement of property boundaries. The need to protect the English position created a requirement for defensible towns and ports through which the plantation's proprietors and tenants could export the produce of their estates. The challenges facing the English proprietors in Ulster were also to have a bearing on American colonial history and understanding of the venture that produced the landing at Jamestown in 1607.

Embracing both the town and the county, the survey provides by far the fullest single picture of the Londonderry plantation in the first half of the seventeenth century and is remarkable for the fine set of colour maps and picture plans. It was commissioned in 1621 by Sir Thomas Phillips, Governor of Coleraine, and formed part of the evidence which he submitted to King Charles I (r. 1635–49) in support of his charge against the London proprietors that they were not fulfilling their legal obligations towards the plantation. The maps were drawn by Thomas Raven, perhaps the most gifted cartographer to make his home in early seventeenth-century Ireland and one of the small number of cartographers employed by the English administration.

The survey depicts the lands, buildings and fortifications, and provides tantalising clues to the shape and organisation of the Irish landscape of the day. Included are drawings of the plantation city of Londonderry, encircled by walls and with its street layout carefully planned, and also of Coleraine and the fort at Culmore. The survey lists the number of stone and timber houses, thatched houses and cabins, watermills and churches built or repaired. It also represents the first attempt at complete population statistics, including British men, armed and unarmed, natives and 'idle persons', that is young men dwelling with their parents, and servants. No other plantation in Ulster was to be surveyed in such a detailed fashion until William Petty's 'Down Survey' of the 1650s.

The survey exists in two known manuscripts. The one at Lambeth contains Sir Thomas Phillips's signed petition to Charles I and is presumed to be the original version. The second manuscript, in the archives of the Drapers' Company (prominent investors in the Plantation), represents a slightly revised version. The Lambeth manuscript is among 42 volumes of the Irish papers and collections of George Carew (1555–1629), who was created Earl of Totnes in 1626. It opens with a lavish display of his coat of arms. Much of Carew's career was spent in Ireland, where, as President of Munster from 1600 to 1603, he ruthlessly suppressed the Munster rebellion. In 1624 he was one of four Commissioners appointed by King James I to report on Sir Thomas Phillips's indictment of the proprietors of the Londonderry plantation. The final document in the volume represents the outcome, the King's approval of a programme of reform known as the 23 Articles. Carew's papers on Irish history passed to the antiquary Sir Thomas Stafford, who drew on them for his history of the Munster rebellion, *Pacata Hibernia* (1633). The collection subsequently passed to Archbishop Sheldon and from him to Lambeth Palace Library.

*Nicholas Poole-Wilson*
*Bernard Quaritch Ltd, London*

T. W. Moody, *The Londonderry Plantation 1609–41* (Belfast, 1939)
J. S. Curl, *The Londonderry Plantation 1609–1914* (Chichester, 1986)

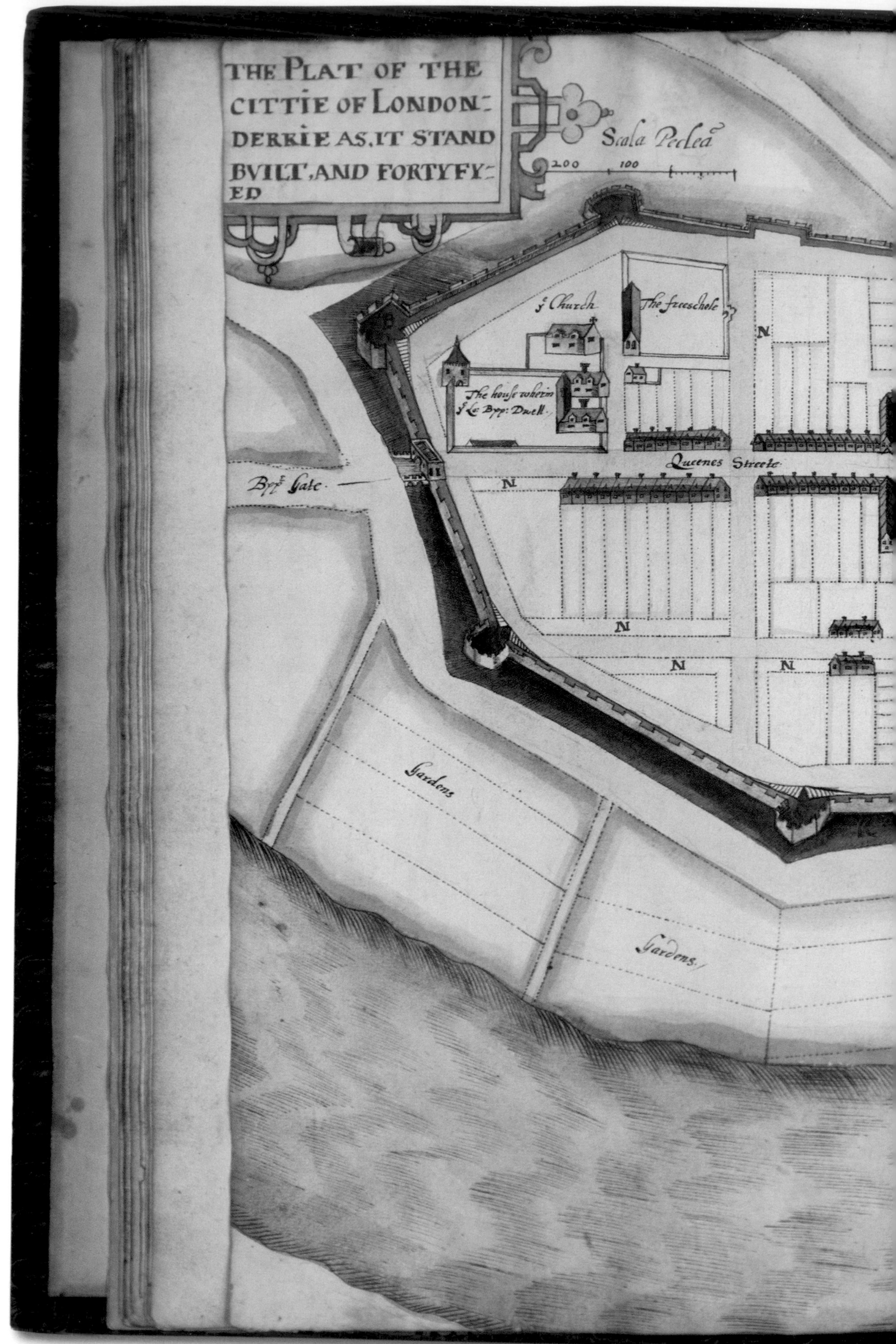
THE PLAT OF THE CITTIE OF LONDON-DERRIE AS, IT STAND BVILT, AND FORTYFYED
Scala Pedea
200
100
ye Church
The freeschole
The house wherin ye Lo: Byp: Dwell
Queenes Streete
Byps Gate
N
Gardens
Gardens

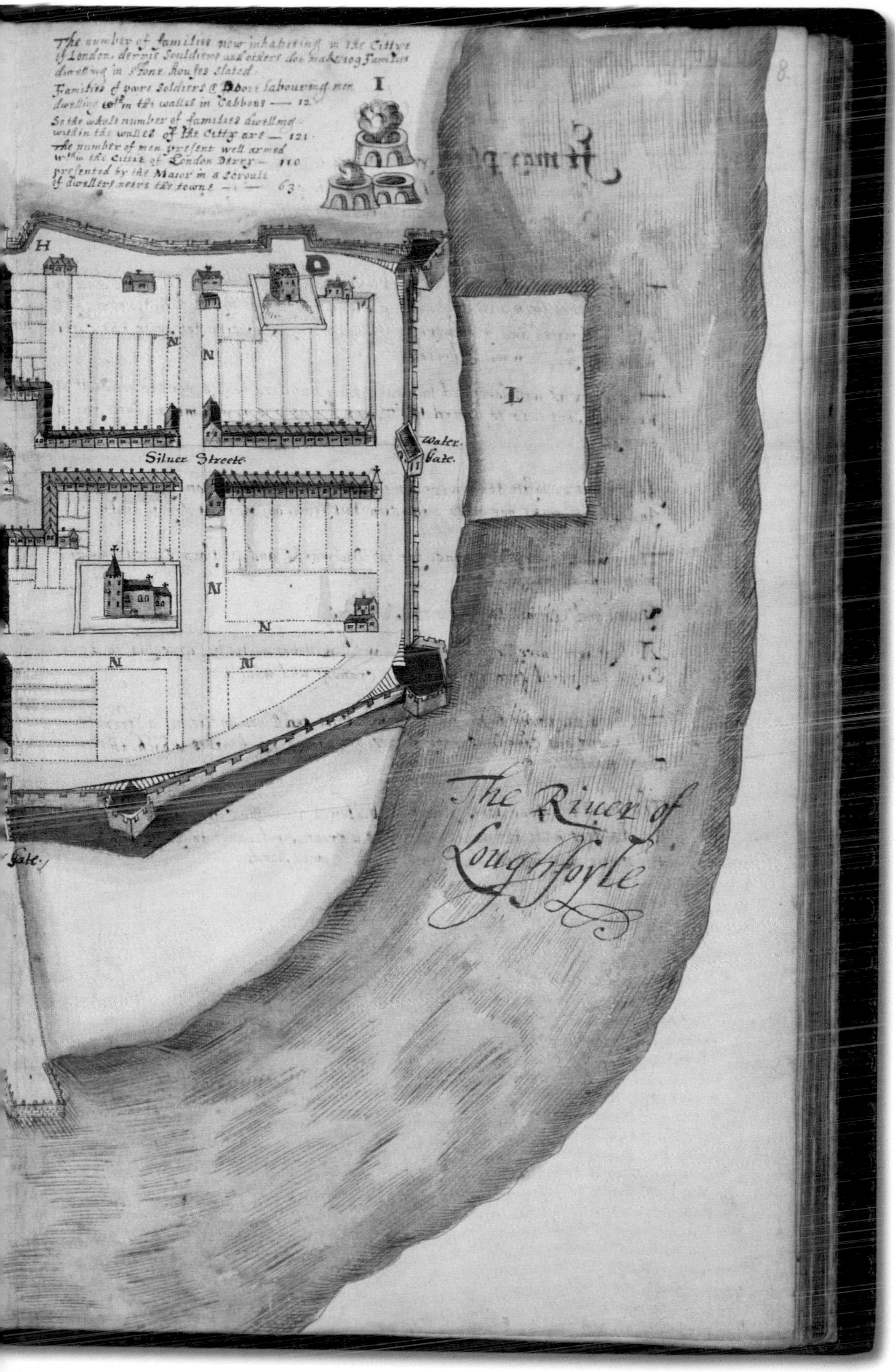
The number of families new inhabiting in the Cittye
of London derrie Souldiers and others doe make 109 families
dwelling in Stone houses slated
Families of poore Soldiers & poore labouring men
dwelling within the walles in Cabbons — 12
So the whole number of families dwelling
within the walles of the Citty are — 121
The number of men present well armed
within the Cittie of London Derry — 110
presented by the Maior in a Scroule
of dwellers neere the towne — 63
I
H
D
N
N
L
Silver Streete
Water Gate
N
N
N
N
Gate
The River of Loughfoyle
8

# 40 Archbishop and King in the Caroline Church

**MS 943, pp. 245–98; reports on the Province of Canterbury by Archbishop William Laud, annotated by King Charles I, 1633–39**
Illustrated: (*opposite*) p. 285, report dated 2 January 1638/39

**Medal commemorating Laud's execution**
*c.*1671; silver; diameter 55 mm
Illustrated: (*right, above*) obverse; (*right, below*) reverse

*shown actual size*

William Laud, Archbishop of Canterbury from 1633 to 1645, is a dominant figure in the history of the post-Reformation Church of England. In the 1630s he attempted to shift the practice and priorities of the Church, moving it away from a sermon-centred piety, forbidding discussion of the Calvinist interpretation of Predestination and cracking down on Puritan Nonconformity. More positively, Laud enforced the observance of the Prayer Book, and encouraged the beautification of churches in which divine worship was accompanied with greater ritualism and a stronger sense of sacred space, especially the newly introduced railed altars. Laud's work was highly controversial, and he was denounced as an agent of Rome, so in 1640, when Charles I's regime was overwhelmed by public hostility, Laud had to be sacrificed. He was imprisoned in the Tower of London, tried for treason in 1644, and executed on 10 January 1645. However, the ideals which Laud championed did not die and returned, in muted form, after the Restoration of Charles II (r. 1660–85).

The Laudian Reformation was the achievement of both the Archbishop and his Supreme Governor, Charles I. In 1629, having consulted Laud and other bishops, the King issued a series of instructions to reform the Church. He ordered bishops to return to their sees, protect their lands, ordain with care, police the pulpits and, via the two Archbishops, report to him in January each year. The annual reports for Canterbury province survive from 1632 to 1639, one written by Archbishop Abbot and the remainder by his successor Laud. Most of them were carefully annotated by Charles I, indicating his personal commitment to reform. There was no precedent in the Protestant Church of England for the compilation of such reports. They allowed Laud and the King to monitor the work of the bishops, and represent a wonderful source to trace the impact of Laudianism across the country.

The illustration comes from Laud's report for 1638, with three comments written by the King in the margin. At the top, Charles has underlined, and endorses, a recommendation from Laud that those who remain excommunicated by the Church should be absolved if they are penitent but cannot afford the fees for absolution. The other two comments by Charles show his impatience with bishops (St David's and Gloucester) who had been absent from their dioceses, as the episcopate were his key agents for change. These reports constitute some of the best evidence of the partnership of King Charles I and Archbishop Laud in running the Church in the 1630s.

To some contemporaries, Laud died a martyr for the Church of England. A silver medal commemorating his execution was issued around 1671. It was the work of Jan Roettiers (*c.*1631–1703), chief engraver of the Royal Mint. The obverse shows Laud in academic cap and robes, while the reverse links the martyrdom of Laud to that of King Charles I with the inscription *praecursor Sancti Caroli* (the precursor of St Charles). Nevertheless, in death as in life, Laud remained controversial. When his body was brought back to Oxford in 1663 for re-internment in St John's College Chapel, the authorities thought it prudent that the cortège enter the college under cover of darkness and through the back gate.

*Kenneth Fincham*
*University of Kent*


J. Davies, *The Caroline Captivity of the Church* (Oxford, 1992)
A. Lacey, *The Cult of King Charles the Martyr* (Woodbridge, 2003)
P. Barber, *London in Miniature – Medallic Panoramas of London 1633–1975* (London Topographical Society, 29, 2006), pp. 26–28
K. Fincham (ed.), 'Annual Accounts of the Church of England 1632–1639', in M. Barber and S. Taylor (eds), *From the Reformation to the Permissive Society* (Church of England Record Society, 17, 2010)

Holy Orders at all, or at least not a Priest. For soone as he was discovered, he slipt out of ye Diocess, and ye Bp thinke's yt he now serves in a Peculiar under ye Deane and Chapter of Wells. I will send thither to knowe ye certainty, and see ye Abuse punished: if I can light upon ye Person.

The Bp further certifyes me yt there are very many within yt small Diocess who stand Excomunicate, and divers of them onely for not paymt of ffees; And againe yt many of these are not able to paye them. I think it were not amiss yt once every yeare in Lent ye Chancellor were comanded to take an Accompt of all ye Excomunicats in ye Diocess, and to cause all to be absolved yt shall be fitt for Absolucon, and particularly to see yt noe man be suffred to continue Excomunicated, where nothing but Poverty hinders ye paymt of Dutyes or other ffees. The Bp likewise informes me yt Monumts even of obscure and meane Persons are growne very common in those Partes, and prejudiciall both to ye walles & Pillars and liberty of Churches, wch ye Bp oppose's as much and as fairely as he can, but all is too little.

this ye have very
at reason, for it is
fit that the Sen=
ce of Excomuni=
on should stand,
er then it needs
t

Landaff:

There were in this Diocess the last yeare but two Refractory Ministers knowne to ye Bp, Mr Wroth, and Mr Erbury. The former hath submitted, but ye other would neyther submitt, nor satisfye his Parishioners to whom he had given publike offence. Soe he resigned his Vicarage, and hath thereby left ye Diocess in peace.

St Davids.

For this Diocess ye Bp humbly crave's yor Maty pardone for his longer stay in London then ordinary, & professes his excuse formerly made to your Maty to be most true, viz: That he was forced to it by extremity of Sicknes falling upon him in those partes, and forcing his change of Ayre. That Diocess hath been a little out of quyet this yeare by some Mens medling wth those nice questions, which yor Maty hath forbidden should be comonly preached in ye Pulpitt. But ye relacon being somwhat imperfect, I shall informe my selfe farther and then give yor Maty such Accompt as I receyve.

is no wunder that
this relation is
erfect since the
ickness gives him
excuse for absence

Bangor

In this Diocess ye Bp certifyes me two considerable things, and both of them are of difficult cure. The one concerne's his Bishopricke where every thing is lett for Lives by his Predecessors, to ye very Mill yt grindes his Corne. The other concerne's ye Diocess in generall, where by reason of ye Poverty of ye Place all Clergymen of hope & worth seeke Preferment elswhere. And he tells me plainly some weake Schollers must be Ordeyned, or else some Cures must be left alltogether unsupplyed.

Glocester

My Ld of Glocester confesseth he hath been absent from his Diocess a good part of this yeare, being kept from his dwelling houses by ye Infeccon at Glocester, which just cause of absence he humbly submittes to yor most gracious Matie.

This is well anufe
have left his desyre
urther absenting
selfe

Concerning yt Diocess ye Bp speakes not much more. But ye Archdeacon at his visitacon finding ye Clergy conformable gave them this grave and fitting Admonicon, viz That noe man should presume

# 41 Inigo Jones at St Paul's

**FP 43 (formerly FP 321); monthly accounts for the rebuilding of the west end of St Paul's Cathedral, signed by Inigo Jones and others**
London; October 1639–September 1640
Vellum, damaged by fire; 450 x 310 mm; ff. 12
Illustrated: (*below; detail*) f. 2r; accounts signed by Inigo Jones, (*opposite*) Daniel King, *The Cathedrall and Conventuall Churches of England and Wales* (London, 1656), pl. 65

The restoration of St Paul's Cathedral was central to William Laud's programme of church reform as Bishop of London and after his translation to Canterbury. King Charles I had already promised £500 per annum for ten years towards the cost of repairs, but in 1634 he determined that he alone would bear the cost of the west front portico. The result was a triumph for its architect, Inigo Jones (1573–1652), and a landmark in the revival in England of ancient Roman architecture.

Separate accounts for the west end were begun in November 1634. The series survives in the archive of the Dean and Chapter in Guildhall Library (MS 25471), but a stray volume for the year 1639–40 came to Lambeth among papers of the Bishops of London from Fulham Palace. It records payment for the inscription marking the royal act of piety in October 1639: 'To Thomas Decritts [De Critz] for … makeinge the Letters in the frieze with black upon Goulde.' Inigo Jones signs the monthly accounts as surveyor, and the young John Webb, also acting as Jones's draughtsman, is paid for engrossing the books: 30 years later he will be unstopping the very same lettering that had been plastered over in the time of the Commonwealth. In the same October, Ambrose Andrewes works on the 'Modell of the great Cornish'; by May 1640 the 'Basement of the Peddistall under the Piramides' is in hand; and in June provision is made for 'the Straight Rayle of the Portico' and task-work undertaken on 'inrichments of the great Architrave' and 'great Marble Dore Case'.

Here in the richest detail we learn the construction of 'that goodly Chur<c>h St *Paules* … & that beautifull Portico (for structure comparable to any in Europ …)' and lament with Evelyn the appearance of its 'sad ruine' after the Great Fire of 1666. Although greatly admired by Sir Christopher Wren, the portico was lost as the new Cathedral rose from the ashes.

*Joseph Wisdom*
*St Paul's Cathedral Library, London*

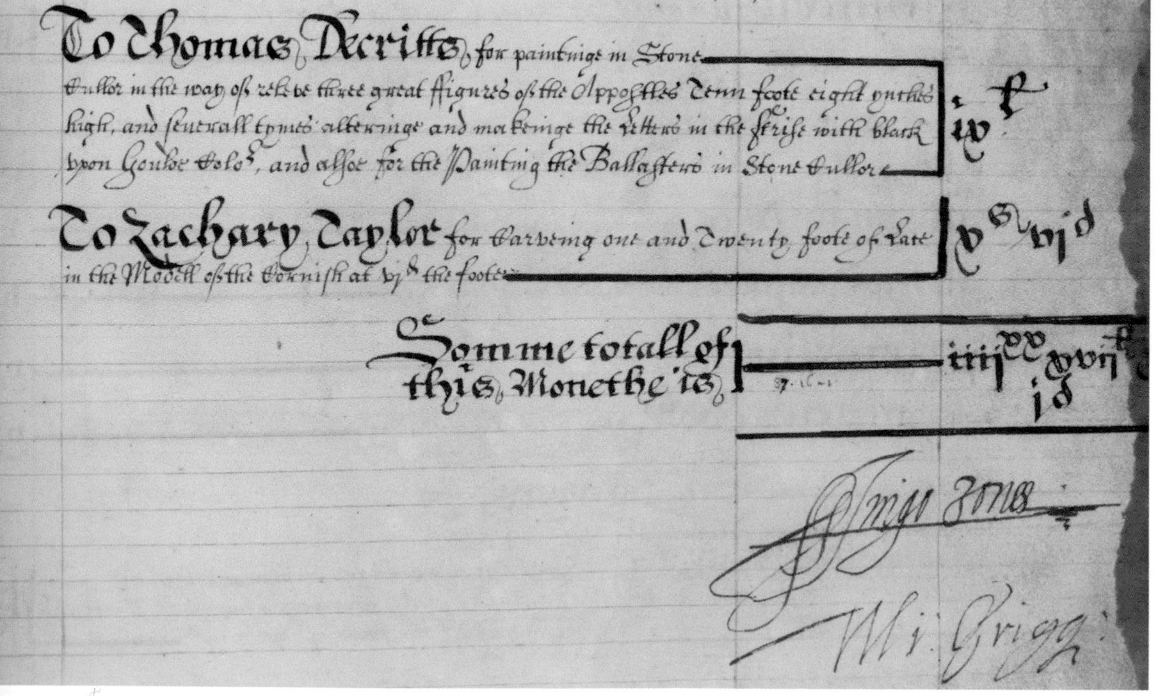

To Thomas Decritts for paintinge in Stone Culler in the way of releive three great figures of the Appostles tenn foote eight ynches high, and seuerall tymes alteringe and makeinge the letters in the frise with black upon Goulde colors, and alsoe for the Painting the Ballasters in Stone Culler — iv li

To Zachary Taylor for Carveing one and twenty foote of [illegible] in the Modell of the Cornish at vj s the foote — vj li vj s vj d

Somme totall of this Monethe is — iiij c xvij li [illegible] j d

Inigo Jones

Wi. Grigg


John Evelyn, *Diary*, ed. E. S. De Beer, vol. 3 *Kalendarium, 1650–1672* (Oxford, 1955), p. 458
Gordon Higgott, 'The Fabric to 1670', in *St Paul's: The Cathedral Church of London* ed. D. Keene, A. Burns and A. Saint (New Haven, 2004), pp. 171–89

The West Prospect of the Cathedral Church of S.t Paul.

Ecclesiæ Cathedralis S.t Pauli latus occidentale.

Daniell King sculpsit,

The manner and forme of the Arch-Bishops Triall in the House of Peeres.

PROVERBS 11. 8.

*The Righteous is delivered out of Trouble, and the wicked commeth in his stead.*

*A.* The Arch-Bishop of *Canterbury.*
*B.* The Gentleman Vsher with his Black-Rod.
*C.* The Leiutenant of the Tower. *D.* The Bishops Councell.
*E.* The Clarke that reades the Evidence.
*F.* The Table where the Books and Papers given in evidence lay.
*G.* The Members of the House of Commons, and Mr. *Prynne* standing in the midst of them, *H.* Mr. *Henry Burton.*
*I. I. I.* The witnesses, Mistris *Bastwicke*. Mr. *Baker* the Messenger.
*K. K. K.* The People and Auditors, within and without the Barre.
*L. L.* The LORDS. *M. M.* The Judges, and Assistants.
*N.* The Speaker of the Lords House. *T.* The Hangings of 88. *S.* Mich. *Sparke.*

# 42 Arch-Enemies: William Prynne and William Laud

**William Prynne, *A Breviate of the Life of William Laud, Arch-bishop of Canterbury, extracted (for the most part) verbatim out of his owne Diary and other Writings …* London; F. L. for Michaell Sparke; 1644**
290 x 195 mm; pp. v, 35
Illustrated: (*opposite*) frontispiece, engraving by Hollar of Laud's trial; (*right; detail*) front endpaper, inscription by Charles I

The lives of William Prynne (1600–69) and William Laud (1573–1645) illustrate the waxing and waning of fortunes in the era of the English Civil War. *A Breviate of the Life of William Laud* is based on the diary that Prynne seized from Laud in the Tower of London in 1643 in an attempt to find evidence to bring him to trial. Lambeth's copy was owned by King Charles I and the inscription which it contains is a poignant memento of the King's own captivity.

Prynne was a prodigious pamphleteer who incited official opprobrium with his attacks on Laud's innovations in the Church and on Laud himself as the 'Pope of Canterbury'. Tried and found guilty twice in the Star Chamber, he suffered a cruel penalty: in 1633 his ears were cropped and in 1637 the initials 'S. L.' ('Seditious Libeller') were burned into his cheeks as a symbol of his crime. For Prynne, this stood for *Stigmata Laudis*, which he made into a pun as 'Laud's scars'. He returned from imprisonment in November 1640 in time to witness Laud's downfall and to exact revenge. In the following month Laud was impeached for high treason, accused of popery, facilitating arbitrary government and alienating the King from his subjects.

Laud's trial began in 1644, with Prynne taking an active part. Laud described him as 'relater and prompter and all, never wearying of anything, so he might do me mischief'. The *Breviate* was published while the trial was in progress, in a maladroit attempt to discredit the Archbishop through his own words. Prynne's 'new discoveries' of 'sundry plots and workes' were intended to support the charge that the Archbishop had treasonably sought reunion with Rome, but critics found the diary less convincing. In the Preface, Prynne states that the Providence of God kept him through his sufferings and selected him to be both 'seizer and peruser' of Laud's papers and prosecutor of his trial. In the trial scene that accompanies the work, Wenceslaus Hollar depicts a solemn and claustrophobic House of Lords; Prynne is shown standing among the group of Members of Parliament identified with the letter 'G'.

However, despite Prynne's access to the Archbishop's diary and private correspondence, he could not prove the charges, and the use of unreliable witnesses made the trial a flagrant abuse of justice.

Parliament found it necessary to pass a bill of attainder to allow his execution, which took place on Tower Hill in January 1645. The ebullient Prynne went on to recount the trial proceedings in *Hidden Workes of Darkenes* (1645) and more fully in *Canterburies Doome* (1646), both of which are bound with Lambeth's copy of the *Breviate* in a volume decorated with the arms of Archbishop Sheldon.

The *Breviate* was printed just four years before King Charles I's own trial and execution. Bereft of political authority and an exile in his own kingdom, Charles wrote the words 'Dum spiro spero. C. R.' ('While I breathe I hope') on the front endpaper. Perhaps, mindful of his sacrifice of his trusted Archbishop, he wondered who, or what, could alter his own fate.

*Jennifer Higham*
*Lambeth Palace Library, London*

J. Bliss and W. Scott (eds), *The Works of the Most Reverend Father in God, William Laud*, 7 vols (Oxford, 1847–60)
E. W. Kirby, *William Prynne: A Study in Puritanism* (Cambridge, MA, 1931)
W. M. Lamont, *Marginal Prynne 1660–1669* (London, 1963)
C. Carlton, *Archbishop William Laud* (London, 1987)
H. Trevor-Roper, *Archbishop Laud, 1573–1645*, 3rd edn (London, 1988)
K. Sharpe, *The Personal Rule of Charles I* (London, 1992)

## 43 King Charles the Martyr Expurgated

**MS 322; *Basilika. The Workes of King Charles the Martyr***
London; James Flesher for R. Royston; 1662
355 x 225 mm
Illustrated: (*opposite*) half-title page, engraved by A. Hertocks; (*overleaf*) engraving of King Charles the Martyr, by A. Hertocks after Philip Fruytiers, 1662, illustrating the *Eikon Basilike*

Books as well as people suffered at the hands of the Inquisition. One of the Library's most unexpected treasures is a copy of the works of King Charles I that still bears the marks of its ordeal. Published in 1662 to mark the triumphant restoration of the monarchy and the re-establishment of the Church of England, this copy was seized on board an English ship on its way to Portugal and handed over to the Inquisition in Lisbon, where it was thoroughly censored before being passed on to the English merchant Barnaby Crafford. He gave it to the English preacher in Lisbon, Zachary Cradock, afterwards Provost of Eton, who brought it back with him to England and presented it to the Library at Lambeth in 1678.

Of the handful of seventeenth-century English books that passed through the hands of censors in Spain and Portugal, the most famous is the copy of the Shakespeare Second Folio (now in the Folger Shakespeare Library) that was expurgated by an English Jesuit, William Sankey, to make it suitable for students in the English College at Valladolid. Shakespeare suffered heavily at the censor's hands, with many passages blacked out in ink and one entire play, *Measure for Measure*, cut out of the volume altogether.

By comparison, King Charles I appears, at least at first glance, to have got away fairly lightly. The objectionable passages are crossed out with a series of diagonal pen-strokes, leaving the text clearly legible, in a manner reminiscent of the Russian jamming of English-language radio stations during the Cold War, where the intention was not to render the programme inaudible but to create a background hum as an inescapable reminder of the censor's presence. References to Charles as a 'Martyr' or as 'Defender of the Faith' are crossed out, as is a reference to William Laud as 'Archbishop of Canterbury and Primate of all England'. The censorship is heaviest in *Eikon Basilike*, where virtually every reference to 'the Church' or 'religion' is systematically deleted. References to the Irish 'Rebellion' of 1641 are also crossed out, as if to imply that the uprising was not a rebellion, as King Charles I was not a lawful king. Individually, these corrections are very small – often only a single word in a sentence – but, cumulatively, they undermine the basic assumptions of the text and serve to remind the reader that an alternative interpretation of English history is possible.

Not long after its arrival at Lambeth, this copy attracted the attention of the diarist Samuel Pepys (1633–1703), who wrote to the librarian, Edmund Gibson (1669–1748) in October 1700, asking to borrow it. Gibson replied that it could not be loaned out of the Library, but that Pepys was welcome to come to Lambeth to consult it. Pepys, by then in his late sixties, was worried about the chilly riverside air, writing to Gibson that 'my health and the season being such as they are, I am jealous your Library may be too cold for me'. Luckily Gibson was able to reassure him, promising that he would 'order a Fire to be made betimes tomorrow morning in a private Room, where the Book shall be ready for you'. Was this, one wonders, a special privilege accorded to a potential benefactor? Did Gibson have hopes of persuading Pepys to bequeath his own splendid library to Lambeth? If so, he was to be disappointed. But two centuries later, the book still remains at Lambeth, hardly changed from when Pepys saw it, testimony to the care and attention of Gibson and his successors.

*Arnold Hunt*
*British Library, London*

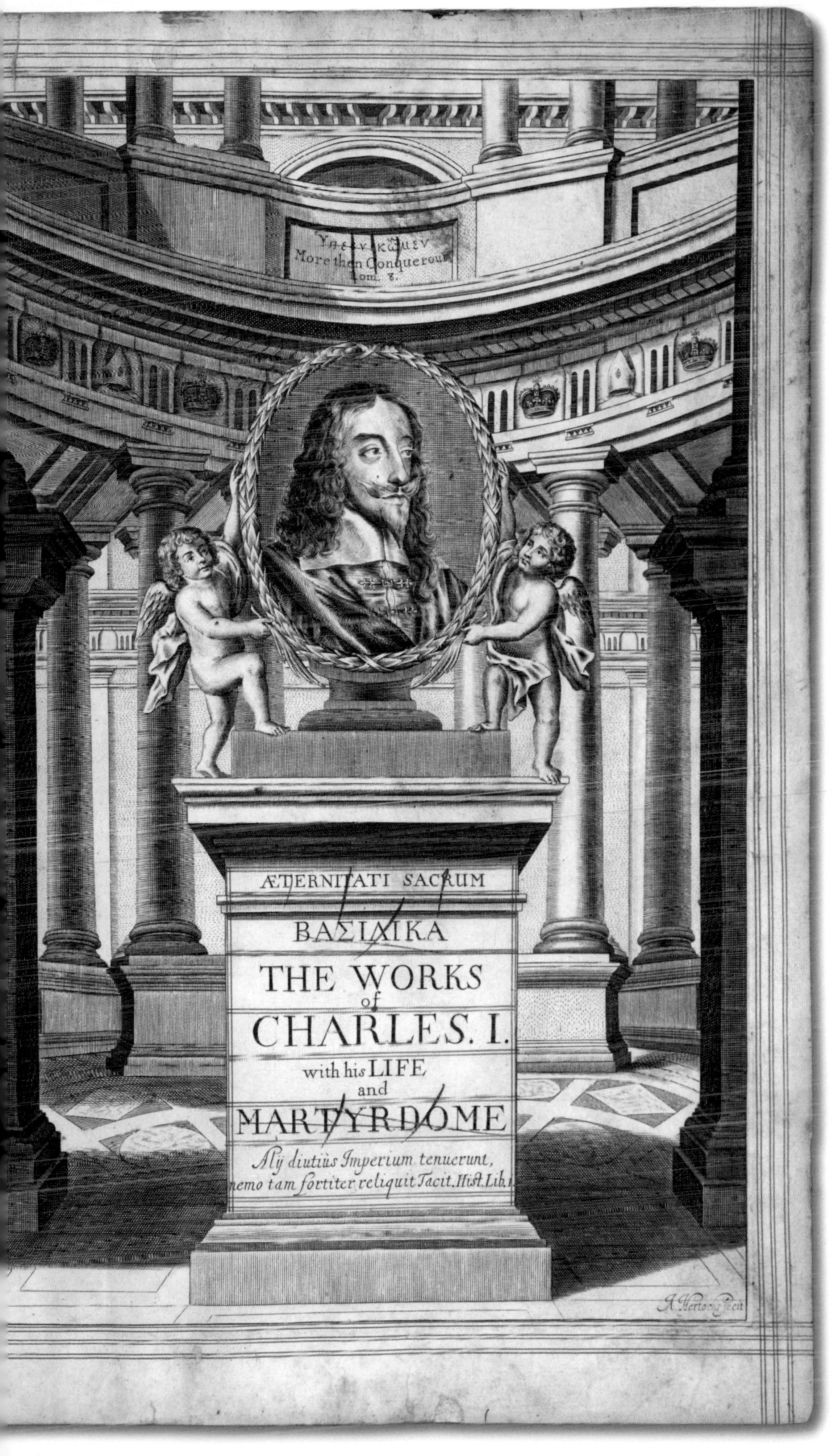
ΥΠΕΡΝΙΚΩΜΕΝ
More then Conquerours
Rom. 8.
ÆTERNITATI SACRUM
ΒΑΣΙΛΙΚΑ
THE WORKS
of
CHARLES. I.
with his LIFE
and
MARTYRDOME
Alij diutius Imperium tenuerunt,
nemo tam fortiter reliquit Tacit. Hist. Lib. 1.
A. Hertocks fecit

BEATAM
CÆLI SPECTO
ASPERAM AT LEVEM
In verbo tuo
Spes mea.
CHRISTI TRACTO
SPLENDIDAM AT GRAVEM

NESCIT NAVFRAGIVM VIRTUS.
CLARIOR E TENEBRI
IMMOTA TRIUMPHANS
CRESCIT SUB PONDERE.
MUNDI CALCO.

# 44 The Popish Plot

***The Papists' Powder Treason***
London; Richard Northcott; 1679
Engraved broadside; 495 x 360 mm
Illustrated: (*opposite*)

**Godfrey dagger**
Steel blade, gilded, with silver hilt; made in London by 'RF',
1678 or 1679; 334 x 55 mm
Illustrated: (*below*)

The Popish Plot of 1678–79 was one of the most extraordinary episodes in English history, when the unscrupulous perjury of Titus Oates (1649–1705) convinced Parliament and the people of the existence of a Roman Catholic conspiracy to assassinate King Charles II and overthrow the Protestant Establishment. Hundreds of Catholics were imprisoned and 24 were executed in the reign of terror which followed.

The plot gained credibility from the murder of Sir Edmund Berry Godfrey, the magistrate to whom Oates had first taken his story. Catholics were blamed for the death, amid hysterical fears that a general slaughter of Protestants was in prospect. Publications such as the popular broadside *England's Grand Memorial,* which portrayed the crime, hailed Godfrey as a martyr.

In London the murder was also memorialised through the sale of thousands of daggers in remembrance of Godfrey and for the protection of Protestants. A fine example in the Library's collection has a steel blade, gilded and engraved with skulls, the date 1678, and the words '*memento Godfrey*'. It is unique in having a silver hilt, with the maker's mark 'RF', and was possibly a 'special edition' for the spectacular pope-burning procession in London on 17 November 1679. This is the subject of a further engraving at Lambeth, *The Solemn Mock Procession*, which includes six Jesuits marching with bloody daggers upraised.

Anti-Catholicism drew on long memories. In 1678 there were rumours of another Gunpowder Plot and a deputation was sent to search the cellars of Parliament. The following year saw the publication of *The Papists' Powder Treason*, of which Lambeth holds one of only two known copies. It is thought to have been first issued in 1612 to mark the seventh anniversary of the Gunpowder Plot, but was withdrawn on the death of Henry, Prince of Wales, whom it features. Its moment came again in 1679.

*The Papists' Powder Treason* depicts a triumphal arch adorned with scenes, inscriptions and figures, including King James I, his Queen, Anne of Denmark, and the royal children, Henry, Charles and Elizabeth. Between them is 'Iacob's stone, erected in aeternal memorie of the divine bountie in England's preservation from ye hellish powder-plot, intended for the blowinge up of ye parliament house, 1605'. There is a scene of Parliament in session, and, below it, at the base of the arch, the conspirators are shown taking counsel, while Guy Fawkes, lamp in hand, enters a room stocked with barrels of gunpowder. A final scene shows the hunting down of the conspirators, while the chariot of justice maintains a steady course through the arch, crushing the wicked beneath its wheels.

During the Popish Plot the chariot of justice did indeed prove unswerving, but those whom it crushed were Oates's hapless victims. Only as the Plot unravelled, bringing Oates himself to trial in 1684, was there an opportunity – as the jury was reminded – to free English justice from reproach.

*Richard Palmer*
*Lambeth Palace Library, London*

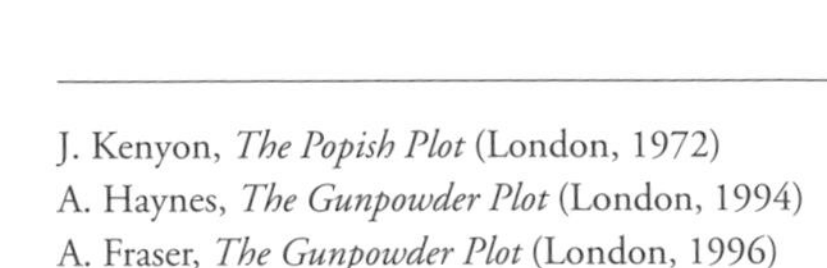

J. Kenyon, *The Popish Plot* (London, 1972)
A. Haynes, *The Gunpowder Plot* (London, 1994)
A. Fraser, *The Gunpowder Plot* (London, 1996)

THE PAPISTS POWDER TREASON
IACOB'S STONE ERECTED IN ÆTERNAL MEMORIE OF THE DIVINE BOVNTIE IN ENGLANDS PRESERVATION FROM Yͤ HELLISH POVDER=PLOT, INTENDED FOR THE BLOWINGE VP OF Yͤ PARLIAMEͭ HOWSE, 1605.
THINE IS THE KINGDOME
GVY FAVX.
Psal. 94. 23.
Least wasting Tyme (Sire of obliuion)
By foggs Infernall might obscure the fame,
Of a deliuerance to be thought vpon,
Whiles reuolution shall giue Time his name,
Deuotion this triumphall Arch doth raise,
To eternize Iehouas glorious praise.
A voice in th'eare, (though ne're so shrill it rings)
Resolues to aire, whence first it formed was:
Whiles obiects of the eye, impressions bringe,
Sometimes more durable, then lasting brasse;
Then let theis lines (like lime) all eyes hould fast,
In memory of this Saluation past.
A malecontented crue, distast the state,
And to subuert it forraigne counsaile take,
Brought from abrode by Faux yͭ renegate.
The Parliament (which law's dislikt did make)
Must be blowne vp, by powder vnder set,
When King wͭʰ all yͤ chiefest states be met
For this yͤ Traitors, arm'd meete in the Vaulte,
Sweare secrecie, seal'd by the Eucharist,
(Least some one might reueale this close assault)
Confessed all by a King-killing Priest;
Where yͤ light shuning messenger doth bring,
There holy Fathers Bull them pardoning.
Mounteagles warning letter is receaud,
Read, shewd yͤ Kinge, scand by yͤ counsel wise,
The Kinge concludes, the rest were all deceau'd:
That (Terrible blowe) shewes that they doe deuise
With gunpowder to blowe vp all the state
In Parliament, except God them frustrate.
Then masked Faux wͭʰ his blinde sconce appears,
Whose powder flaskes, swifte Nemesis reueales,
By helpe of yͤ Kings Scepter wͭʰ shee beares,
Whose sharpe eye sees: whose pious heart appeales
To God for aide, who wͭʰ his bridle staies,
Threats wͭʰ his scourge, & in yͤ end repaies.
An hunting match is sett against the daie,
Of theire intended Tragedie at courte,
Diuers greate Horsse by sleight are tane away
To furnish out this theire pretended sporte.
Theis Nimrods sente yͤ royall bloud of Kings
Whiles into their owne ginns, heauns King them brings
The Kinge like Ezechias, doth vnfould
This cursed threatning Scroule before yͤ Lord,
Beseeching him this Plot may be contrould:
Hath gratious answer, that it is abhord;
Then wͭʰ his Queene & Royal childreͭ her,
Yeelds publique thākes to God on bended knee.
The like both States assembled doe professe,
With all the Comons, whoe participate,
So greate a Mercy, in so greate distresse:
Striuing the Authors praise to propagate.
Gods goodnes sitts aboue & doth behould
How Iustice her euen Charriot wheeles are rould
Drawne by a patient Oxe & Lion fierce;
Mercy wͭʰ Iudgment yoaked safely guide
Her vpright heart, whose single eye doth pierce
Twixt right & wrong, leaning to neither side;

# 47 The Eruptions of Vesuvius

**Sir William Hamilton,** ***Campi Phlegraei: Observations on the Volcanos of the Two Sicilies***
Naples; 1776–79; 3 vols
445 x 335 mm
Illustrated: (*opposite above*) pl. 3, the Bay of Naples;
(*opposite below*) pl. 38, a visit with the King and Queen of Naples, 1771

Visitors to Lambeth Palace Library might be surprised to discover that it contains a handsome book that powerfully evokes the court of Naples and the eruptions of Vesuvius in the eighteenth century. It came to the Library in 1996 from Sion College.

Sir William Hamilton (1730–1803) and his activities as antiquary, connoisseur and natural historian have enjoyed greater renown following the superb exhibition 'Vases and Volcanoes: Sir William Hamilton and his Collection' (British Museum, London, 1996). This exhibition helped to remedy his unjustly one-sided reputation as the compliant husband of Nelson's mistress Emma. He was appointed Envoy Extraordinary to the Kingdoms of Naples and Sicily in 1764 and lived in Naples for over 35 years, not returning to England until 1800. He was a key figure at the Neapolitan court and his home and museum at the Palazzo Sessa was a point of call for every Grand Tourist who visited Naples.

An inveterate collector, Hamilton sold his first collection of pictures, bronzes and terracottas in London in 1761. After his move to Naples, excavations at Herculaneum and Pompeii encouraged his fascination with Antiquity: he collected sculpture, bronzes, gold jewellery, carved gemstones and painted Greek vases. His first collection of Greek vases was catalogued by Pierre François Hugues D'Hancarville in four sumptuous volumes from 1766 to 1767: Hamilton was to sell the collection to the young British Museum in 1772. Fittingly, Hamilton was elected a member of the Society of Dilettanti in 1777, and his introduction is commemorated in the two well-known group portraits painted by Joshua Reynolds: Hamilton is depicted seated before a table on which is placed the folio catalogue, opened to reveal the image of one particular vase, the original of which stands on the table.

Hamilton's enquiring mind caused him to become fascinated by Vesuvius. After a long period of near quiescence, Vesuvius began another period of special activity, with great eruptions, all of which Hamilton witnessed, in 1767, 1779 and 1794. He had first noticed changes in the mountain's behaviour in 1765 and thereafter observed its behaviour closely. In all, he climbed the mountain over 70 times, sometimes acting as guide to visiting dignitaries, and even conducting the King and Queen of Naples to view a fiery flow of lava in 1771. His friend the Earl of Bristol was severely burned by a volcanic rock on one such occasion. He described his findings in a series of letters, published in 1772 and entitled *Observations on Mount Vesuvius, Mount Etna and other Volcanoes in a Series of Letters addressed to the Royal Society.*

His volcanic letters were well received and so Hamilton decided to bring out an illustrated edition that could compare with his catalogue of Greek vases. He chose Pietro Fabris (1740–92) as his artist and the result was three folio volumes of exceptional beauty. The pictures that Fabris produced under Hamilton's supervision, more than 50 hand-coloured gouache illustrations, have a remarkable vitality. Simple and direct, they are mainly designed to illustrate the geological features of the landscape, but they are drawn with a fine sense of artistic imagination and dramatic action.

*Charles Sebag-Montefiore*
*Honorary Treasurer, Friends of Lambeth Palace Library, London*

B. Fothergill, *Sir William Hamilton, Envoy Extraordinary* (London, 1969)
I. Jenkins and K. Sloan, *Vases and Volcanoes: Sir William Hamilton and his Collection* (London, 1996)

III.

# 48 The Court of Arches

Records of the Court of Arches, thirteenth to twentieth century, including:

**N. 1, Black Book of the Arches**
Latin and English; vellum, bound in leather with wooden boards and metal bosses; 320 x 225 mm
Illustrated: (*below left*) binding; (*below right*) f. 42r, Statutes of Robert Winchelsey, Archbishop of Canterbury, 1295

***The trial of Andrew Robinson Bowes, Esq. for adultery and cruelty; first held in the Arches Court of Doctors Commons; and in consequence of an appeal, determined in a Court of Delegates ... when the ... Countess of Strathmore obtained a divorce***
London, 1789
Illustrated: (*opposite*) frontispiece

In 1776 Mary Eleanor Bowes, Countess of Strathmore, an aristocrat of great wealth, who had had many love affairs, met Andrew Robinson Stoney. Although said to be pregnant by another lover, she soon married him. Stoney – supposedly the model for Thackeray's anti-hero, Barry Lyndon – was a fortune hunter. Discovering that a trust prevented him from controlling his new wife's wealth, Stoney (then known as Bowes) forced her with violence to reverse this arrangement. She brought an action against him alleging cruelty and adultery, but was abducted and subjected to further abuse. The case caused a sensation in the popular press; cases so scandalous were rushed into print, often with engravings of telling incidents. Bowes was eventually imprisoned and fined, while the Countess was granted a legal separation and recovered her estates.

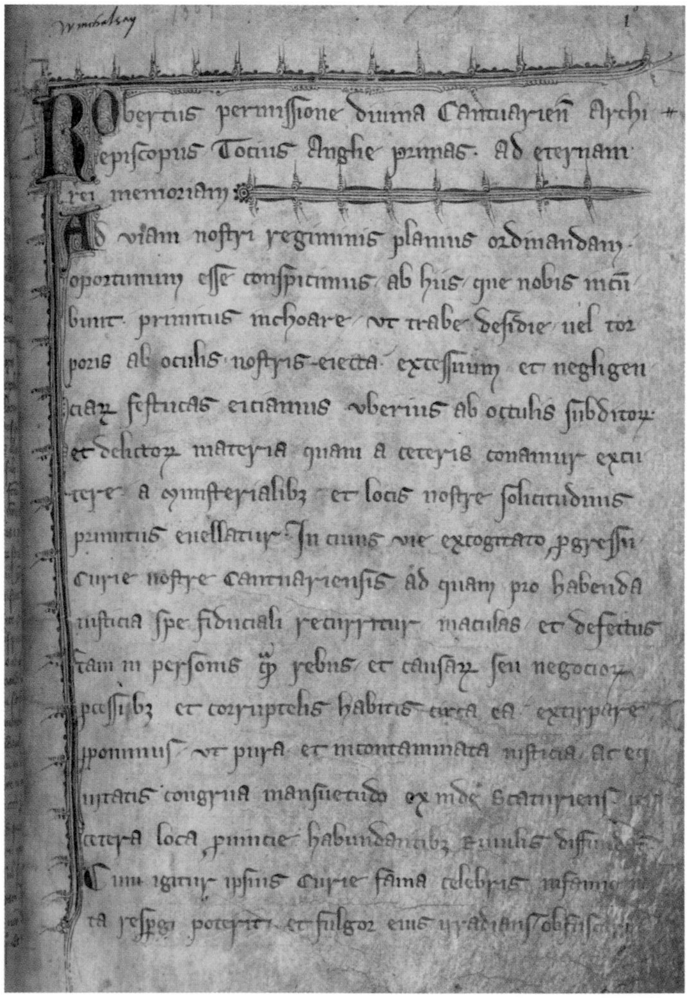

Documents on the case survive at Lambeth among the myriad records of the Court of Arches – the principal ecclesiastical court in England, which had jurisdiction far beyond the clerical sphere. The procedure of ecclesiastical law centred not – as in common law courts – on oral evidence but on written testimony, generating a vast body of records. In divorce suits, the vices of both parties relating to sex, drink and money were intimately described by neighbours, servants and other witnesses. Lunacy, frigidity or impotence might be alleged and household arrangements, material and personal, laid bare. One victim warned potential litigants that one 'must expect to have as much filth as a scavenger's cart will hold emptied upon him'. Proceedings could also be costly. A suit between the Earl and Countess of Portsmouth cost £4,000, and the itemised bill is over 100 feet long.

Although originating in the medieval period, few early records of the Court survive, as the rest were consumed by the Great Fire of London in 1666. One important survivor is the Black Book of the Arches, which provided statutes and precedents concerning procedure to which the court referred, giving authoritative texts dating back to the time of Robert Kilwardby, Archbishop of Canterbury from 1273 to 1278.

From the 1660s onwards, the archive covers some 10,000 cases: a rich picture of the lives of the nobility (some of them not behaving with much nobility), and others of humbler birth. However, by the mid-nineteenth century, Doctors' Commons, where the court sat, was described by Charles Dickens as 'a lazy ... nook near St Paul's ... a little out-of-the-way place, where they administer what is called ecclesiastical law, and play all kinds of tricks with obsolete old monsters of Acts of Parliament'. Legislation in the 1850s curtailed the jurisdiction of the Church courts. The archive of the Court of Arches was abandoned in a disused well, later to be disinterred and cherished as one of the most precious sources for English social history.

*Rachel Cosgrave*
*Lambeth Palace Library, London*

D. M. Slatter, 'The Records of the Court of Arches', *Journal of Ecclesiastical History*, vol. 6, no. 2 (October 1953), pp. 139–53
J. Houston (ed.), *Index of Cases in the Records of the Court of Arches at Lambeth Palace Library 1660–1913* (Index Library, vol. 85, 1972)
L. Stone, *Road to Divorce: England, 1530–1987* (Oxford, 1990)
M. Barber, 'Records of the Court of Arches in Lambeth Palace Library', *Ecclesiastical Law Journal*, vol. 3 (1993–95), pp. 10–19
F. D. Logan, *The Medieval Court of Arches* (Canterbury and York Society, vol. 95, 2005)

# 49 The First Church in Australia

**Moore Papers, vol. 1, ff. 9–95, Richard Johnson, account of his chaplaincy**
Sydney, New South Wales; 1793–94
Illustrated: (*below*) Moore Papers, vol. 1, f. 20v, page from Johnson's account; (*opposite*) f. 95, plan of the first church; (*overleaf*) Arthur Phillip, *The Voyage of Governor Phillip to Botany Bay* (London, 1789), plates opposite pp. 46, 106, 150

When the First Fleet reached Sydney Cove in 1788, the officers, marines and convicts sent to establish a penal colony in New South Wales had endured an epic voyage of eight months and thirteen days. The real challenge, however, lay ahead, as the colonists strove to forge a viable settlement. The chaplain, Richard Johnson (1755–1827), an evangelically minded clergyman and a friend of John Newton and William Wilberforce, faced an especially difficult task. Charged with the mission, as he saw it, of reforming 'those poor and abandoned people ... possessed of souls that are immortal', the soil on which he had to sow his seed proved stony indeed.

Johnson had received support from the first governor of the colony, Arthur Phillip, but, after his departure in 1792, Johnson's position became unbearable. The new administrator, Francis Grose, viewed Johnson as 'one of those People called Methodists … a discontented troublesome character', and seized every opportunity to undermine his standing and frustrate his ministry. Under Grose's administration (1792–94) the moral tone of the colony sank to a new low. In a letter to Archbishop John Moore, Johnson recounted the laxity of the officers and soldiers, living in 'open adultery or fornication', attending divine service in states of intoxication and neglecting the spiritual welfare of the prisoners. In such circumstances respect for his clerical status was almost wholly lacking. He wrote: 'I declare that I cannot walk along the street or road, but I am almost sure to have my eyes and ears insulted with some wicked gesture, action or language.'

Yet what troubled Johnson most was the colonial government's failure, after five years' settlement at Port Jackson, to erect a suitable building in which to conduct church services. Faced with Grose's contempt for such a project, Johnson set out, in March 1793, to build a church with his own labour and at his own cost:

> *… for days together I have myself been in the woods, stripped and working as hard as any Convict in the Colony – night after night, and almost all hours of the night, I have been upon the water or in the woods exposed to rain, cold, hunger etc. For what? Why for no other Reason, End, or Interest, than to provide a comfortable Place for myself and fellow Creatures to assemble together in order to worship God in a manner as becometh Christians.*

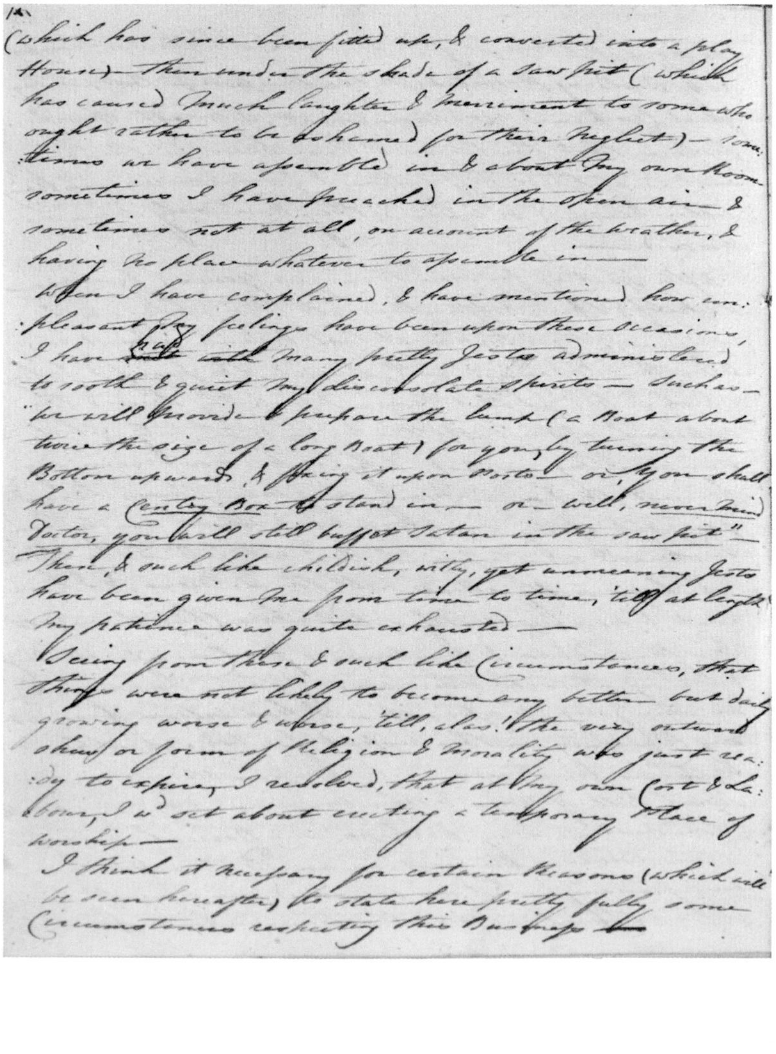

In 1794 Johnson sent a detailed account of his tribulations to William Wilberforce. Now part of the Moore Papers in Lambeth Palace Library, it provides a fascinating glimpse of life in the fledgling colony, and includes the plan of the first church in Australia, the fruit of Johnson's labours, completed in August 1793. This structure was burnt in an act of arson five years later, an event that must have

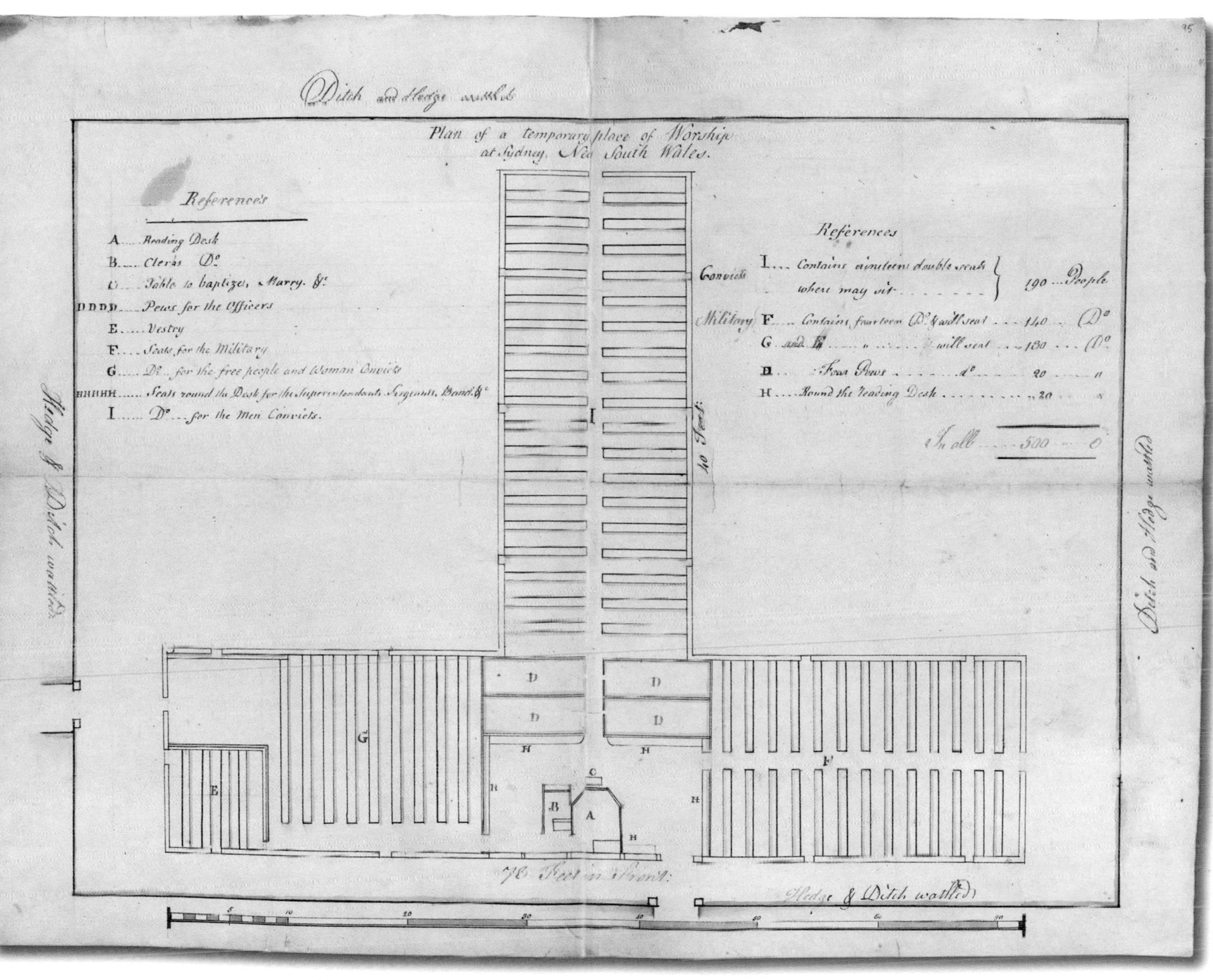


distressed Johnson deeply. Yet, by the time of his departure for England in 1800, under the more benevolent rule of Governor John Hunter, Johnson witnessed the laying of the foundation stones of not one, but two stone churches for the colony. If his efforts for many years seemed in vain, he had in the end established the Church of England in a new world.

*Aaron Hope*
*Lambeth Palace Library, London*

J. Bonwick, *Australia's First Preacher* (London, 1898)
W. H. Rainey, *The Real Richard Johnson* (Melbourne, 1947)
N. K. Macintosh, *Richard Johnson: Chaplain to the Colony of New South Wales; His Life and Times 1755–1827* (Sydney, 1978)
D. Chapman, *1788: The People of the First Fleet* (Sydney, 1986)
P. Emmett, *Fleeting Encounters: Pictures and Chronicles of the First Fleet* (Sydney, 1995)
B. Kaye et al. (eds), *Anglicanism in Australia: A History* (Carlton, 2002)

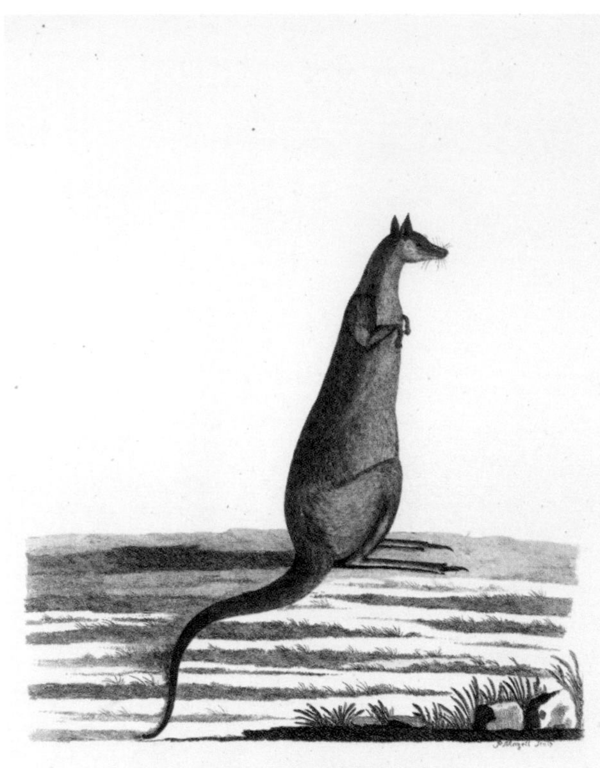

THE KANGOOROO.

*Published as the Act directs June 13, 1789, by J. Stockdale.*

WULPINE OPOSSUM.

*Publish'd Aug. 21, 1789 by J. Stockdale.*



*R. Cleveley delin.t*

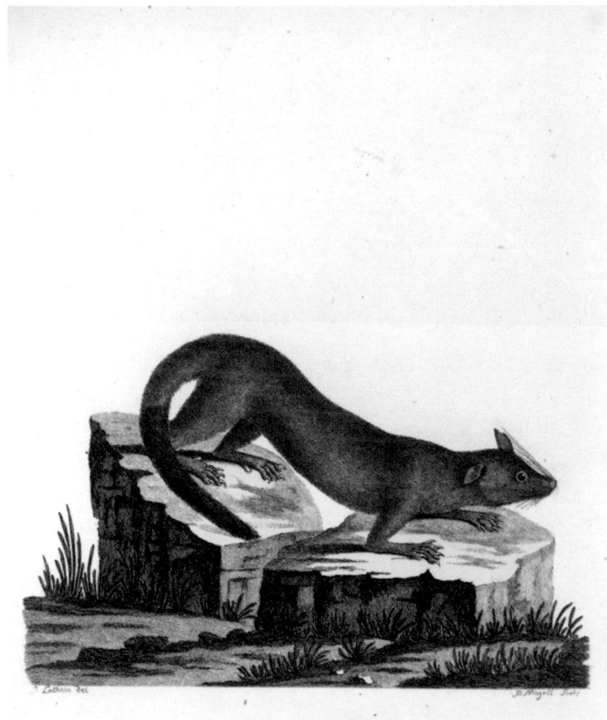

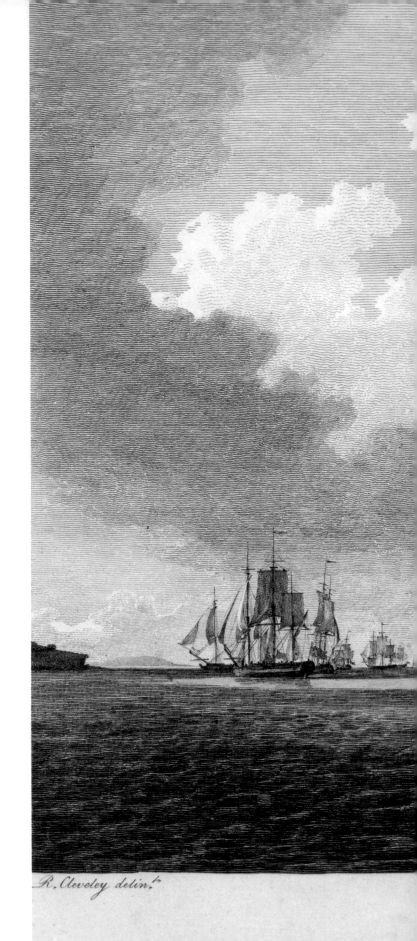

T. Medland sculp.

IEW OF BOTANY BAY.

Published June 17. 1789, by I. Stockdale.

# 50 The Malady of King George

**MSS 2107–2139; records of the Queen's Council during the incapacity of George III**
1811–20
Illustrated: (*below; detail*) *The Royal Procession in St Paul's on St George's Day 1789*, engraving by J. Neagle after E. Dayes (London, 1793), by courtesy of Professor Stephen Taylor; (*opposite left*) MS 2117, f. 27r, medical report of 14 October 1811; (*opposite right*) MS 2107, f. 234r, letter from Queen Charlotte to the Queen's Council, 9 October 1811

On 23 April 1789 King George III (r. 1760–1820) went in solemn procession to St Paul's for a service of thanksgiving to mark his recovery from the mental derangement which had brought intense personal suffering and created a political crisis. His recovery, all the same, did not prove permanent. The illness of 1788–89 was followed by further episodes in 1801 and 1804. The last ten years of his long life – 1810 to 1820 – were a time of severe affliction, marked by sleeplessness, incessant agitation, delusions, loss of reason, a rapid pulse and other symptoms of physical and mental disorder.

The Regency Act of 1811 vested the care of the King's person in Queen Charlotte and established a Council to assist her. At its head was Charles Manners-Sutton, Archbishop of Canterbury. The Council supervised every detail of the sick room and oversaw the medical attendants. Having the responsibility to declare whether the King was well and competent, the Council required daily reports

27

To the Queen's Council

His Majesty pass'd yesterday upon the whole quietly – He sometimes played upon His Harpsichord & Flute, but was almost constantly engaged with his own distemper'd fancies –

His Majesty slept only three hours in the night, and when He awoke, He was even more turbulent than usual, so as very soon to require the Restraint to be impos'd – At our visit this morning, His Majesty was so irritable, that we could not venture to feel His Pulse, or to enter into conversation with Him —

Henry Halford
M Baillie
R. Willis.

Windsor Castle
Octr 14 – 1811

234

The Queen has this moment received the communication from Her Council, inclosing for Her Information a Copy of the Instruction given by them to the Consulting Physicians, and H. M. has observed with satisfaction that they have so explicitly stated to them & also made known to the Physicians actually in attendance the Conditions upon which alone the Queen could Consent to the former having access to the Kings Apartment.

Windsor
the 9th Octbr.
1811.

Charlotte

from the physicians and quarterly replies to questionnaires on the King's health and his chances of recovery. The resulting archive is one of the most remarkable at Lambeth. Here are preserved the 3,075 daily reports, each carefully dated and numbered by the Archbishop. Here, too, are the public bulletins – shorter and more benign – along with letters from the Queen, politicians and the physicians whose differing views on the nature of insanity and on therapy perplexed Queen and Council alike.

The medical reports portray the pitiable state of the King, 'lost in mind, perverted in his ideas ... irritable and violent'. He was prone to delusions: that he was immortal and could call up the dead; that the whole of England south of the Humber was to sink; that the Duke of Clarence would marry the Princess of Wales and sail to Botany Bay. He conversed endlessly with imaginary bystanders and acquaintances long dead. Sleepless, angry and agitated, he would sometimes throw his food away or display a 'perverse disposition to uncleanliness'. Often he was confined in a straight-waistcoat, given opiates to calm him and put to bed by force.

The King's medical treatment was entrusted initially to three physicians, Sir Henry Halford, Matthew Baillie and William Heberden junior. Heberden believed that the King's mind should be soothed by familiar company, conversation and amusement, and that he should have liberty to live as normally as possible. Under Heberden's influence, the King was at first allowed to ride at Windsor and to see his family. However, in May 1811, with the King in the grip of a fresh paroxysm, the Queen and her Council turned to Robert Willis, whose father had been credited with the King's recovery in 1789, and put him in charge. Willis instituted a regime based on the isolation of the King from any stimulus or excitement, and on restraint and coercion to correct 'wrong ideas'. Under this system of forced and monotonous confinement, King George III lived out his twilight years, old, blind and increasingly deaf, comforted only by his flute and his harpsichord, once owned by Handel. Medical report 3,075 logs his end, with a note by the Archbishop: 'His Majesty expired at 32 minutes past 8 o'clock p.m., January 29th [1820]. C. Cantuar'.

*Richard Palmer*
*Lambeth Palace Library, London*

C. Chenevix Trench, *The Royal Malady* (London, 1964)
I. Macalpine and R. Hunter, *George III and the Mad-Business* (London, 1969)

# 51 The First Lambeth Conference

**Lambeth Conference records**
Illustrated: (*opposite; detail*) MS 1728, f. 27, group photograph of the Conference by Mason & Co., 27 September 1867; (*right*) MS 1680, f. 23, photograph of C. T. Longley, Archbishop of Canterbury, by C. L. Dodgson, 7 July 1864

The photograph of the bishops attending the 'Pan Anglican Synod' at Lambeth from 24 to 27 September 1867 records an iconic moment for the Anglican Communion, being the first time all bishops in communion with the see of Canterbury were invited to Lambeth Palace for 'brotherly consultation'.

Of the 151 Anglican bishops 148 were invited (three were not: Colenso of Natal, who was considered a heretic; Hinds, formerly of Norwich, who was disgraced for marrying his housekeeper; and Nixon, formerly of Tasmania, who had retired to Italy), and 76 attended. In the photograph, taken on the last day of the Conference, the preponderance of American bishops is notable – 20 out of 76, the largest national group. The other bishops were all British or British expatriates. Eighteen English and Welsh bishops were present, but only Chester and Sodor and Man from the province of York. There were eight Canadian bishops, six Scottish, five Irish, four from New Zealand, four from southern Africa, three from the West Indies, and one each from India and Australia. Three retired bishops, from Hong Kong, Ceylon and New Zealand, supplemented colonial experience. The shortness of the notice, and long, slow and expensive journeys from India and Australia, discouraged their bishops from attending. Some English and Irish bishops were absent because they suspected their fellow bishops wished to legislate for the Communion, and might undermine English Church–State relations.

The photograph was taken after the final, acrimonious, Conference session, which overran by nearly two hours. Bishop Gray of Cape Town (sitting on the step in front of the Archbishop of Canterbury, looking miserable) had attempted to introduce a motion, with the support of Samuel Wilberforce of Oxford (just to the right of the Archbishop in the photograph) to elect a new Bishop of Natal, despite Colenso having been confirmed as Bishop by the English courts. Gray was angrily opposed by Tait of London (just to the left of the Archbishop), Sumner of Winchester (just to the left of Tait) and Thirwall of St David's. Selwyn of New Zealand (to the right of Wilberforce) had joined in, criticising the English bishops for not condemning Colenso's heresy. The bishops are all carrying their hats and umbrellas ready to hurry off to a public meeting, where Gray, to Tait's fury, implied that the Conference had endorsed the appointment of a new Bishop of Natal, and thereby Colenso's condemnation and deposition.

Archbishop Longley, the convenor of the Conference, had been Bishop of Ripon where his Archdeacon of Richmond was the father of Charles Lutwidge Dodgson (Lewis Carroll), who had been at Rugby and Christ Church, Oxford, with Longley's eldest son. The families were close friends. Dodgson, the author of *Alice in Wonderland*, was a distinguished portrait photographer. Longley's daughters were among his earliest child friends, and he wrote his *Legend of Scotland* for them. During 1864 Dodgson used Lambeth Palace as his studio. It is claimed that Dodgson photographed Archbishop Longley more often than any other man.

*W. M. Jacob*
*University of Wales Lampeter*

W. R. Curtis, *The Lambeth Conferences* (New York, 1942)
A. M. G. Stephenson, *The First Lambeth Conference: 1867* (London, 1967)
A. M. G. Stephenson, *Anglicanism and the Lambeth Conferences* (London, 1978)
W. M. Jacob, *The Making of the Anglican Church Worldwide* (London, 1997)
W. M. Jacob, 'The First Lambeth Conference and the Anglican Communion', *Lambeth Palace Library Annual Review* (2008), pp. 54–68
Lambeth Palace Library, Longley Papers, vol. 9, f. 2, another copy of the Conference photograph, with key to sitters

# 52 The Incorporated Church Building Society

**ICBS Archive, comprising minute books and 15,234 files, 1818–1994**
Illustrated: ICBS 7232, plan for the enlargement of St Mary, Fishponds, Gloucestershire, by John Pollard Seddon (1827–1906), 1871, 620 x 470 mm

By the start of the nineteenth century, England's church organisation had been overwhelmed by population increase and redistribution. The Church was unable to respond because it was in a parliamentary straitjacket, and heavy war taxation made State aid unlikely. A Church Building Society was therefore launched in February 1818, essentially by lay church-members, to promote through voluntary subscriptions the building, enlargement and repair of Anglican churches. Their groundwork encouraged the Government, later in the same year, to grant a million pounds for building new churches under the aegis of a Church Building Commission.

The Society, some of whose leading members also served on the Commission, was careful to work within the frame of the Established Church, and its standing was enhanced by incorporation in 1828 by Act of Parliament. It would not undertake to build churches, but gave grants up to £500 towards a new building. Crucially, unlike the Commission, it supported the repair and enlargement of existing churches, work of great importance, as many parish churches were in poor condition or offered little accommodation for the poor. However, as State aid dried up around 1830, the Society contributed more widely towards new churches. Its rules required that the additional accommodation provided should be designed in an economical way and be available without charge, so the poor could use it. The Society continued independently until 1982, when its administration was taken over by the Historic Churches Preservation Trust.

The Society required applicants to supply data in a regular form, along with plans and drawings of the proposed work. A vast archive was thus built up, the greater part of which is held at Lambeth Palace Library. The plans and drawings are accessible online, but many are supported by forms, reports and letters, sometimes voluminous, a source that has been little explored by historians. There are also minute books detailing the Society's comments on, and responses to, applications.

Some 400 of the files relate to the Society's first four years, from 1818 to 1822. Often a unique record, these are mostly for repairs or enlargements; but W. George's St James, Pontypool, a new church, has a plan and elevation and even a sketch-plan of the town. With succeeding years new church applications become more numerous, especially in the Victorian years, though there are still many enlargements and rebuilds. Plans and elevations proliferate through the rest of the century, from Lowder's Holy Trinity Bath (1837), through George Gilbert Scott's simple design for Shippon, Berkshire (1856), J. P. Pritchett's Emmanuel, Saltburn, Marske (1870s), with five plans and a perspective, and James Fowler's grand, but never completed, Holy Trinity, for leafy suburban Snaresbrook (1880s), to Fellows Prynne's All Saints, Sydenham, in the twentieth century.

After the First World War, there are fewer plans: Temple Moore's St Mary's, Sculcoates (1920) has illustrations from architectural periodicals and an appeal booklet; Gerald Wellesley's ambitious SS Mary and George, High Wycombe (1935–38) has photographs of a model and copies of newspapers with illustrations. After the Second World War, repairs predominate, and plans are scarcer still, as fewer new churches were built. In the 1960s, Cachemaille-Day's contemporary-styled St Alban's, Wednesfield, offers plan and section; and H. Millson's more traditional St John Baptist, Tilbury Dock, a rebuilding, has nine photographs of exterior and interior. In the 1970s, one of the few perspectives is of A. Platt's deplorable portakabin-like extensions to St Augustine's, Broxbourne.

This wonderful archive, readily accessible for all to use through www.churchplansonline.org, is an inexhaustible treasure for students of architectural and parish history.

*M. H. Port*
*Queen Mary College, University of London*

T. V. Parry, *The Incorporated Church Building Society 1818–1851*, M.Litt. thesis (Oxford University, 1984)
M. H. Port, *600 New Churches. The Church Building Commission 1818–1856* (Reading, 2006)

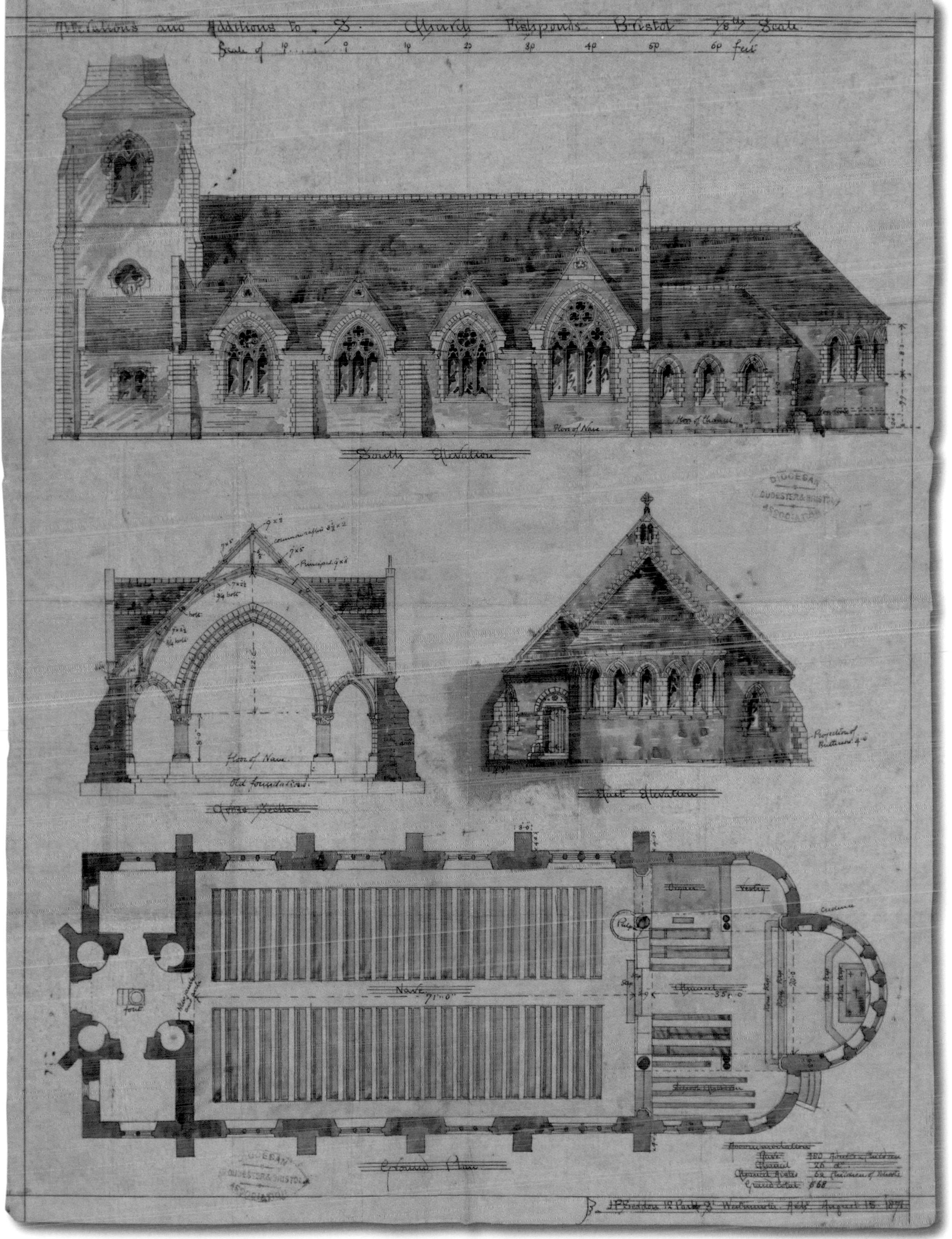
Church Fishponds Bristol
South Elevation
Floor of Nave
Floor of Chancel
Principal
Floor of Nave
Old foundations
Cross Section
Projection of Buttresses 4'-0"
East Elevation
Organ
Vestry
Pulpit
Font
Nave 71'-0"
Chancel 35'-0"
Ground Plan
DIOCESAN
GLOUCESTER & BRISTOL
ASSOCIATION

# 53 The Gladstone Diaries

**MSS 1416–1455, 2758–2774; diaries and papers of William Ewart Gladstone (1809–98)**

Illustrated: (*right*) portrait of Gladstone by Millais, 1885, replica by C. H. Thompson, presented by Lord Gladstone; (*below*) MS 1451, pp. 60–61, defeat of the first Irish Home Rule Bill, 7 June 1886; (*opposite*) MS 1455, the final diary entry, 29 December 1896

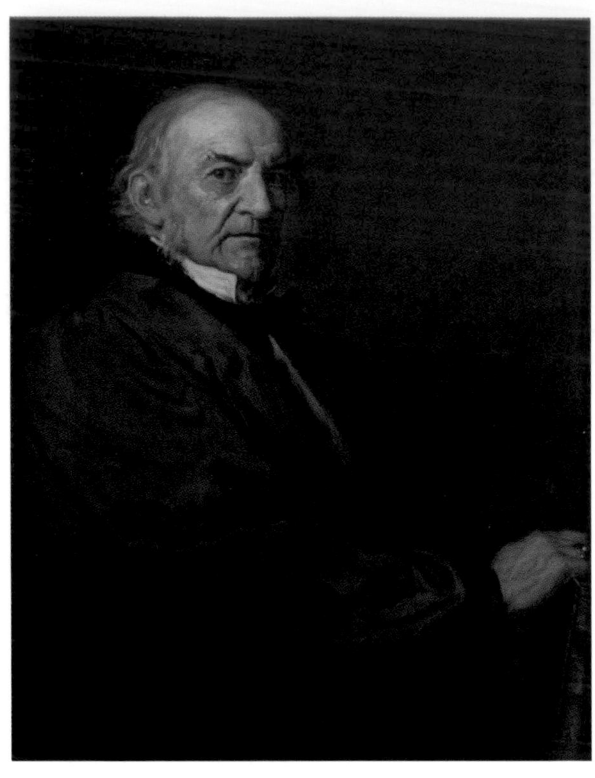

Within 41 tiny notebooks, etched out in minute script, lie the skeletal remains of one eminent Victorian's intense and complex world. Described by former Lambeth Librarian, Claude Jenkins, as 'one of the most remarkable "human documents" ever composed', Gladstone's journals were his diurnal companions for over 70 years. They were his 'account-book of the all-precious gift of time', designed not for publication but for self-examination, improvement and reference.

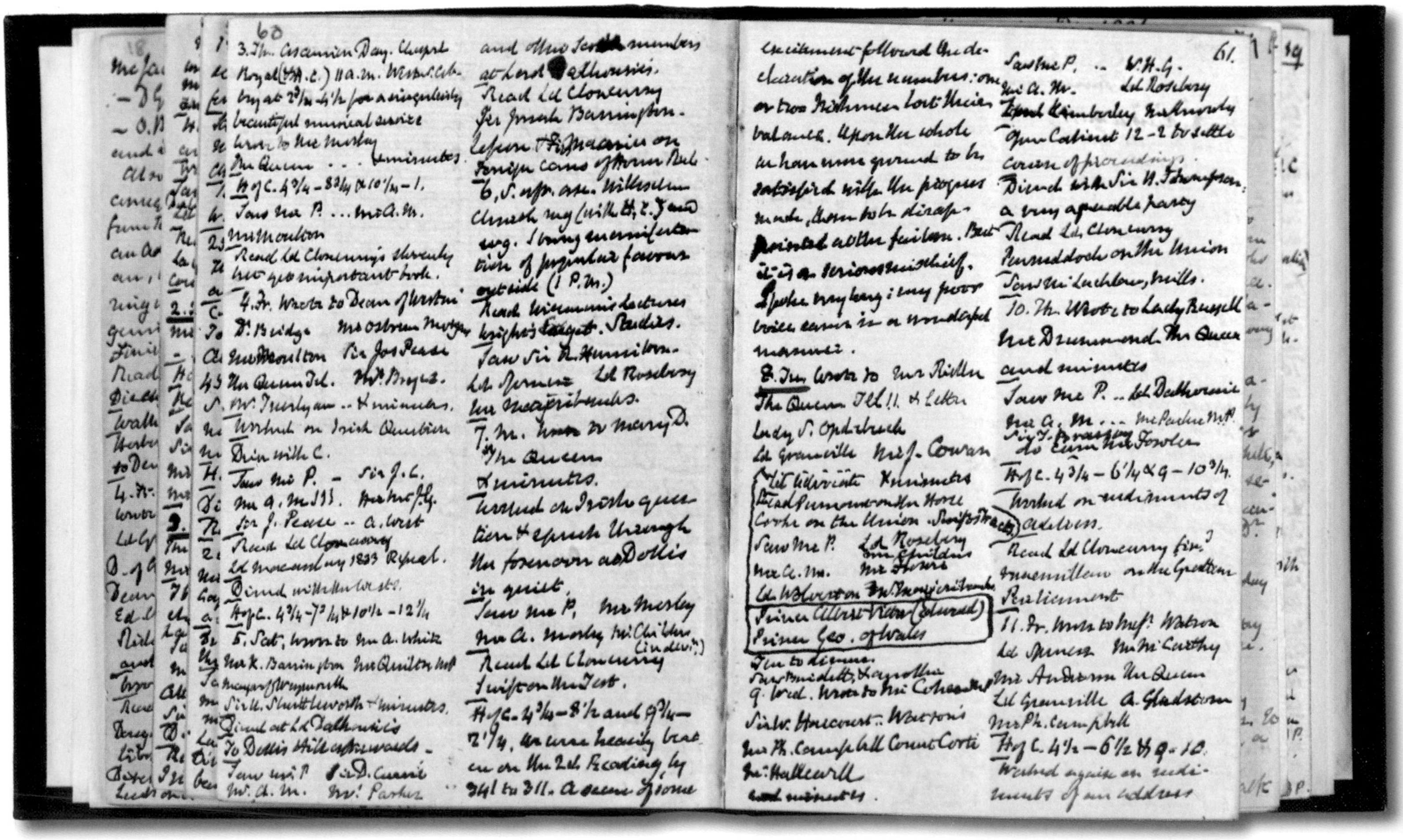

The first surviving entry, written at Eton, dates from 16 July 1825, and the last from 29 December 1896, his 87th birthday and a traditional retrospective moment. There are over 25,000 entries, mostly brief, factual, and unreflective: letters written, people seen, books read, church services and parliamentary debates attended. Nevertheless, the content is not prosaic. Personal landmarks, such as his marriage in 1839 and the births of his children, intermix with events of national significance such as Wellington's funeral in 1852 or the rejection of Irish 'Home Rule' in 1886.

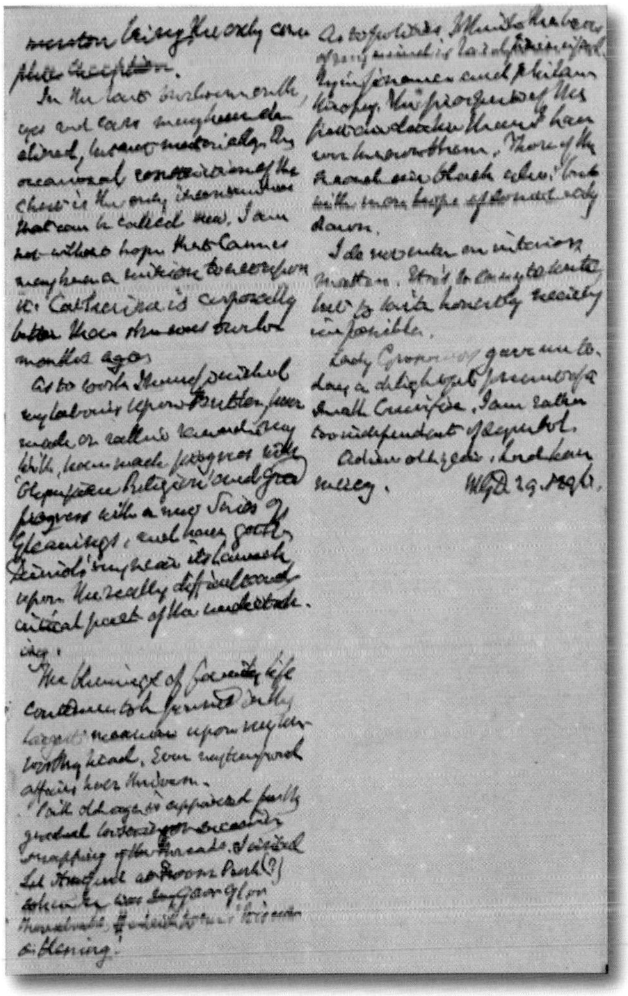

Gladstone's journal was also a site for inscribing secret thoughts and desires (often in foreign-language code). These included his guilt-ridden pornography reading, and his morally ambiguous 'rescue work' with prostitutes. Gladstone counteracted such temptations by verbal and physical chastisement, recording both in his journal. Although rescue work was a widespread philanthropy, Gladstone's involvement provoked concern during his life and threatened to escalate into scandal in the 1920s.

Gladstone had anticipated posthumous attacks and had written a 'Declaration' in 1896 pledging 'that at no period of my life have I been guilty … of infidelity to the marriage bed'. Captain Peter Wright's assertion that Gladstone's custom was 'to pursue and possess every sort of woman' culminated in a court battle in 1927 in which Gladstone's sons successfully defended his reputation. They had decided against offering the journal or 'Declaration' as evidence, but remained committed to the archive's preservation. In this they demonstrated both historical prescience – realising the journal's indispensability for understanding their father – and a family trait: Gladstone had written in 1837: 'Let keeping be the general rule, only burn such scraps as cannot be subjects of interest or future reference.' Nevertheless, the question remained where the 'Arcana' (the family's collective name for Gladstone's journals, private memoranda, and rescue-work correspondence) could safely be preserved.

In 1926, Cosmo Lang, then Archbishop of York, provided a solution. Trapped in Hawarden during the General Strike, he proposed entrusting successive Archbishops of Canterbury with guardianship. This resonated with Gladstone's lifelong Anglicanism and promised to safeguard both the source and Gladstone's reputation from prurient selection and misrepresentation until the entire journal could be published.

The collection was deposited at Lambeth in July 1928, with a later donation (MSS 2771–2774) arriving in 1938. Here the journals have remained, save for two sojourns in Oxford: the first in Claude Jenkins's Christ Church wine cellar to evade the Blitz, and the second – following the acquiescence of Archbishops Fisher and Ramsey – to be painstakingly edited for publication by M. R. D. Foot and the late H. C. G. Matthew between 1968 and 1994.

*Ruth Clayton Windscheffel*
*Faculty of Theology, University of Oxford*

J. Morley, *The Life of William Ewart Gladstone*, 3 vols (London, 1903)
P. E. Wright, *Portraits and Criticisms* (London, 1925)
M. R. D. Foot, 'Introduction', in *The Gladstone Diaries*. Vol. 1: *1825–1832* (Oxford, 1968), pp. xix–xlix
W. E. Gladstone, *The Gladstone Diaries*, ed. M. R. D. Foot and H. C. G. Matthew, 14 vols (Oxford, 1968–94)
R. J. Olney, 'The Gladstone Papers 1822–1977', in J. Brooke and M. Sorensen (eds), *W. E. Gladstone*. Vol. IV: *Autobiographical Memoranda 1868–1894* (London, 1981), pp. 118–30
H. C. G. Matthew, 'Gladstone and his Diaries', *Flintshire Historical Society Journal*, 35 (1999), pp. 167–75

# 54 Signing the Pledge

**Temperance collections, including the archives of the Church of England Temperance Society and the UK Band of Hope Union**
Illustrated: (*below*) *Church of England Temperance Chronicle*, vol. 21, 1892, p. 3, drunkards in court, an offender is let off pending a report from a Police Court Missioner; (*opposite above*) UK Band of Hope Union, *Temperance Pictorial Diagram no. 4, Reapers* [1893], 880 x 1150 mm; (*opposite below*) Band of Hope badges and prize medal

Few campaigns for social change in Victorian Britain were fought more earnestly than the temperance crusade. It sought to awaken the public conscience to the evils of drink: the self-destruction of the drunkard; the disappearance of wages into public houses and beer shops; and the descent of families into pauperism and crime. Local temperance societies mushroomed during the 1830s on the new principle of teetotalism, and were increasingly linked to national leagues and alliances pursuing a variety of aims, sometimes as radical as State prohibition. From the 1870s the Churches gave official backing to the temperance cause, and here the Church of England led the way.

A report on intemperance by the Convocation of Canterbury in 1869 set out to shock. It gave evidence of the 'frightful extent' of intemperance among the labouring classes, causing more deaths annually than Waterloo, filling prisons and workhouses, making the streets unsafe and crippling the national economy. A Church of England Total Abstinence Society had been formed in 1861, but its principle of abstinence proved a stumbling block. It was relaunched as the Church of England Temperance Society at a grand meeting in Lambeth Palace Library in February 1873 under the chairmanship of Archbishop Tait (1811–82). It now comprised separate sections for teetotallers and for the more moderate supporters of temperance.

Fully incorporated into Tait's vision of the role of the national Church, and keenly supported by his successors (including Frederick Temple, a committed abstainer), the Society went from strength to strength. By 1899 it was the largest temperance society in the country, with 7,000 branches and up to 200,000 members. In many localities it was the Church agency most in touch with the working class. Its thrift banks, sick and benefit societies, funeral guilds and coffee stalls for working men led it into broader fields of welfare work and encouraged new initiatives. One of these, its Police Court Mission, founded in 1876 to work with drunkards before the court and to help them not to reoffend, gave birth to the modern probation service.

Training children to shun alcohol was central to the temperance cause. Bands of Hope, linked to churches and chapels of all denominations, spread throughout England between 1847 and 1855, when a national organisation, the UK Band of Hope Union, was founded. By 1897, when Archbishop Temple preached a jubilee sermon, more than 2.5 million children were enrolled, linked by pledges of abstinence and a temperance catechism.

Temperance talks with lantern slides, singing and recitations were the staple fare of meetings, and there were parades, concerts and competitions with the award of prizes. The Union provided speakers, sample addresses and visual aids of every kind, such as the twelve pictorial diagrams published in 1893 with an accompanying manual entitled *Abstinence and Hard Work*. Designed to show that work was best performed without intoxicants, these portrayed teetotal laundries and abstaining navvies, miners and even printers. In place of beer or cider, thirsty harvesters were urged to drink cocoa. The Union also published a wide range of temperance literature, including the monthly *Band of Hope Review*, a vividly illustrated children's magazine packed with cautionary tales, and the *Band of Hope Chronicle* for adult supporters.

REAPERS.
Harvest work under the burning sun is very exhausting, and causes great thirst. Experience proves that beer and cider do not satisfy thirst or support strength so well as tea, cocoa, milk, or oatmeal-and-water. The latter, which is a favourite drink, is the best.


These journals form part of the rich material on temperance held at Lambeth. Ranging from minutes to improving novels and prizes, pledge books, badges and even an embroidered tablecloth, the collection documents one of the most widespread and influential movements in English social history.

*Richard Palmer*
*Lambeth Palace Library, London*

L. L. Shiman, *Crusade against Drink in Victorian England* (London, 1988)
B. H. Harrison, *Drink and the Victorians*, 2nd edn (Keele, 1994)

# 55 'To check the plague of immorality': The Mothers' Union

**The Mothers' Union archive, comprising 530 boxes, 1886–1990s**
Illustrated: (*right*) MU/MSH/3/15, proposed sign for Mary Sumner House by Morris Singer Company, 1947; (*below*) MU/OS/5/13/33, photograph of Mothers' Union worker with members in Uganda, *c.*1920; (*opposite*) MU 417, Mothers' Union stall at the Ideal Homes Exhibition, Olympia, 1951

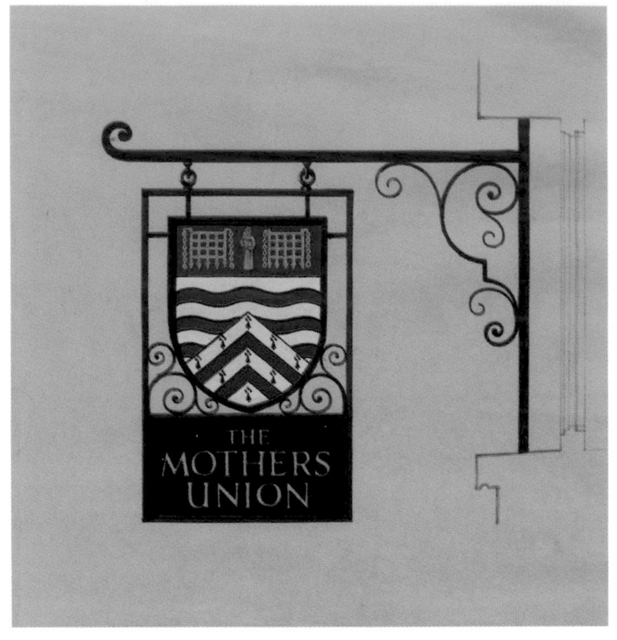


Popular perception of the Mothers' Union centres largely around banners and church bazaars, but its archive reveals a very different picture. In 1876 Mary Sumner (1828–1921) founded the society to defend the institution of marriage and promote Christian family life, an aim which has engaged its members in a range of religious, social and political issues down to the present day.

The morality of society has always been a central concern. Whether discussing the birth rate, divorce law reform or the moral dangers of riding pillion on a motorcycle, the Mothers' Union tackled the issues through consistent application of its Christian principles. It was reluctant to engage in politics, yet its concern for family life was so great that it found itself voicing opinions in the

most controversial of political debates. One such topic was socialism, for which the Union once reserved some of its fiercest attacks: 'out to destroy religion' was the verdict on Socialist Sunday Schools in the 1920s. The Mothers' Union undoubtedly moulded the political views of many recently enfranchised women.

Under the auspices of the Watch and Social Problems Department, a committee was formed in 1926 to examine the regulation of obscenity in the media and arts. Long before Mary Whitehouse campaigned in this field, the Mothers' Union was reproaching the film and television industries for 'incentives to murder, violence and promiscuity'. Its condemnation of the cinema, however, was not outright: an advocate of increased funding for British films, the Union praised the medium as an educational tool through which one could learn anything from fruit preserving to sex education. Health care was another concern. In an era before the National Health Service, the society offered medical advice on topics from chilblains to infant blindness through its journal and also campaigned for government action such as the 1927 Registration of Nursing Homes Act.

The Mothers' Union had established branches in British colonies by the 1890s and went on to expand worldwide, working particularly with women in developing countries. While its workers taught literacy, handcraft skills and Christian values, they witnessed struggles for independence and changes in political regime: the killings under Idi Amin in Uganda, insurrection of the Mau Mau in Kenya and forced relocation of families in Tanzania are all included in the reports sent home.

Equally important was the role of the Overseas Department in educating home members in unfamiliar cultures. Long before the twinning of towns in Europe, the Mothers' Union was forging similar links between branches in different countries. Using slides sent by workers abroad, the Overseas Department provided both exhibition material for use in parish halls across Britain and speakers specialising in overseas affairs.

Throughout its history the Mothers' Union has gone where others feared to tread, tackling social ills and teaching skills to some of the least developed communities. The resulting archive of administrative records, photographs and printed literature reflects the ambitious scope of the society's interests in Britain and around the world.

*Rachel Freeman*
*Lambeth Palace Library, London*

V. Lancaster, *A Short History of the Mothers' Union* (London, 1958)
C. Moyse, *A History of the Mothers' Union: Women, Anglicanism and Globalisation 1876–2008* (Woodbridge, 2009)

# 56 The Davidson Papers

**Correspondence and papers of Randall Davidson, Archbishop of Canterbury**

Illustrated: (*below*) MS 4820, a drawing by Sir Bernard Partridge for a *Punch* cartoon showing Davidson during the Prayer Book controversy, 1927; (*opposite*) Davidson Papers, vol. 23, f. 25, photograph of Randall Davidson, Archbishop of Canterbury (left), with Cosmo Lang, Archbishop of York, robed for the coronation of George V, 22 June 1911

Randall Thomas Davidson (1848–1930) became Archbishop of Canterbury in 1903 with strong credentials for the role. He had served as chaplain to Archbishop Tait (and married Tait's daughter, Edith), Dean of Windsor, and Queen Victoria's domestic chaplain. He had held the bishoprics of Rochester and Winchester. When in 1928 he retired from Canterbury (the first Archbishop to do so), he had held the office for longer than anyone since the Reformation.

The papers of the Archbishops of Canterbury, which include correspondence, diaries, sermons, newspaper cuttings and photographs, are an invaluable resource not only for ecclesiastical affairs but also for political and social history, and the papers of Archbishop Davidson are among the Library's richest. They run to over 800 volumes, indicative of his long tenure of office and large workload, which he tackled by working for over sixteen hours each day, following Archbishop Tait's example. Interest in the papers began early on, with George Bell, Bishop of Chichester, publishing an epic biography of Davidson in 1935, which begins 'the author of this work has been greatly assisted … by the ample records and admirably arranged correspondence which Archbishop Davidson left behind him'.

The papers reflect the many facets of the Archbishop's role. As well as recording his administration of the Diocese and Province of Canterbury (both of which saw major alterations, the former through boundary changes and the latter through the removal of Wales from the Province upon Disestablishment in 1920), the papers provide in-depth documentation on wider developments. Davidson oversaw the 1919 Enabling Act, which set up the Church Assembly and Parochial Church Councils, and the revision of the Prayer Book, which was completed in 1927, although subsequently rejected by Parliament. The papers also reflect the Archbishop's role in spiritual leadership of the nation, in areas such as public morality.

Davidson was keen to uphold the national role of the Church, and played an active part in the House of Lords, exerting significant political and social influence. The papers include correspondence with all the Prime Ministers of the period. Much concerns ecclesiastical preferment (a key involvement of Davidson since his years as confidential adviser to Queen Victoria), but his engagement in mainstream politics is apparent as well. Twenty-five volumes of papers on educational reform provide one example, and there is also documentation on the General Strike of 1926, when he issued an appeal to all sides in an attempt to move towards a settlement.

On the world stage Davidson was also a significant figure, not least through his leadership of the Anglican Communion and his active role in ecumenism. No fewer than 36 volumes of correspondence concern the Great War. Davidson visited the Western Front on several occasions, and was concerned with issues such as the welfare of servicemen, conscientious objection, the plight of German nationals and

prisoners, and the use of poison gas. Fourteen volumes of correspondence are concerned with Russia, reflecting Davidson's sympathy for the Orthodox Church in the period after the Revolution. Papers on the League of Nations (4 vols), India (5 vols) and Ireland (4 vols) further exemplify the international richness of the collection.

Personal papers deposited separately provide a deeper insight into Davidson's life. The Library holds almost 100 of his personal diaries, as well as those of his parents, Henry and Henrietta.

*Matti Watton*
*Lambeth Palace Library, London*

R. T. Davidson and W. Benham, *Life of Archibald Campbell Tait, Archbishop of Canterbury* (London, 1891)
C. Herbert, *Twenty-five Years as Archbishop of Canterbury (Randall Thomas Davidson)* (London, 1929)
G. K. A. Bell, Bishop of Chichester, *Randall Davidson, Archbishop of Canterbury* (Oxford, 1935)
E. Carpenter, *Cantuar: The Archbishops in their Office* (London, 1997)

# 57 The Golden Cockerel Gospels

*The Four Gospels*
Waltham St Lawrence; Golden Cockerel Press; 1931
342 x 245 mm
Illustrated: p. 69, Jesus at Gethsemane, from the Gospel of St Matthew, by courtesy of the Estate of Eric Gill

When Robert Gibbings (1889–1958) took over the ailing Golden Cockerel Press in 1924, he wrote to fellow members of the Society of Wood Engravers to see if they would like to collaborate on books. Over the next eight years he built up one of the grandest of the fine presses of the twentieth century, and his publishing programme was dominated by wood-engraved illustrations. The artists with whom he worked are a roll-call of contemporary talent, but the largest number of titles, after Gibbings's own work, were illustrated by an artist who initially turned down his invitation (supposedly because Gibbings was not a Catholic) – Eric Gill (1882–1940).

After his initial reluctance was overcome, Gill's friendship with Gibbings became a model of collaborative harmony. When they reached the high point of their partnership, *The Four Gospels*, differences were settled by each deferring to the other. Gill gave way on the text: as a Catholic he wanted the Douai translation, but the Authorised Version was chosen. However, his preference for unjustified setting prevailed over Gibbings's for straight right-hand margins.

Early announcements of the *Gospels* had given Caslon as the typeface to be used. But Gibbings prevailed on Gill not only to engrave over 60 pictorial subjects and decorated letters for the book, but also to design a new, exclusive typeface as well. The Golden Cockerel Roman, cut and cast by the Caslon foundry for hand setting only, shows a likeness to Perpetua, which Gill had recently designed for the Monotype Corporation, but has its own rugged beauty and a greater weight which makes it the perfect companion for bold black-line engravings. Many of the later Golden Cockerel books were in the 14 point size, but for the *Gospels* the magnificent 18 point was used.

When the type arrived in the workshop, it was set and proofed in galleys, and pasted up in pages, with selected chapter headings set in larger sizes of the titling alphabets. Gibbings and Gill then discussed how the big engravings would be arranged. In general, the model of medieval manuscripts was followed, with large historiated words for the openings. Aside from the pages of text, each gospel had a full-page engraving of the Evangelist's symbol. Every detail that might mar the noble simplicity of the pages, such as chapter and verse numbers, was jettisoned. Early plans to print some initials in red and blue were changed to having everything in a wonderfully rich black, making a superb impression on the Bachelor hand-made paper. The printing of this masterpiece of the twentieth-century book arts was begun on 20 February and completed on 28 October 1931. Gibbings took care to name in the colophon the Press's craftsmen, the compositors Frank Young and Harry Gibbs, and the pressman Albert Cooper.

*Sebastian Carter*
*Typographical Historian*

J. Dreyfus, *A Typographical Masterpiece: An Account … of Eric Gill's Collaboration with Robert Gibbings in Producing the Golden Cockerel Press Edition of 'The Four Gospels' in 1931* (San Francisco, 1990)
M. J. Andrews, *The Life and Work of Robert Gibbings* (Bicester, 2003)

COMETH JESUS WITH THEM UNTO A PLACE CALLED GETHSEMANE, AND SAITH UNTO THE DISCIPLES, SIT YE HERE, WHILE I GO AND PRAY YONDER. AND HE TOOK WITH HIM Peter and the two sons of Zebedee, and began to be sorrowful and very heavy. Then saith he unto them, My soul is exceeding sorrowful, even unto death: tarry ye here, and watch with me. And he went a little farther, and fell on his face, and prayed, saying, O my Father, if it be possible, let this cup pass from me: nevertheless not as I will, but as thou wilt. And he cometh unto the disciples, and findeth them asleep, and saith unto Peter, What, could ye not watch with me one hour? Watch & pray, that ye enter not into temptation: the spirit indeed is willing, but the flesh is weak. He went away again the second time, and prayed, saying, O my

# 58 George Bell and T. S. Eliot

**Papers of G. K. A. Bell, Bishop of Chichester**
373 vols
Illustrated: (*below; detail*) T. S. Eliot, *Murder in the Cathedral*, London, 1935, presentation inscription from Eliot to Bell, 4 June 1935; (*opposite above*) Bell papers, vol. 357, f. 187, portrait photograph of Bell, 19 January 1943; (*opposite below*) vol.156, f. 94r–v, letter from Eliot to Bell, 20 July 1935, by courtesy of Faber and Faber Ltd

This amiable, ironic inscription, on the flyleaf of one of the most celebrated plays written in Britain in the twentieth century, discloses the quiet but purposeful relationship which brought *Murder in the Cathedral* by T. S. Eliot (1888–1965) to life. As Dean of Canterbury from 1924 to 1929, the dedicatee, George Kennedy Allen Bell (1883–1958), had worked to inspire a rebirth of Christian drama in England. There were by then a number of societies and organisations working out the same argument. Many churches were used to pageants or nativity plays; medieval mystery plays were soon being revived and performed. The Dean of Canterbury cut a conspicuous figure in this bustle.

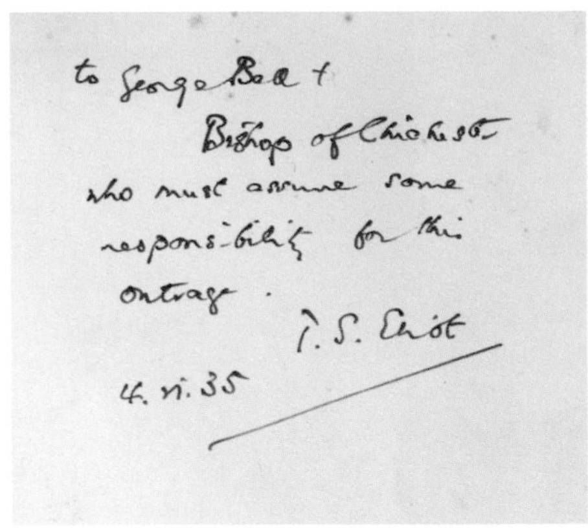
to George Bell
Bishop of Chichester
who must assume some
responsibility for this
outrage.
T. S. Eliot
4. vi. 35

Bell found ready allies among writers such as Laurence Housman and John Masefield. Masefield's work, *The Coming of Christ*, was a nativity play of a kind and at Canterbury it marked the dawn of a new era when it was performed at the cathedral itself in 1928. After 1929, when Bell became Bishop of Chichester, a pattern of new commissions emerged, and within it the literary voices of a new generation: T. S. Eliot, Charles Williams, Dorothy L. Sayers and Christopher Fry. Many of these plays were consciously poetic in language: beauty and dignity in language declared reverence. Bell himself was devoted to poetry, as reader and writer, too. Eliot's work was particularly well known to him and the poet became a visitor to the Bishop's Palace. Eliot's 1933 pageant, 'The Rock', owed much to an invitation from Bell. According to Eliot himself the venture which became *Murder in the Cathedral* emerged in a conversation in the garden of the Bishop's Palace in Chichester one afternoon in the summer of 1934. By now an established poet, Eliot turned playwright. The first performance of his new 'outrage' took place in Canterbury in June 1935.

The decision to write a play about the martyrdom of Thomas Becket, King Henry II's 'turbulent priest', was no accident in a world in which Church and State were at odds. Indeed, Bell himself was coming to represent the strain. A committed ecumenist and internationalist, he had by 1935 become known as the ally of the refugees who fled Hitler's Germany and the friend and advocate of those who remained there to resist Nazism as best they could. His public protests against the obliteration bombing of German cities during the Second World War established his reputation as a controversialist and some insisted that he lost any opportunity to become Archbishop of Canterbury because of it. Bell feared that if the defeat of Nazism entailed the destruction of ideals and principles, museums, galleries and libraries no less, the prospects for rebuilding civilisation might perish, too.

Bell's extraordinary career may be traced in the great collection of papers which he bequeathed to Lambeth Palace Library. The correspondence with Eliot offers a glimpse, at least, of its richness. Among records left by campaigns, committees and conferences a reader may also discern a quiet, but enduring devotion to the Arts. Bell's widow later recalled that one of the last things on which he had worked was not a letter or a memorandum, but a sonnet. When the BBC broadcast an appreciation of this rare spirit in 1959, Eliot participated in the tribute, praising him not only as a great Christian who possessed a 'dauntless integrity', but one who remained, above all, a loveable man.

*Andrew Chandler*
*George Bell Institute, University of Chichester*

G. K. A. Bell, *The Church and Humanity* (London, 1946)
R. C. D. Jasper, *George Bell, Bishop of Chichester* (London, 1967)
A. Chandler, *Piety and Provocation: A Study of George Bell, Bishop of Chichester* (Chichester, 2008)

94

# FABER & FABER

Limited

PUBLISHERS

DIRECTORS
G.C.FABER (CHAIRMAN)
C.W.STEWART
R.H.I.DE LA MARE
F.V.MORLEY (U.S.A.)
T.S.ELIOT (U.S.A. ORIGIN)

TELEPHONE: MUSEUM 9543
TELEGRAMS: FABBAF, WESTCENT, LONDON

24 RUSSELL SQUARE
LONDON, W.C.1

20 July 1935.

The Rt. Revd. the Lord Bishop of Chichester,

The Palace,

Chichester.

My dear Lord Bishop,

By good chance your letter found me this morning at my office, just before leaving for the country. I am going down into Sussex for the weekend, and thence to Gloucestershire and Wales, and shall not be in town again until the 10th August. So I shall be unable to accept your kind invitation to lunch on July 29th.

But as for a Pageant Play, that is something which I know I cannot do. I can write words for such plays, when the visual design, the scenario and the construction are in the hands of someone like Martin Browne; and this is all that I did for "The Rock". For a Pageant Play I am convinced that the prime necessity is a producer of imagination, rather than a poet or even a dramatist. I am partly incompetent simply, and partly incompetent because I am not much interested in that off-shoot of drama. Then again, I find that I have to be very parcimonious of my time. Only by unscrupulously restricting my engagements during the winter months - both business andsocial - am I able to get one piece of original work done; and if I undertook such a job as this, even under Browne's supervision, I should be postponing for a year anything of my own. And I am no longer young enough to be able to postpone things, especially as a great deal of my life has been wasted in the past. I write rather fully, and put the case rather strongly, because I should not like you to feel that I am ungrateful: for I am aware that without your initiative and support I should not have had the most valuable opportunities of writing "The Rock" and "Murder in the Cathedral". But I feel that what I should try now would be "religious drama" somewhat in the sense of, let me say without appearance of being over-ambitious, <u>Polyeucte</u>.

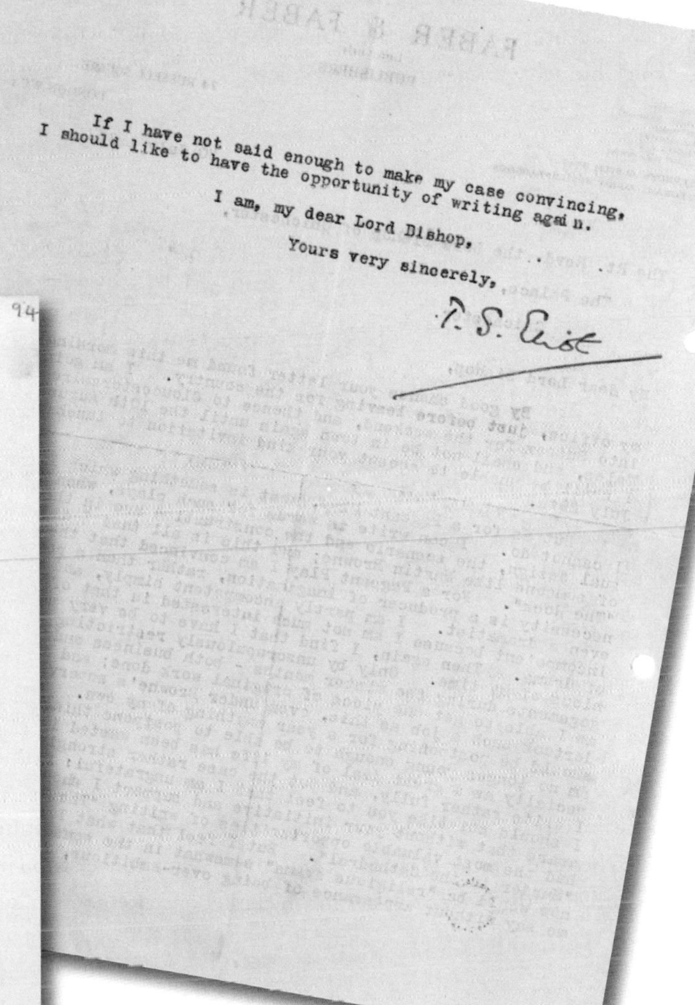

If I have not said enough to make my case convincing, I should like to have the opportunity of writing again.

I am, my dear Lord Bishop,

Yours very sincerely,

T. S. Eliot

# 59 The Coronation

**Archives, manuscripts and printed books from the Lambeth collections**
Illustrated: (*below; detail*) Francis Sandford, *The History of the Coronation of… James II*, London, 1687, plate showing the crowning performed by Archbishop Sancroft; (*opposite*) *The Holy Bible*, Oxford, 1953, the Coronation Bible of Queen Elizabeth II, binding designed by Lyntton Lamb and executed by Sangorski and Sutcliffe

The Archbishop of Canterbury has played a leading role in the coronation of the monarch since Anglo-Saxon times. He administers the coronation oath, anoints with holy oil, invests with the regalia and finally places St Edward's crown on the sovereign's head.

The form and order of the coronation are ancient in origin but not immutable, and the archbishop has played a major part in drawing up the rites and ceremonies. At Lambeth there are orders of service for all coronations since the seventeenth century: manuscript and printed services, annotated drafts and final copies used for the rite itself. Frequently they include notes by the archbishop of the day on what was intended and what actually took place. They include, for example, a manuscript compilation 'out of the rites of the Coronation called Liber Regalis as allso other bookes of good recorde in Coronation Order', translated for the first time into English for the coronation of King James I in 1603. A copy of the service for King George II (r. 1727–60) in 1727 was annotated by Archbishop Wake with notes of numerous mistakes: the first anthem was never sung due to 'the negligence of the choir of Westminster', a following anthem was 'in confusion' and 'Zadok the Priest', first composed for this occasion, was sung in the wrong place.

The presentation of the Bible was first introduced into the service for William and Mary in 1689. The Bible originally became the perquisite of the dean of Westminster, but Lambeth holds the elaborately decorated copies used at the coronations of Kings Edward VII, George V, George VI and Queen Elizabeth II. Most unusual at Lambeth are the prompts printed in gigantic type and attached to the reverse of banners to assist the failing eyesight of Archbishop Frederick Temple in 1902.

As well as the official texts, Lambeth holds archival material on the preparations and proceedings of various coronations. Claude Jenkins, Lambeth Librarian from 1910 to 1952, played a leading role in devising the 1911 text and was still involved in 1953. The papers reflect the intimate relationship between the archbishop and the monarch, as in Lang's prayers with King George VI and Queen Elizabeth on the eve of his coronation and the private prayers drawn up by Fisher for their daughter Elizabeth: 'For the Queen: a little book of private devotions in preparation for Her Majesty's Coronation; to be used from first of May to second of June 1953.'

The collection includes splendid descriptive works, including Francis Sandford's history of the crowning of King James II (r. 1685–88), which is illustrated with full-page plates of the ceremonies. There are copies of the coronation sermons, discontinued only in 1902, which made important political statements. There are Books of Common Prayer specially published and illustrated for coronation years, and the annotated Prayer Book used by Archbishop Tenison at the crowning of Queen Anne. The holdings form a living archive of the coronation, ancient and still continuing.

*Christina Mackwell*
*Lambeth Palace Library, London*

---

Roy Strong, *Coronation: A History of Kingship and the British Monarchy* (London, 2005)

# 60 The Ecumenical Century

**Ecumenical archives, including papers of the Archbishops of Canterbury, the Lambeth Conference and the Council on Foreign Relations**
Illustrated: (*below*) MS 2084.2, the Common Declaration (Latin version) signed by Archbishop Ramsey and Pope Paul VI, 1966, vellum, 423 x 570 mm; (*opposite above*) Ramsey Papers, vol. 324, item 151, photograph of the signing of the Common Declaration, 1966, by courtesy of L'Osservatore Romano; (*opposite below*) Council on Foreign Relations OC12, photograph of the signing of a communiqué on Anglican–Orthodox dialogue by Archbishop Ramsey and Athenagoras, the Ecumenical Patriarch, 1967

With its traditions both 'catholic' and 'reformed', the Anglican Communion has a special role in ecumenism, based on the conviction that its *via media* may serve as an instrument for Christian unity. For centuries the Archbishop of Canterbury has led the ecumenical endeavours of the Church of England and the Anglican Communion. The collections at Lambeth reflect early initiatives such as Archbishop Abbot's contacts with Orthodoxy after 1617, and Archbishop Wake's correspondence concerning the union of the English and Gallican churches from 1717 to 1720.

With gathering pace from the primacy of Archbishop Tait (1869–82) onwards, the Archbishops' papers show progressive

HAC in Urbe Roma, unde a Sancto Gregorio PP. I missus est in Angliam Sanctus Augustinus, conditor Sedis Cantuariensis, quam omnes, qui nunc sunt, Anglicani quasi centrum suae Communionis christianae habent, Sanctissimus Dominus Paulus PP. VI et Reverendissimus et Honoratissimus Dominus Michael Ramsey, Archiepiscopus Cantuariensis, Communionis Anglicanae gerens personam, inter se convenerunt, ut fraterno animo salutem sibi impertirent.

Cuius congressionis in fine Deo omnipotenti gratias agunt, quod, Spiritu Sancto afflante, per hos annos proxime elapsos novus sensus christianae fraternitatis inter Ecclesiam Catholicam Romanam et Ecclesias Communionis Anglicanae est exortus.

Eadem congressione, die XXIII mensis Martii anno MCMLXVI habita, novus quidam efficitur gradus pertinens ad progressionem fraternae necessitudinis rationum, in christiana caritate innixarum, atque sincerorum conatuum, quibus obstacula, perfectam communionem ecclesiasticam impedientia, superentur.

Praecepto igitur Christi Domini obtemperare cupientes, qui discipulis suis mandavit, ut se invicem diligerent, declarant se in sinu Dei miserentissimi, eiusdem ope, ea cuncta deponere, quae huic praecepto caritatis praeteritis temporibus sunt refragata, et ad mentem Apostoli se accommodare, qui dixit: "quae quidem retro sunt obliviscens, ad ea vero, quae sunt priora, extendes meipsum, ad destinatum persequor, ad bravium supernae vocationis Dei in Christo Jesu" (Phil. 3, 13-14).

Edicunt se exoptare, ut fideles utriusque Communionis eodem sensu reverentiae, bonae existimationis, amoris fraterni ducantur. Quam mutuam necessitudinem fovere ac provehere volentes, proponunt, ut inter Ecclesiam Catholicam Romanam et Communionem Anglicanam sedulo instituantur colloquia, quorum veluti fundamenta sint Evangelium et antiquae Traditiones utrisque communes, quaeque ad illam unitatem, pro qua Christus oravit, in veritate perducant.

Colloquia illa non solum argumenta theologica comprehendent, veluti Sacram Scripturam, Traditionem, Liturgiam, sed etiam res illas, quae in vitae usu seu praxi ex utraque parte difficultates habent. Paulus PP. VI ac Archiepiscopus Cantuariensis noverunt quidem gravia obstacula, quae impediunt, ne perfecta communio fidei et vitae sacramentalis restituatur; nihilominus consentientes studiose agere constituunt, ut ex utraque Communione alteri alteros cum auctoritate attingant circa ea omnia, ad vitam ecclesialem spectantia, in quibus mutua opera apta sit ad consensionem et caritatem augendam, atque coniti, ut universae illae graves quaestiones solvantur, quae in mundo nostrae aetatis in Christum credentibus occurrunt.

Hac mutua opera, adiuvante Dei Patris gratia et Sancti Spiritus lumine, citius ad effectum deducatur precatio Domini Nostri Jesu Christi, qua pro unitate discipulorum suorum oravit, et hac progressione, quae fit ad unitatem, pax in humana consortione roboretur, quam solum concedere potest is, qui donat pacem, "quae exsuperat omnem sensum"; haec vero pax una cum Benedictione Dei omnipotentis, Patris et Filii et Spiritus Sancti, cum omnibus hominibus maneat semper.

Romae, apud Sanctum Paulum extra moenia, die XXIV mensis Martii, anno MCMLXVI.

+ Michael Cantuariensis:　　Paulus PP. VI

engagement with sister Churches at home and abroad. From the nineteenth century too come the papers of pioneers of Anglican–Orthodox relations, John Mason Neale, William Palmer, William Birkbeck, whose knowledge of the Russian church was unmatched in England, and Athelstan Riley, whose papers are enriched with journals and photographs of his travels to Mount Athos and elsewhere.

The Missionary Conference at Edinburgh in 1910 inspired a century of ecumenism, and the collections display the immensity of the effort, the achievements and the disappointments. Included are records of the Lambeth Conference, which issued its influential 'Appeal to All Christian People' in 1920. One of the outcomes at home was a series of conversations between the Church of England and the Free Churches, which were taken further after 1946, when Archbishop Fisher delivered his 'Cambridge Sermon' calling on the Free Churches to 'take episcopacy into their system'.

In 1933 the Church of England Council on Foreign Relations was formed, with separate committees on the various branches of Christendom overseas. The Library holds over 250 boxes of its records, as well as the papers of its first chairmen, Bishops Arthur Headlam and George Bell, and its first secretary, John Douglas. They are supplemented by papers of ecumenists such as John Wordsworth, Bishop of Salisbury, whose endeavours laid the ground for the agreements on intercommunion with the Church of Sweden from 1920 to 1922, J. A. Robinson, Dean of Wells, who participated in the Anglican–Roman Catholic conversations at Malines from 1921 to 1925, and John Moorman, Bishop of Ripon, including his diary of the Second Vatican Council. The archives of Anglican societies extend the range, including those of the Anglican and Eastern Churches Association and the Society of St Willibrord, which helped towards the Bonn Agreement of 1931, establishing full communion between the Anglican and Old Catholic Churches.

The personal breviary of Pope John XXIII, given by him to Canon Donald Rea in a spontaneous gesture in 1959, is one of many poignant items reflecting growing friendship between the Churches. So too are records of the visits by the Archbishop of Canterbury to other Church leaders. Archbishop Fisher's visit to Pope John XXIII in 1960, momentous as it was, was deliberately kept low key. Archbishop Ramsey's visit to Pope Paul VI in 1966 was more official, and is recorded in photographs and in the Common Declaration which they signed. No less moving because of the depth of their common feeling was the meeting of Archbishop Ramsey and Athenagoras, the Ecumenical Patriarch, at Lambeth in 1967, when they signed a communiqué establishing Anglican–Orthodox dialogue.

In 1981 the Council on Foreign Relations was reorganised and its work brought more closely into association with the ministry of the Archbishop. Papers from this later period, yet to be released for research, document the continuing work for Christian unity, which Archbishop Ramsey once defined 'not as the bringing together of ecclesiastical systems as they stand … but the renewal together of Churches in every part of the world in holiness, truth and mission'.

*Richard Palmer*
*Lambeth Palace Library, London*

# Index

Note: the abbreviation 'LPL' is for Lambeth Palace Library

First published in 2010 by
Scala Publishers Ltd
Northburgh House
10 Northburgh Street
London EC1V 0AT, UK
Telephone: +44 (0) 20 7490 9900
www.scalapublishers.com

Hardback: ISBN-13: 978 1 85759 627 4
Paperback: ISBN-13: 978 1 85759 637 3

Content editors: Richard Palmer and Michelle P. Brown
Project editor: Esme West
Copy editor: Rosalind Neely
Designer: Yvonne Dedman
Photographer: David Cooper, except pp. 8, 10, 22–23, 45, 82–83, 93, 97, 112, 136, 140, 159 (medals) and 162

Printed and bound in Spain
10 9 8 7 6 5 4 3 2



British Library Cataloguing in Publication Data
A catalogue record for this book is available from the British Library.

The editors express warmest thanks to all who have helped with this book, especially the contributors; the staff of Lambeth Palace Library (particularly Clare Brown, Janet Atkinson, Gabriel Sewell, Krzysztof Adamiec and Mary Comer); David Cooper (for the photography and for transferring copyright of the images to the Library) and his wife Gill; the Trustees of Lambeth Palace Library; the Lambeth Palace Library 400th Anniversary Committee and its Chairman, Declan Kelly; Jenny McKinley and Esme West (Scala Publishers Ltd) and the book's designer, Yvonne Dedman; the Bridgeman Art Library (see no. 21); the National Portrait Gallery (see nos 35 and 46); Professor Stephen Taylor (see no. 50); the Estate of Eric Gill (see no. 57); Faber and Faber Ltd (see no. 58); and L'Osservatore Romano (see no. 60).

*Right:* Border detail from MS 186; A London Liturgical Psalter, f. 1r (see no. 17)